Religious Explanation and Scientific Ideology

Toronto Studies in Religion

Donald Wiebe, General Editor
Trinity College
University of Toronto

Vol. 17

Published in association with
the Centre for Religious Studies
at the University of Toronto

PETER LANG
New York • San Francisco • Bern • Baltimore
Frankfurt am Main • Berlin • Wien • Paris

Jesse Hobbs

Religious Explanation and Scientific Ideology

PETER LANG
New York • San Francisco • Bern • Baltimore
Frankfurt am Main • Berlin • Wien • Paris

Library of Congress Cataloging-in-Publication Data

Hobbs, Jesse.
    Religious explanation and scientific ideology/ Jesse Hobbs.
       p.   cm. — (Toronto studies in religion; vol. 17)
    Includes bibliographical references and index.
    1. Explanation—Religious aspects. 2. Explanation. 3. Knowledge,
Theory of (Religion) 4. Religion and science. 5. Science—Philosophy.
I. Title. II. Series.
BL51.H7163   1993   210—dc20   93-6954
ISBN 0-8204-2197-9   CIP
ISSN 8756-7385

Die Deutsche Bibliothek-CIP-Einheitsaufnahme

Hobbs, Jesse:
Religious explanation and scientific ideology/ Jesse Hobbs. - New York;
Berlin; Bern; Frankfurt/M.; Paris; Wien: Lang, 1993
    (Toronto studies in religion; Vol. 17)
    ISBN 0-8204-2197-9
NE: GT

The paper in this book meets the guidelines for permanence and durability of
the Committee on Production Guidelines for Book Longevity of the
Council on Library Resources.

Printed in the United States of America.

for Beverly

ACKNOWLEDGEMENTS

There are many people whose efforts contributed to making this work possible. I would like to express special thanks to Robert Barrett, Roger Gibson, Gary Varner, Dorothy Fleck, Jerome Schiller, Paul Martin, Jeff Zents, and Robert Canfield; and to Beverly, for her loyal support.

CONTENTS

PREFACE

Can premises mentioning the existence of God ever be cited legitimately in explanations of matters of fact? In the philosophical literature, explanation is portrayed almost exclusively as the province of science, so the fact that God could never be recognized as an entity or used in an explanation in scientific contexts would seem to preclude that possibility. Neither would religious explanations be sanctioned by the noncognitive reconstructions of religious discourse that have been fashionable since Wittgenstein.

My argument is essentially a limited defense of cognitive pluralism. I claim that the cognitive values, goals, and methodological precepts informing scientific practice, although having much to recommend them, are not the only values, or the only way of structuring values, which can be held rationally. To be sure, some of the explanatory values employed by science are applicable to all theoretical contexts, including nonscientific ones. These include such values as clarity, consistency, and evidential support. But other cognitive values used in science do not have adequate global credentials to adjudicate all questions of explanatory practice. In this group I include control, replicability, and (to a limited extent) prediction. In other words, I maintain that the limits on scientifically acceptable explanations are generally narrower than the limits on rationally acceptable explanations.

It is easier to define the rationality at stake here negatively rather than positively. I do *not* mean by rationality what economists and decision theorists mean, viz., enlightened self-interest. The rationality in question is not means/end rationality but epistemic rationality, or a matter of what beliefs are legitimate given the evidence available to the believer. Although I have no general theory of rationality to offer, I assume that what makes a belief epistemically rational is more-or-less the same regardless of the subject matter—there are no separate rules for religion, science, or anything else. In lieu of a formal theory, I take the ultimate arbiter of cognitive values to be any and all judgments of rationality whose basis in epistemology and/or common sense seems secure or uncontroversial. Although not a panacea, common sense is an excellent antidote for religious and scientific hubris.

Science offers us a splendid understanding of a great many events, but even more events remain to be explained, especially in the social and psychological realm. What posture is reasonable toward phenomena which science thus far has been unable to explain? Certain scientific principles work to preclude the legitimation of nonscientific explanations for such events. For example, scientists may reject nonscientific explanations by offering a "promissory note" in exchange for maintaining a higher, scientific standard of explanatory acceptability. That is, they promise to explain the phenomenon sooner or later, and urge us to be patient until then. Inferences to the best explanation also have legitimate scientific employment, but are often used (or abused) ideologically to rule out explanations not sanctioned by science. Besides these there are doctrines of reductionism, physicalism, materialism, and naturalism that fall under the general rubric of *scientism:* "Science tells us what there is, and that's *all* that there is." Determinism is another commonly held position which, like the others, is relatively innocuous within scientific contexts, because its denial is effectively ruled out by the structure of scientific inquiry (see 5.1.2). But in contexts in which the sovereignty of science is disputed, these methodological principles have an ideological aspect that effectively and unnecessarily precludes alternative explanations. By what set of values does one determine which explanation is "best" when one is making an inference to the best explanation? If we think of religion and science as different cultures, it is safe to say that answers to this question are often parochial, or cross-culturally insensitive.

If rational acceptability is broader than scientific acceptability, nevertheless its relation to religious acceptability is less clear. I am mindful that rationality is often valued less highly in religious contexts than in scientific ones, which is entirely proper. But without the restraint of rationality, one would be left in a normative vacuum so far as cognitive values are concerned, and noncognitive models do not adequately capture the semantics of religious discourse. Therefore, I "rationally reconstruct" religious discourse, hoping that this might be an improvement over prevailing practice, even as philosophers often prefer to discuss a rationally reconstructed science rather than actual scientific practice. Hence I adopt the stance that if a religious practice can be shown to be irrational in some far-reaching, fundamental way, it ought to be abandoned. In speaking of religious *explanation* and of scientific *ideology* then, I do not mean to imply that there are no such things as religious ideologies or scientific explanations—rather, I take their existence for granted. My claim is that there is enough explanatory power contained within religious beliefs to be philosophically interesting and enough ideological content within science to foster widespread belief to the contrary.

My position is that one can reconstruct from religious contexts a system of cognitive values with broad application that takes exception to a number of scientific norms. These norms pertain to:

(1) the ranking of outstanding problem areas in importance
(2) the usefulness of anecdotal material
(3) the status of teleological explanations
(4) the degree to which pragmatic considerations govern theorizing
(5) standards for explanations in nonscientific areas.

Item (2) requires special emphasis here because so much of the evidence for God encompassed in revealed theology is anecdotal in nature, including most of the contents of the historical texts of western religions, as well as virtually all religious experience. Most of the apparent difference in how anecdotal material is valued probably stems from the fact that scientists are accustomed to having more reliable evidence to go on, while religious people are not. Yet the difference is no less real.

Explanations constructed in accordance with this new set of values would still be weaker, methodologically speaking, than scientific explanations typically are, and the use of anecdotal material would be part of the reason why. Although they may occasionally compete with scientific explanations successfully as accounts of the same phenomenon, more often religious explanations will be appropriate for phenomena that science does not explain. Teleological explanations (in terms of the intentions or purposes of God) for phenomena that are explained scientifically in non-teleological terms may also be rationally acceptable.

The Pivotal Value of Truth

Although the *truth* and *rationality* of religious claims are distinct issues, they often become intertwined in practice. Hence, one cannot defend the rationality of religious explanations without raising questions regarding their truth. Philosophical interest in the truth of religious claims generally revolves around the correspondence conception of truth. This is because it is fairly evident that people generally *can* hold that God exists coherently along with most of what educated people believe. Similarly, though establishing that religious practices have pragmatic value is nontrivial, we want to say that they have such value independently of their truth. So the coherence and/or "pragmatic truth" of religious claims are nonissues in comparison to whether there is anything in reality corresponding to the contents of religious beliefs or religiously interpreted perceptions. Yet the correspondence theory of truth has come under vigorous attack in recent years. While recognizing that even with appropriate qualifications the viability of the correspondence theory cannot be taken for granted, I adhere to the commonsensical view that, for the majority of religious claims, questions of correspondence can be made intelligible and have answers, even if we don't know what they are.

Therefore, I reject polemical critiques of science, such as Paul Feyerabend's. A political solution to the conflicts between science and religion, such as he advocates, would have little prospect of arriving at or being based on truth.[1] His appeal to the people's right to self-determination sounds like empty rhetoric, since even societies founded on explicitly democratic principles, such as our own, often do not realize self-determination in practice. Feyerabend suggests that anyone talking about "the truth" thereby reveals himself to be an ideologue intent on having his personal truth proclaimed universal. I do not have answers to many of the questions I will be raising herein, but if there is any truth to the matter, I would not want to adopt a policy whose effect would be to make it more inaccessible; and this would be the effect of politicizing research or, as Richard Rorty suggests, replacing inquiry with conversation.[2] Similarly, I regard Antony Flew's critique of religious discourse as too ideological to be acceptable. Flew claims to be justified in presuming atheism since the burden of proof is now on the religious believer, or so he argues.[3] But burden-of-proof arguments seem more the tool of the rhetorician than the serious inquirer, and presumptions are something to be entered into cautiously, not a means of settling a dispute.

It has been commonplace since the work of Thomas Kuhn to allege that there can be neither evidence nor perception except within the framework of some worldview or other. Indeed, some philosophers of religion have embraced this development as legitimizing ideological religious positions, untestable worldviews, and irrefutable interpretations of the contents of perception. I seek to avoid ideological commitments insofar as possible,

---

[1] *Farewell to Reason* (London: Verso, 1987), pp. 40, 59, 308.

[2] *Philosophy and the Mirror of Nature* (Princeton Univ. Press, 1979), pp. 372, 377.

[3] "'Theology and Falsification' in Retrospect," in *The Logic of God*, ed. by Diamond and Litzenburg, 269–83 (Indianapolis: Bobbs-Merrill, 1975).

and support the position articulated by Kuhn himself that incommensurability is remediable. Lines of incommensurability are those across which discussants *are* failing to communicate, or *are* talking past one another, not where communication is impossible.[4] Even if everything can be seen only from the standpoint of one worldview or another, that does not preclude worldviews from being flexible enough to permit suspension of judgment on particular disputed issues. Given any two worldviews, it may not be necessary to find a metaphysically neutral ground from which to evaluate them, so long as one can find enough *common ground* to make arbitrating them possible. So I do not see incommensurability as a sanctuary for religious discourse, but an obstacle to be overcome in inquiring into the truth of the matter.

This perspective will help us sidestep some of the stale terminology in which these issues are often cast. A little common sense is enough to dispel the more extreme forms of foundationalism and coherentism, for example, so it seems that foundationalism simply is not the issue. Critics of religion frequently point out that religious experiences are incapable of providing a "logical ground" for ontological claims regarding the existence of ostensibly experienced entities such as God. True enough, but since no experience of any kind is capable of providing a "logical ground" for any ontological claim involving the external world, and we all believe in the external world anyway, this argument has no philosophical force against religious ontological claims.

The "framework" or "worldview" issue is another red herring—it is to be hoped that the *contents* rather than the form of religious evidence, beliefs, and explanations will ultimately save or doom them. Nor do I see "objectivity vs. subjectivity" or "faith vs. reason" as useful ways of drawing up the battle lines between science and religion. Though I take what Plantinga calls an *evidentialist* stance, it is not that I leave no room for faith. Rather, I see in science significant opportunities for exercising faith (2.2), and hence I see faith and reason as complementing rather than contradicting one another in practice. On the whole, however, I wish to emphasize that one can go much further in the religious domain with evidence and argument than many suppose. If I am right about this, rationality enjoins us to go as far as we can on that basis. This is a controversial claim, but most religious traditions recognize the principle of not trusting human life to faith healers until empirically more promising remedies are exhausted.

---

[4] "Reflections on My Critics," in *Criticism and the Growth of Knowledge,* ed. by Lakatos and Musgrave (Cambridge Univ. Press, 1970), pp. 232–3, 267–8, 276–7.

Incorrigibility, and the Perceptual Metaphor

In keeping with my policy of avoiding ideological postures whenever possible, I am wary of philosophical treatments of religion given by Basil Mitchell and his followers, who interpret as benign Kuhnian and Lakatosian justifications of incorrigibility.[5] Only an unconverted dogmatist would elevate his opinion on a controversial issue without further ado into the functional equivalent of an analytic truth. Indeed, a common positivistic complaint against religious claims is the absence of any state of affairs that can count against them. Following the Quine-Duhem thesis, it is *possible* to hold any element of a theoretical system true "come what may," but this doesn't make such a policy rational. It would seem to be a greater demonstration of faith in God to maintain one's position in the face of a recognizable risk of being proven wrong, than through a policy of explaining away any and every occurrence which apparently conflicts.

Perhaps only a weaker claim was intended that one may not be acting irrationally if one does not question certain core beliefs, so long as one's research program is making adequate theoretical and empirical progress, and one has a plan for extending the program and defending it against competitors.[6] Such programs may be rationally acceptable, but I must hasten to add that, at best, satisfying Lakatosian strictures on progressiveness is necessary for the rationality of one's research program—it is hardly sufficient. Any academic worth her salt will try to develop and extend her theory in some such manner, yet intellectual history is strewn with the wreckage of research programs gone bad. It seems unlikely that all were rationally defensible.

Other philosophers such as Alvin Plantinga and Nicholas Wolterstorff, while eschewing incorrigibility, nevertheless adopt terminology that obfuscates their essentially ideological commitments. Plantinga claims to be a new kind of foundationalist in that he maintains the two-tiered noetic structure whereby certain beliefs are "properly basic" or known non-inferentially while other beliefs are known only inferentially. Unlike classical foundationalists, however, he denies that properly basic beliefs are incorrigible, or immune from revision.[7] Properly basic beliefs then include the existence of

---

[5] *The Justification of Belief* (New York: Macmillan, 1973). See also his contribution to "Theology and Falsification," in *New Essays in Philosophical Theology,* ed. by Flew and MacIntyre (London: SCM, 1955).

[6] Cf. Nancey Murphy, *Theology in the Age of Scientific Reasoning* (Cornell Univ. Press, 1990).

[7] "Reason and Belief in God," in *Faith and Rationality,* ed. by Plantinga and Wolterstorff,

other minds, that I am being appeared to greenly, or that I see a tree or a horse, as well as religious interpretations of the contents of perception. Yet it seems highly doubtful that God's immateriality, omniscience, omnipotence, and moral perfection are directly perceivable. Given how few *religious* people even claim to perceive directly God's omnipotence or his signature on creation, God's existence hardly seems epistemically basic, and is considerably less certain than other traditional foundational aspects of knowledge. Why else is there so much dispute over the existence and nature of God, and not over arithmetic, or whether the sky is blue?

The overtly ideological character of Wolterstorff's book is manifest in its title—*Reason within the Bounds of Religion.* While Wolterstorff focuses on theoretical beliefs rather than perceptual beliefs, or "matters of fact," he follows Plantinga in dividing them into two categories: those that function as "control beliefs," regulating the acceptance or rejection of all other theories, and those that are subject to this regulation but do not obviously regulate other theories in turn. He then elevates beliefs regarding how one's fundamental religious commitment ought to be realized into control beliefs.[8] Although Wolterstorff doesn't deny that other theoretical beliefs might sometimes come into play in accepting or rejecting control beliefs, drawing the distinction would be pointless if one weren't giving control beliefs a privileged position in one's noetic structure.

I lump these two theories together because they both have the effect of privileging beliefs that are controversial—beliefs that one would have to suspend judgment upon in examining the comparative merits of religious and scientific rationality. Believing that God's goodness or creative power are evident in the contents of perception is not like believing in other minds or the existence of trees and horses, because one does not find the world full of people who sincerely deny the existence of other minds, trees, and horses, but there are many such people who dispute the existence of God. If some beliefs are more certain than others, then it is fitting that they be more immune from revision, or given an enhanced epistemological status, but Wolterstorff nowhere argues that fundamental religious beliefs are more certain or better grounded epistemologically than the beliefs they are used to regulate. Rather, he justifies their control function in terms of our commitment to them rather than in terms of their evidence, but this kinds of move makes

---

16–93 (Univ. of Notre Dame Press, 1983).

[8] *Reason within the Bounds of Religion,* 2nd ed. (Grand Rapids, MI: Eerdman's, 1984), pp. 70–84.

an investigation into the rationality of such commitments effectively impossible. Nor can one easily ascribe objective *certainty* to the existence of God without maintaining that nonbelievers are simply obstinate, irrational, and/or immoral in failing to recognize it. Although this may be true of individual cases, it seems implausible as a general rule.

The Link Between God and Explanation

I accept as a kernel of truth in Anselm's ontological argument for the existence of God that it would be more appropriate to attach the word 'God' to some entity that exists in reality than to something that exists in the understanding alone, no matter how wonderful the latter may seem. Still, prior usage in the Western tradition constrains the kinds of real entities that can qualify as God. Thus, it seems necessary to restrict our discussion of God to entities satisfying five conditions:

> immateriality
> intelligence
> ability to act
> creator of the world
> worthiness for worship.

If no entity satisfies all of these, then there is no God.

From the foregoing, it should be evident that I also treat God as a theoretical entity, a view that Plantinga has worked hard to depopularize. If it is not self-evident that a particular experience is a perception of God or caused by God, but a matter of inferential relations among other beliefs, then drawing such a conclusion will always involve a modicum of interpretation. If one had no prior experience of God, and if prior experience were the only basis for interpreting one's perceptions, one would *never* be able to draw the conclusion that God caused or was the object of a particular experience. But this same epistemic predicament would also apply to tables and chairs—anything that has ever been experienced for a first time. Hence there must be some latitude for going beyond the evidence in epistemic contexts, whether in the form of "conjectures and refutations," working hypotheses, or some other means for exploring explanatory possibilities. Perhaps learning through a process of trial and error is at the root of all perceptually based cognition, so that without such inferences one could never generate useful information or expand one's knowledge.

This latitude is what entitles one at least to try out God as a possible explanation for religious experiences. One might posit God as a theoretical entity with such unobservable attributes as omnipotence, omniscience, moral perfection, etc., for the purpose of explanation, whereas one could never justify this on the basis of perception alone.[9] I do not claim that philosophers are mistaken in emphasizing directly perceived aspects of God's existence; if there is a mistake, it is in contrasting these with explanatory and theoretical aspects of God's existence. The contrast is inspired by the positivistic distinction between observational entities and theoretical entities (1.2.4), according to which the latter are not directly observed but are posited in order to explain directly observed effects. This dichotomy is no more tenable than other positivistic dichotomies, however. One cannot truly perceive God unless the existence of God is part of the explanation of the perception, any more than one can perceive a tree if the tree is not part of the explanation of the perception. Hence, making God observable is insufficient to deny God explanatory status, or make cognitive values that apply directly to explanations inapplicable in religious contexts. Moreover, once God's explanatory status is recognized, a theory of God's nature is inevitably necessary to give substance to the resulting explanations, and much of God's nature is not directly perceivable even if God is. Whether one prefers omnipotence, omniscience, and moral perfection; or ability to act, intelligence, and goodness, most of God's defining properties are unobservable.

Perhaps the existence of God is the best explanation for some religious experiences, although this is not a claim I intend to argue for herein. I do maintain that it would not be rational to postulate God as the best explanation if one did not also consider other potentially undermining explanatory possibilities. Otherwise, in one's quest to acquire information one would have forfeited the capacity to recognize errors, or avoid falling into them. In other words, if it is necessary to make a trade-off between the need to acquire information and to avoid error in any epistemic context, as recent work in naturalistic epistemology suggests (chapter 2), the rationality of such a trade-off still depends on neither of these desiderata being shortchanged. This is why one cannot simply dismiss a competing hypothesis, such as that nothing more than a drug-induced hallucination is involved, by saying as does C. D. Broad, "One might need to be slightly 'cracked' in order to have some peep-hole into the super-sensible world."[10] This may sometimes be

---

[9] I am not sure that any logical sense can be made of 'omniscience' or 'omnipotence', or whether a more backed-off conceptualization of God wouldn't be preferable in any case, but this is not a major thrust of the present work.

[10] "Arguments for the Existence of God, II," *Journal of Theological Studies* 40 (1939): 164.

true, but when it isn't, how are we to discover that fact? We must take seriously the possibility that particular religious explanations are unfounded and lead to erroneous inferences.

Nevertheless, this brings us back to the original point that when different value systems become involved in evaluating proposed explanations, they may not yield a univocal result. I doubt that a mere oversight caused God to be left out of the scientific explanatory scheme, or that it happened only because scientists are irrational or stubborn, even if, like everyone else, they sometimes are. Explanations invoking religious entities do not harmonize well with the scientific value structure, since God is supernatural while scientific values embody the desideratum that explanations be given in naturalistic terms.

Concluding Remarks

We have already touched upon topics of religious belief, religious experience, religious explanation, and theism. Each is intimately related to the others in religious epistemology, however the focus of what follows will be on religious explanation. This is not because it is the most important of these topics so much as because it is the most neglected, in spite of its amenability to treatment by analytical methods. Contrary to an all-too-widespread view, religious explanations are not merely an intellectualist corruption of religious practice. Their successful competition with other explanations under suitably designed ground rules can yield reason for belief in God, even as belief in a theistic God would naturally lead one to proffer religious explanations. They open the door to the possibility of a rational basis for religious practice, from which both religion and our understanding of religion can profit.

A note on the system of parenthetical references employed herein: decimal numbers in parentheses refer to sections of this book that discuss the topic in more detail; whole numbers in parentheses are page references to some other book or article being discussed. A previous footnote within the same section or subsection identifies explicitly which work this is.

CHAPTER 1

EXPLANATIONS IN SCIENCE

1.1 INTRODUCTION

The goal of this study is to determine whether and to what extent explanations of matters of fact employing religious premises can satisfy reasonable criteria of adequacy stemming from a normative account of explanation. "Religious premises" will be limited herein to those invoking the existence of God. Since this study is primarily philosophical—not historical, psychological, or anthropological—I examine the topic normatively rather than descriptively. That is, I am not content to catalogue religious practices with respect to giving explanations, or analyze how the term 'religious explanation' is customarily used. Customary practice or usage may be defective. Not all proposed explanations are equally good or worthy of acceptance, and I want to distinguish those that are not from those that are.

A normative account of explanation need not have universal pretensions. Universalist accounts hold that there is some feature (e.g., unification or causation) common to all legitimate explanations, by virtue of which they are explanatory. Such accounts may also maintain that a uniquely correct explanation exists for any event or why-question. If one were to ask, for example, "Why did President Kennedy die?" a universalist might not credit such explanations as, "A bullet pierced his skull," or "Lee Harvey Oswald shot him to death" as all legitimate or equally legitimate. I do not pretend to offer a universalist account, but follow a pluralistic approach. In other words, I find these explanations satisfactory, but still wish to rule out such explanations as: "The South wanted to put its man in the White House," or

"The planets were in a very inauspicious alignment." Pluralism does not mean "anything goes."

Having a normative account requires having some principled means of distinguishing adequate explanations from inadequate ones. Although there exists no completely satisfactory way to draw this distinction in practice, to a first approximation adequate explanations are based on theories that are reasonably well-established or have a viable claim to truth, and are constructed in accordance with a method having a track record of reliability, or a good chance of developing one. For example, there is a tradition of explaining any and all events by saying "God willed it," or by invoking God wherever there is a gap in our secular knowledge. It is doubtful that all such "God of the gaps" explanations are true, but even if they were this method would encourage the construction of explanations independently of any theories or evidence that might help one discriminate the will of God. Its tendency to squelch more productive and informative avenues of inquiry is undesirable pragmatically, nor would many religious people follow this method in attributing evil events or sinful actions to the will of God. So heading in this direction would start us off on the wrong foot.

The human enterprise that furnishes the greatest number and highest quality of explanations is science, hence when philosophers seek standards of acceptability for explanations they often look to science as an example to be imitated. In so doing it is customary to "dress up" science normatively by way of *rational reconstruction.* That is, one does not just want to describe how scientists give explanations, but to say how they do it *when on their best behavior.* If religious explanations could fit the same patterns as the best scientific explanations, there would be no question of their adequacy, however most agree that the best religious explanations fall short of this ideal. This fact in itself does not imply that religious explanations are never legitimate. A primary focus of this book is on many considerations that weigh in favor of broadening our standards of legitimacy beyond the scientific ideal—i.e., I claim that some nonscientific genres of explanation should be taken seriously. But let us start by restricting our attention to scientific explanations, or the explanations that approach closest to the ideal.

'Religion' itself is a word that covers a variety of sins. Where in religion ought one to look for explanations? It seems inappropriate to call on the traditions of natural theology, since the conceptions of God that usually result from this approach are not easily connected to particular states of affairs in the world, although they have resulted in many interesting arguments attempting to prove either the existence or nonexistence of the God thus conceived. A more naturalistic approach would explain in developmental terms why people brought up in a culture pervaded by belief in God come to believe in God themselves, and apparently are justified in so doing.[11] The purpose of this essay is neither to argue that God exists nor to explain why people give religious explanations. The former is more a question of evidence rather than explanation, whereas the latter is not a religious explanation at all (it does not invoke the existence of God), but a naturalistic explanation of a religious practice. Plenty of books argue the evidence for or against God, and I see no need to rehearse the arguments here. My task also is not to explain anything, but to examine the adequacy of proposed explanatory practices. So it seems necessary to turn to revealed theology, or religious experience in its broadest construal, as a source of explanatory practices to reconstruct. Explanations grow out of experience it seems, and the most parallels between theology and science are also found here. Like most who offer religious explanations, I conceive God as an agent who directly affects the world, at least occasionally, in a way that is out of the ordinary.

The first order of business, however, is to turn to the sciences and the difficulties attending normative accounts of explanation. In this chapter two general models of scientific explanation will be set forth, with some discussion of their details and implications. Examples will also be given illustrating the kinds of constraints and desiderata commonly used to argue the adequacy of explanations, and specific patterns of explanation relevant to later chapters will be introduced. One terminological note before proceeding: I try to avoid arcane slur-words such as 'pseudoexplanation' for explanations that fail to meet reasonable tests of adequacy. Thus, I use 'explanation' and 'adequate explanation' interchangeably except when the context makes it clear that finer distinctions are needed, following the tradition that inadequate explanations really aren't explanations at all.

1.2 THE D-N MODEL AND ITS PROBLEMS

Explanation came into its own as an area of philosophical inquiry with the introduction of the Deductive-Nomological (D-N) model by Carl Hempel and Paul Oppenheim in 1948. Although deeply flawed and much maligned, this model has been remarkably durable as a standard account of explanation because of its simplicity and intuitive appeal. Discussing the D-N model here

---

[11] See, for example, Michael Arbib and Mary Hesse, *The Construction of Reality* (Cambridge Univ. Press, 1986).

will call attention to the intuitions upon which most subsequent philosophical work on the subject has been based, and once these intuitions are in hand, they may be applied directly in evaluating specific explanations.

On the D-N account an *explanation* (*any* explanation, since it is a universalist account) consists of (1) an *explanandum,* or sentence describing the event or state of affairs to be explained, and (2) an *explanans,* or set of sentences being offered to account for it. The explanans can be further divided into (a) factual statements describing boundary conditions C_1, C_2, ..., C_m, and (b) one or more universally quantified theoretical statements or *covering laws* L_1, L_2, ..., L_n, all of which jointly entail the explanandum.[12] A reductive explanation (5.3) that merely accounts for one law in terms of another may contain no statements of type (a), but Hempel and Oppenheim insisted that all explanations contain at least one statement of type (b), and made it clear that the law must be essential to the entailment relation for the explanation to be adequate—hence the D-N model is often referred to as "the covering-law model." Two noteworthy facts about the D-N account are its argumentative, linguistic structure—what is being explained is a sentence rather than an event, since explanation is deduction—and that it ignores contextual factors, such as the circumstances in which explanations are sought. Speech acts associated with asking and answering questions, and the explanation's relation to anyone's beliefs or knowledge are also ignored. In fact, D-N explanations must meet only one empirical criterion of adequacy: the statements in the explanans must all be true.

1.2.1 Some Initial Objections and Rebuttals
The D-N account fails in many ways, but I will focus only on its most significant shortcomings. These include:

    (1) the level of idealization at which the model deals with explanation
    (2) the lack of safeguards against irrelevance
    (3) the asymmetry of causal laws which has no counterpart in entailment relations
    (4) the requirement that the statements in the explanans be true
    (5) the implied conception of science in terms of product rather than a process
    (6) the syntactic conception of scientific theories implicit in the covering-law concept.

In its defense, the D-N model was not intended to capture all worthwhile explanations, however universal its pretensions. The reasoning was roughly

---

[12] "Studies in the Logic of Explanation," *Philosophy of Science* 15 (1948): 135–75. Page references herein are to the reprinted version in Hempel's *Aspects of Scientific Explanation* (New York: Free, 1965).

that it would be a major accomplishment to explicate a broad class of explanations well, even if the model needs supplementation by other models. Thus, Hempel denied that it is an objection to his model that it does not include the kinds of explanations one gives to a Yugoslav auto mechanic of what is wrong with one's car (413). Hempel and Oppenheim also acknowledged in their original paper that a supplementary model would be needed for statistical explanations—explanations in which the relation of explanans to explanandum is probabilistic rather than deductive. A perfectly good explanation of why a person is Lutheran may be that she is Norwegian and most Norwegians are Lutheran. But this is not a basis for *deducing* that the person is Lutheran, since it only renders the conclusion probable.

Another common objection is that the D-N model sanctions many trivial or vacuous explanations. To the question "Why do the rails of a railroad appear to converge in the distance?" the D-N model permits the answer "Railroad tracks *always* appear to converge in the distance." Such explanations are uninformative, and a more useful story can be told about how this effect arises in the perceptual process that reduces a three-dimensional world to a two-dimensional retinal image. Note the similarity of these objections to those previously raised for "God willed it" explanations. In fairness, the D-N model also sanctions the fuller stories, and merely fails to address questions of degrees of adequacy, or which explanation is most appropriate in particular circumstances. Anyone who doesn't like the first answer can always force a more detailed one by asking again, "Well, why do railroad tracks *always* appear to converge in the distance?" Hence this seems less an objection to what the D-N model does than to what it leaves undone.

Most of the objections to the D-N account cannot be so easily defused, however—a fact that gains added significance by the positivist dynamic within which the model was offered. The purpose underlying the positivistic practice of *explication* was to take a vaguely-defined, haphazard practice and find some way of representing the essentials of it in a clear and precise "regimented" vocabulary assimilable within first-order predicate logic. The goal was to replace obscure and ambiguous talk about the world with clear and precise talk about language—i.e., words displace the world as the center of attention—in the belief that many philosophical conundrums may thereby be avoided. Philosophers imputed enough importance to this goal to excuse proposed explications of a great many faults of infidelity. In practice, Hempel's universalist pretensions spoke more loudly than his cavils, and many philosophers assumed henceforth that explanations just *are* sets of statements conforming to the D-N model. This made the easily committed errors of the covering-law model particularly difficult to correct.

1.2.2 Problems of Relevance and Asymmetry

One drawback to the D-N model is its lack of relevance conditions on the sentences in the explanans. Suppose, for example, an explanation employs the covering law 'If *L* and *C*, then *E*', and suppose that *B* stands for Kierkegaard's statement (coined to make fun of those who objectify truth as a value), "Bang, the earth is round." It seems that 'If *L* and *C*, then *E* and *B*' would also be a covering law, and imply everything the original one did, yet intuitively there is something wrong with an explanation of why the car doesn't start that mentions the fact that the earth is round. Pragmatically, irrelevance vitiates explanations because if the person giving the explanation does not know enough about the phenomenon to know what is relevant to it, she probably doesn't understand it well enough to explain it either. Hempel recognized irrelevance as an objection to any explanation, but the pragmatics of explanation resist logical treatment, and his efforts to explicate relevance logically were unsuccessful.[13]

Causal explanations of events are offered so frequently that any model failing to accommodate them would be seriously inadequate, yet the D-N model indeed fails in this respect. Here I assume that causes precede their effects in time and physically necessitate them. Hempel's account models causal necessity with logical necessity—the sentences in the explanans describing the causes are formulated as logically sufficient conditions for the explanandum. The problem is that logical necessity has a symmetry that is not shared by causal necessity. Suppose, for example, that two causally related events could be characterized so that their descriptions are deductively related. In other words, if *p* were the cause of *q*, the effect, then 'If *p* then *q*' would be deductively valid. If it were, then by contraposition one could infer 'If ¬*q* then ¬*p*', but one still could not say that the absence of *q* *caused* the absence of *p* since it did not precede it—hence it also seems incapable of explaining it. The altitude of the sun and the height of the flagpole causes its shadow to have a certain length, and one can deduce that length from the other two values; but one can also deduce the altitude of the sun from the other two values, yet it seems that nothing pertaining to the flagpole is relevant to bringing it about that the sun has the altitude it has, or helps to explain that altitude. From an epistemological standpoint, giving the height of the flagpole and the length of its shadow may explain how one *knows* what the sun's altitude is, and this kind of explanation has its place. But explaining where our knowledge of a phenomenon comes from is distinct from

---

[13] See his *Philosophy of Natural Science* (Prentice-Hall, 1966), pp. 48–9.

explaining the phenomenon itself. Science's success in the latter endeavor is what theories of explanation normally aim to capture.

1.2.3 The Requirement of Truth

The D-N model's empirical condition of adequacy—that the statements in the explanans be true—has also been criticized as overly restrictive. Newton's laws cannot be true, strictly speaking, since they have been superseded by Einstein's theories of relativity, yet they continue to function explanatorily in science as well as in common sense. It has been argued in Hempel's defense that (i) the D-N model does not attempt to account for informal discourse; and (ii) the fact that Newton's laws have pedagogical or instructional value is irrelevant to their ultimate status as scientific explanations. When cited by practicing physicists, Newton's laws may be taken elliptically as convenient substitutes for Einstein's more cumbersome equations, and would be replaced by them in a more formal setting or when the difference matters. Such a construal of scientific activity takes on quite an other-worldly air of what would or could be done if it were necessary—although somehow it never is. But where does this leave all of the explanations given in terms of Newton's laws during the 250 years prior to Einstein? What if Einstein's theories turn out not to be true either? We would be unable to distill out of all of the accomplishments of modern mechanics a single genuine scientific explanation!

Several solutions have been proposed for this problem, none entirely adequate. One could say that the D-N model merely sets an ideal for explanations, and whether anything actually realizes it is not important. This was the approach Hempel and Oppenheim took in their original paper, denying both the truth of Newton's theories, and the adequacy of explanations based on them (248). But this takes much of the normative force out of their account, given the dictum often attributed to Kant that 'ought' implies 'can'. If one cannot achieve this ideal of truth, why ought one try? If truth is a regulative ideal that can be "looked to from any distance," then one will be unable to rule out, say, religious explanations that look to it from a greater distance than scientific explanations. Yet ruling out "pseudoexplanations" was a primary motivation for the Hempelian model. Alternatively, one could relativize truth to whatever is widely accepted as true at a given time—i.e., interpret truth merely in terms of coherence rather than correspondence to reality. One might even drop the term 'truth' and replace it with 'warranted assertibility'. This approach is complicated by the difficulty of specifying non-arbitrarily whose acceptance is important. Without such a specification, it lacks normative force or philosophical interest; hence it is more common to seek some middle ground between truth *simpliciter* and coherence or assertibility. Some realists follow Karl Popper in replacing the requirement of truth with a requirement of approximate truth or *verisimilitude,* another concept that has proven notoriously difficult to explicate. On the other hand, the anti-realist Bas van Fraassen requires truth only of the theory's observable consequences, being more lenient otherwise. This move still would not account for the explanatory value that most of us perceive in Newton's laws despite the fact that they are known to be false, both theoretically and observationally. Truth remains a sticking point for theories of explanation.

1.2.4   The Dearth of Laws and Correspondence Rules

The statements in the explanans pertaining to boundary conditions are considered *factual* insofar as they are formulated in an *observational* vocabulary—i.e., with terms such as 'green', 'tree', 'now' whose appropriateness is determinable by observation alone. By contrast, statements of laws are usually formulated in a *theoretical* vocabulary, and their truth is more difficult to ascertain. It is now widely recognized that no sharp dichotomy exists between theoretical and observational language, yet the distinction between facts and theories remains a useful way to call attention to different degrees of epistemic transparency. Having distinct observational and theoretical vocabularies makes it difficult, however, to draw deductive inferences combining both, as D-N explanations were meant to do. One must supplement the explanans with correspondence rules or bridge principles linking the languages, usually by giving observational criteria for the application of a law's theoretical terms. Suppose, for example, one wished to use Newton's second law, $f = ma,$ to explain the motion of a projectile. If one starts with the law and the observational record, one still must relate what was seen and heard to the values of m and a in the equation; otherwise one cannot *deduce* the motion from the observations and theories. But there is no standardized way of doing this in practice, nor has any adequate account of bridge principles ever been given. Worse, no such principles have ever been formulated explicitly, let alone employed by scientists. Since the D-N account is ostensibly normative, one can't help wondering whether science really ought to proceed in this way. A common response is that these pragmatic concerns have no ultimate epistemic import—what matters is that correspondence rules could *in principle* be given. But if they aren't in practice, perhaps there are "principled" or normatively forceful reasons why. The otherworldliness of positivism turns many of its tenets into articles of faith—ironic for a movement founded on the principle that positive knowledge ought to replace every kind of faith, opinion, or speculation.

The major normative work of the D-N account lies in the requirement that every explanation include at least one law, which among other things must be a universally quantified statement making no explicit reference to particular persons, times or places. Positivists sometimes cited this requirement to argue that psychological, evolutionary, and social scientific theories are not really scientific at all.[14] But this requirement is so stringent that it would make much of geology, astronomy, and other "hard" sciences unscientific as well. It seems there aren't enough universal laws to go around—one must repeatedly fall back on ceteris paribus generalizations—statements that purport to be true only "other things being equal." Nancy Cartwright points out that even these may not be literally true "other things being equal," but only if other things are *just right*.[15] So again we come up short: where we hoped to find normativity we find only a non-normative idealization.

1.2.5 Idealizations and Practice

To sum up, what began as a normative account of scientific explanation has strayed in many ways into a highly idealized account whose normative value is questionable. By 'idealized' I mean that many simplifying assumptions were made that are not literally true and cumulatively exert a profoundly distorting effect on the philosophy of explanation. Let's recall what these non-normative idealizations include:

> correspondence rules or bridge principles
> the explanandum as a linguistic entity
> explanatory adequacy as all-or-nothing, rather than having degrees
> truth
> relevance
> deduction as a model of causation
> the unimportance of contextual factors
> the unimportance of psychological, pragmatic, and other nonlogical considerations
> the requirement that explanations employ universally quantified laws.

While I cite Kant's 'ought' implies 'can' dictum to illustrate their non-normativity, ultimately my claim that they lack normative force is independent of any commitment to Kant. Granted, simplifying assumptions are essential

---

[14] This view has been defended as recently as 1980 by Alexander Rosenberg, *Sociobiology and the Preemption of Social Science* (Johns Hopkins Univ. Press). See also his "Fitness," *Journal of Philosophy* 80 (1983): 457–73; and Mary Williams and Alexander Rosenberg, "'Fitness' in Fact and Fiction: A Rejoinder to Sober," *Journal of Philosophy* 82 (1985): 738–49.

[15] *How the Laws of Physics Lie* (Oxford: Clarendon Press, 1983), pp. 45–52.

to giving any straightforward account of explanation at all. My point is that the D-N model's excessive level of idealization makes it so stylized an account of science as to approach total irrelevance to scientific explanatory practice. Instead of "dressing up" science so as to bring out its normative essence, the D-N model has altered its essence. Treating considerations as unimportant for the sake of clarity or ease of analysis has yet another undesirable effect: it encourages people to think they really *are* unimportant, when oftentimes they are not.

The foregoing argumentation may be lost on any reader who doubts that a better way exists, so it is to describing such a way that I now turn. Others may prefer to skip the next section, which is the most technical in the whole book.

1.3   WHAT IS A SCIENTIFIC THEORY?

Patrick Suppes asked this question in an article by the same name in which he gave one of the earlier formulations of what has come to be known as the structuralist, or *semantic view*.[16] The then prevailing view was that a scientific theory is an axiomatized, deductively closed set of sentences within a formal language, plus a set of coordinating definitions giving empirical content to the language's non-logical vocabulary. Under the "received" or *syntactic view,* membership of any given sentence in the theory is determined syntactically using its axioms and the logical calculus. If this is what a theory is, then it makes more sense to think of explanations as proofs or deductive arguments, as in the D-N account. But we saw that this conception is highly idealized, nor has any scientific theory ever been fully cast in syntactic form, nor would any apparent purpose be served in doing so. Again, the coordinating definitions that connect one vocabulary with another prove particularly difficult to characterize, yet it is only by virtue of these that theories are *about* empirical phenomena at all. Suppes asks, if coordinating

---

[16]   Patrick Suppes, "What is a Scientific Theory?" in *Philosophy of Science Today,* ed. by Morgenbesser, 55–67 (New York: Basic, 1967). The semantic view has also had Sneed, Wolfgang Stegmüller, Bas van Fraassen, and Fred Suppe among its advocates—see Stegmüller, *The Structure and Dynamics of Theories* (Berlin: Springer, 1976), and *The Structuralist View of Theories* (Berlin: Springer, 1979); van Fraassen, "A Formal Approach to the Philosophy of Science," in *Paradigms and Paradoxes,* ed. by Colodny, 303–66 (Univ. of Pittsburgh Press, 1972); Suppe, *The Semantic Conception of Theories and Scientific Realism* (Univ. of Illinois Press, 1989).

definitions count as part of the theory, why not include the standard statistical methods for testing it, or its experimental design methodology?

Under the semantic view, theories are taken simply to *be* models, typically mathematical.[17] Whatever sentences the model satisfies are the true sentences of the theory. Thus, first order quantificational logic, or metamathematics, is replaced by mathematics as the vehicle through which theories are formulated. The principal virtues of this approach, according to Bas van Fraassen, are its naturalness and the fact that it is truer to scientific practice, or requires fewer idealizations.[18] By itself, mathematics contains no reference to the world, so the semantic view conceives the commerce of science in terms of *theoretical hypotheses* to the effect that such-and-such a theory can be applied in particular circumstances, or is isomorphic with some substructure of the world. What science gives us, then, are a number of models and a range of applications for them. When applying a given model to real phenomena in the world, rather than concerning oneself with translating a theoretical language into observational terms, one effectively looks for "isomorphisms" between the two—structure-preserving one-to-one maps. Reductions of one theory to another are constructed in the same fashion.

When speaking of models in this context, one might imagine the styrofoam balls and wooden sticks chemists sometimes use to "model" molecular structures—indeed, it is hoped that these are isomorphic in some sense to the molecular structures found in nature. But such concreteness is not typical of the models that the semantic view equates with theories. For example, interactions among gas molecules are sometimes compared to colliding billiard balls, but the function of such a comparison is primarily heuristic rather than theoretical. Billiard balls are a useful way of thinking about rigid body motion, but the theoretical work is done by assumptions of non-deformation, elastic recoil, energy conservation, angle of incidence equal to angle of reflection—all of which are more appropriately expressed in mathematical equations rather than visual images. 'Isomorphism' itself is a mathematical concept. The semantic view is a general reconception of this theoretical

---

[17] There are actually two versions of the semantic view, and whether the models are to be understood as theoretical models or models in the sense of model theory depends on the version of the semantic view being used—see Edward MacKinnon, "Scientific Realism: The New Debates," *Philosophy of Science* 46 (1979): 501–32. Herein I assume that the models are theoretical in accordance with the state space version of the semantic view. Not all theoretical models need be mathematical, nor does the view require them to be.

[18] "Empiricism in the Philosophy of Science," in *Images of Science,* ed. by Churchland and Hooker (Univ. of Chicago Press, 1985), p. 302.

work as primarily mathematical rather than logical. It would have the theory underlying the population dynamics of rabbits and lynx be given by a pair of simultaneous differential equations and appropriate boundary conditions rather than by first order logic, and similarly for the linear harmonic oscillator and other scientific theories.

To understand how the semantic view relates to the syntactic view, one can think of a theory qua model as a direct specification of what a system is and what is true of it—a representation of a theory in terms of its "meaning" or truth structure. There corresponds to any syntactically formulated theory a set of all the models that satisfy it, known as its elementary class. Models, in turn, can be defined in terms of the linguistic structures that they satisfy. Given that the two are interdefinable, why prefer one over the other? Any linguistic structure sufficient to axiomatize elementary number theory (which most theories are) admits of "unnatural models," following the Skolem-Löwenheim Theorem. Insofar as science in practice formulates its theories by specifying models, any syntactic formulation will be satisfied not only by the *intended* model, but also by a lot of other unwanted, extraneous models. The semantic view thus suppresses a lot of extraneous "stuff" that the syntactic view would import into its reconstruction of scientific theories and practice. Moreover, under the syntactic view, any change in linguistic formulation constitutes a change in the theory itself, but with the semantic view one can change the domain of application of a theory or model without necessarily changing the model itself. With no predetermined range of applications built in, questions of extrapolation or generalization are left open, permitting greater flexibility in treating scientific discourse.

If the semantic view is such a great idea, why wasn't it around in the heyday of philosophy of science? The traditional objection was to the unclarity of "intended" models, or "meaning" structures. During the first half of this century Russell's paradoxes showed that serious unclarity can exist even in mathematics, from which only the vigorous application of first order logic saved it. But the development of mathematics since then has proven remarkably unproblematic, while logical reconstructions have often created more problems than they solved. Insofar as clarity-minded scientists prefer to cast their theories in mathematical rather than metamathematical terms, and this continues to work well in practice, the fears of traditional logical empiricists now seem exaggerated.

1.3.1 How the Semantic View Broadens our Concept of Science
A model of an individual system, such as the earth's crust in plate tectonics, could constitute an acceptable theoretical account on the semantic view. The

traditional conception of laws as universally quantified statements prohibits the use of singular terms such as 'earth', however. The rationale for this is that scientific laws should not be formulated for Mary or Joe but for people in general, or perhaps a subgroup of people characterizable in terms of predicates or "universals" rather than only by names referring to individuals. However well-meant this rationale may be, the fact remains that we are not in a position to arrive at universal laws applicable to all tectonically active planets, since this would require extrapolating "inductively" from a single instance. Generality may be worth striving for, and geologists do attempt to incorporate as much generality in their models as possible, but there are limits to what can be accomplished.

Logical positivists followed David Hume in using universal generalizations to model causation, but geologists do not need proof-theoretic analyses of causal language to build causal structures into their theoretical models. How can causes be known or modeled apart from universal generalization? Consider an instance of a hammer shattering a piece of glass.[19] Without presupposing knowledge about hammers or glass, the mere coincidence of the glass shattering at the precise moment that the hammer strikes it would lead one to suspect that the hammer caused it. If the glass had not broken until five seconds after the hammer made contact, one would be more inclined to look for other causes, and if it had broken five seconds beforehand one would feel quite certain that the hammer could *not* have caused it. But it would seem quite miraculous that the glass shattered precisely when the hammer struck it, if no causal relationship were involved. This is part-and-parcel of our intuitive understanding of causation.

So far nothing has been said about the universal laws or necessary and sufficient conditions for glass breakage resulting from hammer impact. This shows that universal laws do not have epistemic priority over their instances, regardless of ontological priority. By manipulating hammers and pieces of glass one can quickly learn enough to draw some interesting counterfactual conclusions about related situations, but this knowledge may not fall out neatly in the form of universally quantified statements, especially given that many additional variables would have to be considered. Generalized statements require replacing mention of this particular hammer and piece of glass with general terms—i.e., placing individuals into reference classes. That

---

[19] The idea for this example is due to James Woodward, "Are Singular Causal Explanations Implicit Covering-Law Explanations?" *Canadian Journal of Philosophy* 16 (1986): 268-9. For more on the inadequacies of the Humean or regularity view of causation, see Nancy Cartwright, *Nature's Capacities and their Measurement* (Oxford: Clarendon Press, 1989).

could be done in myriad ways, each resulting in different formulations of the laws involved, which on the syntactic view thereby amount to different theories. Does a wooden mallet count as a hammer? Does the law apply to safety glass? Modeling directly the causal and counterfactual knowledge obtained for the system at hand is less problematic epistemologically, because it can focus on prototypical cases while leaving borderline cases for later.

Note also that manipulation is not essential for acquiring this knowledge, even though it is an especially efficient means. Geologists cannot manipulate crustal plates, but with systematic observations and measurements they can still model causal structures and interactions. Theoretical models of this kind are frequently offered in geology, biology,[20] and the social sciences, but the received or syntactic view sees only the absence of universally quantified statements in ruling them out as pseudoscience. I see no point in haggling over the extension of the word 'science', but why discard a valuable source of knowledge because it fails to live up to an ideal that is not necessary or practicable?

What does it mean to say that the relevant causal factors can be built directly into the model? Consider the following equation modeling the motion of a pendulum: $T = 2\pi(L/g)^{1/2}$ where L is length, T the period of oscillation, and g the acceleration due to gravity at the earth's surface. Although some might deny that this is a causal law strictly speaking, since it is not a transition law, this equation does identify a causal relationship between the length of the pendulum, the force of gravity, and the period of oscillation, and tells us counterfactually how T would change as the others vary. In the above "standard" formulation the equation also permits one to read off dependent and independent variables—i.e., it permits one to determine which variables function as effects and causes—recapturing the causal asymmetry of pendulum motion.

1.3.2 How the Semantic View Affects our Concept of Explanation
How does reconstruing theories as models affect our ability to give explanations? First note that not all models are explanatory—only those identifying causal factors that can support counterfactual inferences. Ptolemy's model of planetary motion was particularly weak in this regard. It gave values for many parameters but was silent on what would happen if the system were perturbed (which nobody thought possible). But in the above case one can

---

[20] See Paul Thompson, "The Structure of Evolutionary Theory: A Semantic Approach," *Studies in the History and Philosophy of Science* 14 (1983): 215–29; Gregory Cooper, "Fitness and Explanation," *PSA 1988* 1: 207–215.

give an explanation of why the glass shattered by saying that the hammer broke it, and be as informative and more likely to be true than the D-N model's "Glass always breaks when struck by a hammer." Knowing what caused the glass to break is not knowing how it caused it, of course. If one wants to know what gives hammers the capacity to break glass, more theory would be necessary, but again it could as well be in the form of a model of the composition of glass and steel and their causal interactions, rather than in the form of universally quantified statements about them.

The semantic view forces some revisions in our account of explanation. Truth values are not a property of models themselves but of the theoretical hypotheses applying them to real-world systems. Even these aren't always judged by their truth. Suppose, for example, that a ladder stands on a frictionless surface leaning against a smooth vertical wall. The foot begins to slide away from the wall. At what angle will the ladder's acquired momentum cause the top of the ladder to leave the wall? LaGrange's formulation of Newtonian mechanics provides the most natural means of conceiving this phenomenon and grounds explanations of it. Yet in reality we do not have frictionless surfaces and Newton's laws are not strictly speaking true, so how do we account for the angles at which the tops of real ladders leave real walls? Cartwright offers what she calls a "simulacrum" account of explanation according to which one singles out the form of the explanation without its content.[21] The model in this case provides the formal mathematics for describing what happens, but constitutes only the beginning of an explanation. To flesh it out, note: (i) if the surface didn't have a low coefficient of static friction, the ladder wouldn't fall; (ii) the coefficient of dynamic friction is what is relevant once the sliding starts, and is less than the static coefficient, so there are reasons for expecting the effect of friction in realistic cases to be manageably small—that is why the assumption of frictionless surfaces is not otiose; (iii) the velocities involved are small compared to c, so the departure of Newton's laws from the presumably true relativistic ones is negligible. Finally, (iv) deviations between the modeled and observed values can themselves be modeled by continuous functions. In other words, if there is only a slight amount of friction, one would expect only a slight discrepancy between the theoretical and observed values—a situation that does not always hold in quantum mechanics and nonlinear dynamics. This permits one to speak of Newton's equations as representing a limiting case, and helps substantiate their explanatory relevance. Ultimately,

---

[21] *How the Laws of Physics Lie,* pp. 152–3. Page references herein are to this work.

a fully adequate scientific explanation can be elaborated by proceeding in this manner.

Cartwright's simulacrum account is itself a theory of explanation without any content, since it fails to address the fundamental question, "By virtue of what is a scientific explanation explanatory?" Is it by virtue of an argumentative or deductive structure, or by fitting a particular phenomenon into a general pattern, or by providing causal laws, or by showing that the phenomenon to be explained was necessary under the circumstances? What her view does is open the door to a certain amount of pluralism, in that more than one model will often be applicable in a given situation. Alternative models may lead to divergent predictions that can be used to decide which is most appropriate in particular circumstances, but the result need not be confirmation or disconfirmation in any straightforward sense. Rather, one ends up circumscribing the particular kinds of situations for which a given model is an appropriate explanatory or predictive tool (135–6). Indeed, models are often designed around specific intended applications—science tolerates much more ad hocness than positivists countenanced—since, as Cartwright has it, scientists prefer to keep the total number of theoretical models small while making more liberal use of corrections, modifications, and other "tailoring" devices to fit them to particular situations (139).

Our purposes do not require having answers to the above questions either, so long as we understand explanation as involving fitting particular events into an "appropriate" theoretical model. In chapter 7 we will begin constructing a religious model of this kind; the intervening chapters ground this endeavor by unpacking some considerations that affect appropriateness.

1.4   THE VIRTUES OF THEORIES

An explanation is no better than the theory upon which it is based, and in science theories are evaluated roughly in terms of their empirical adequacy. To a first approximation, an empirically adequate theory is one that "saves the phenomena," which means that it must be consistent with what is known about the observable world. In particular, the theory's empirical substructures must be isomorphic with the appearances themselves. Van Fraassen holds that producing empirically adequate theories is the overarching goal of all scientific theorizing.[22] For *his* theory to be "empirically adequate," most

---

[22] *The Scientific Image* (Oxford: Clarendon Press, 1980), pp. 12, 64.

of the desiderata that scientists seek in theories must be components of empirical adequacy. These include explanatory power, testability, simplicity, consilience, and applicability to novel phenomena, or ability to issue novel predictions. Van Fraassen segregates these virtues from those of evidential support and other factors that make a theory more likely to be true, referring to the latter as *confirmational virtues* and the former as *informational virtues.*[23] What makes them "virtues"? On van Fraassen's account, they give us more reason to *accept* a theory, but confirmational virtues do so because of their epistemic value, whereas informational virtues do so because of their pragmatic value.

Consider an example due to Cartwright:

　(U)　Undergraduate women will be allowed to live off campus as of age 21.

A rumor that circulated at the University of Pittsburgh in 1963, *U* seemed highly incredible at the time, until the explanation came out:

　(V)　[*U* is true] because the university is in a difficult situation from having overadmitted undergraduates.

Because *V* makes *U* intelligible, *V* seems more probable on the face of it than *U* does by itself. But *V* also implies *U*, so it is impossible that *V be* more likely than *U*. In other words, there are ways of making *U* true even though *V* is false—the university might have other reasons for instituting such a policy—but not vice versa, so *U* cannot be less probable than *V*. Undoubtedly *V* has more explanatory value than *U*, but van Fraassen argues that the added value in *V* is not epistemic but pragmatic—it makes up for our lack of imagination and our consequent unwillingness to test or believe *U* when it stands alone. His point is that explanation primarily has informative, pragmatic value rather than epistemic value. If all one wants to do is maximize the likelihood that what one says is true, the most prudent policy would be to offer no explanations at all.[24]

---

[23] "Glymour on Evidence and Explanation," in *Testing Scientific Theories,* ed. by Earman (Univ. of Minnesota Press, 1983), pp. 165–76. See also "Empiricism in the Philosophy of Science."

[24] Elliott Sober (*Simplicity* (Oxford: Clarendon Press, 1975), pp. 33, 166) draws a similar distinction between "informativeness" and "support," equating safety with emphasis on the latter, or with refusing to go beyond the mere evidence and its deductive consequences. See also Larry Laudan, *Progress and its Problems* (Univ. of California Press, 1977).

Van Fraassen's analysis of the problem is somewhat controversial, but his general point seems correct that different kinds of criteria go into the evaluation of scientific explanations. If the distinction is not always sharp, still most philosophers will grant that some criteria—say, simplicity or testability—are more pragmatically oriented, whereas others—such as evidential support—are more directly tied to the truth or likelihood of a hypothesis. Why should a hypothesis be more likely to be true just because it is simple? Given the complexity of the real world, one would expect simplicity to count against the likelihood of a hypothesis, if anything. Scientists undeniably value simplicity highly, but they don't value *simplemindedness* highly. Similarly, the verificationist plaint about statements mentioning God being untestable was not primarily meant to impugn their likelihood of truth, but their usefulness in talking about the world.

Outstanding conundrums such as the problem of old vs. novel evidence belie any sharp dichotomy between epistemic and pragmatic considerations. The logical force of evidence seems to be the same whether it was produced before or after the hypothesis was formulated, but in practice novel evidence is always thought to provide more impressive confirmation, presumably because it is easier to accommodate existing evidence than anticipate future evidence. Fitting a curve to existing data points is easier than extrapolating beyond the bounds of current research. The epistemic/pragmatic distinction is no better than other Grand Old Dichotomies (or GODS) of positivism, all of which have suffered partial dissolution at the hands of what Clark Glymour derisively calls the "new fuzziness." I call attention to it here because it remains useful, like the now fuzzy theory/observation, objective/subjective, and fact/value distinctions.

Since the pragmatic or informational virtues of a theory justify some kind of pro-attitude toward it without justifying belief—they would not be *virtues* otherwise—what kind of attitude should it be? Those who acknowledge this distinction typically characterize it as *acceptance* rather than *belief*. That is, the existence of informational virtues gives us reason to accept a theory—say, to act on it as a working hypothesis or useful principle—even though we do not think it any more likely to be true. Some deny this distinction, complaining that '*A* believes *X*' means nothing more than that *A* treats *X* in this way, but such a view seems crudely behavioristic and implies a pragmatic theory of truth that is itself questionable (see 3.4). Moreover, the difference between arm's length acceptance and the warm embrace of belief almost certainly has subtle, behavioral manifestations.

Van Fraassen's analysis illuminates another important fact: in seeking a normative account for scientific explanations, one uncovers more "virtues" or *desiderata,* than absolute conditions of adequacy, or *constraints* (see chapter 3). It would be unrealistic to expect, therefore, that what constraints one does find determine a uniquely best explanation for any given phenomenon. Instead, explanations are often evaluated by ranking them vis-à-vis other proposed explanations for the same phenomenon, on the basis of which satisfies the most desiderata, the most restrictive desiderata, or fits the desiderata "best." The next section illustrates how this is typically done.

1.5 EXPLANATION AND HYPOTHETICO-DEDUCTIVISM

Positivists reconstructed science with the aid of a process/product distinction, following Hans Reichenbach's distinction between the context of discovery and the context of "validation" or justification. Reichenbach reasoned in Popperian fashion that it is impossible to reconstruct rationally how scientific discoveries come about, so the best one can do is account for how the ultimate scientific product is justified. Explanations are a paradigmatic scientific product, so even though the emphasis of contemporary philosophy of science has shifted away from science qua product and toward science qua process, theorists of explanation have been in no hurry to follow suit. I think that looking at science as a process can teach us something about scientific explanation, however. Let me draw an analogy from manufacturing.

If science were viewed as a factory whose output is nothing but explanations, it would be incorrect to think of the explanations as assembled the way automobiles are assembled on a production line, so that the finished product does not appear until the very last step, and the dissimilarity of the intermediate products with the finished product is proportional to the number of production steps between. Rather, the production of explanations is more analogous to the production of computer chips in the semiconductor business, which are manufactured in "one fell swoop," one might say, but with that swoop being inherently unreliable. A great number of chips are thus turned out, which are then extensively tested to determine which are good, the flawed ones being discarded upon discovery. Ontologically speaking, the finished products are present from the first step, and the rest of the process is the epistemic one of identifying them. I say this because something like the hypothetico-deductive method is still widely regarded as a fundamental element of scientific methodology. When confronting a particular problem or puzzle, one starts by proposing virtually any hypothesis which is consistent with the observed phenomena and, if true, would imply or otherwise explain it. There is no reliable means of finding good hypotheses—only rules of thumb. Consequently, most hypotheses are faulty, and a lengthy period of testing is necessary to determine which ones to accept and which to reject.

Like any analogy, this oversimplifies things a bit. Hypotheses do get fitted out with additional features during the testing process, and unlike the semiconductor business, there need be no sharply defined point in science at which the testing process is complete and the product "shipped." Rather, when one asks for a scientific explanation of a phenomenon, the tendency is to trot out the "best" one in stock: one draws an "inference to the best explanation." In a sense, science's product is not simply theories or explanations, but *confidence* that these have withstood considerable scrutiny. But confidence in what—that they are true? As noted, if one wanted to maximize the likelihood of uttering truths, one would not offer explanations at all. However strange it sounds, false statements can be both informative and valuable. So it may not be confidence in truth that is at stake so much as confidence that the explanation will perform satisfactorily in service. Pursuing this analogy, one could say that Newton's theories are not so much faulty as they are obsolete—there are more high-powered theories available and a number of problems on which only they will work. But we still have a high level of confidence in the adequacy of Newton's theories to handle many mundane tasks, just as we have for earlier generations of computer chips.

To distinguish explanations as first proposed from those that finally emerge from the testing process, I propose to call the former *proto-explanations* and reserve 'explanation' without qualification for the latter. In general the explanatory fabrications produced by the hypothetico-deductive method will be proto-explanations until they have undergone significant elaboration and testing. In the next two subsections I illustrate functional and dysfunctional ways in which this works in practice.

1.5.1 TAF[25]

A malignant tumor requires an ample supply of blood in order to grow, so where one observes growing tumors one also finds new blood vessels and capillaries growing, a phenomenon called angiogenesis, or neovascularization. Moses Judah Folkman did experiments in the early 70s showing that when small bits of solid tumors were implanted in the corneas of rabbits (the cornea having no blood vessels), blood vessels would grow out to them from

---

[25] The following account is drawn from Barbara Culliton, "Harvard and Monsanto: The $23-Million Alliance," *Science* 195 (Feb. 25, 1977): 759–63; and Judah Folkman and Michael Klagsbrun, "Angiogenic Factors," *Science* 235 (1987): 442–7.

the iris in a matter of days, after which the tumor would grow rapidly. But the bits remained dormant when implanted in the aqueous humor inside the eyeball, where no blood vessels could reach. Drawing an inference to the best explanation, Folkman hypothesized that some chemical agent was being released by the tumor which is responsible for the growth of blood vessels, and called it 'TAF', for *tumor angiogenesis factor*.

At this point, shall we say that TAF exists? Some competing hypotheses were then losing currency, such as that neovascularization is just an inflammatory reaction, or that tumors make their own vascular channels. So one could say that this hypothesis had some competition, and seemed to offer a better explanation of the phenomenon. But it is still incipient insofar as the history of biochemistry is strewn with various "factors" that were posited at one time or another to explain something, only to be discarded later. One need not say that angiogenesis in the rabbit's cornea is purely coincidental to be skeptical of a particular mechanism proposed for it. But what is TAF except a placeholder? So long as one grants that the effect is genuine and almost certainly has a cause, how can the cause not be TAF? Because such an explanation is so sketchy as to be virtually immune to falsification—a common weakness of bare, existentially quantified statements—I call it a proto-explanation. It may function adequately as a working hypothesis, but it is only a "first stab" at explanation.

Folkman looked for TAF for years without success, until he began to be turned down by peer review boards both for funding and for publication. This led him to withdraw his research from the peer review process and swing a $23-million deal with Monsanto in exchange for the rights to any patentable fruits of his labor. Even with the Monsanto money Folkman was unable to make any headway for another six years, until the discovery that heparin-affinity chromatography could be applied to the candidate factors under study. At that point it soon became apparent that there were a lot of angiogenic factors. Of the more directly active, two were ~140 amino acid polypeptides with a 53% absolute sequence homology, but they turned out to be universally present both in cancerous and normal tissues, much in the way that the substances necessary for blood clotting are universally present, but normally in a "turned off" state. So how do tumors cause angiogenesis? The current view is as follows:

(1) they synthesize and release angiogenic factors themselves—some release more than one factor;
(2) they attract macrophages—"white blood cells" that function in the repair of damaged tissue—and activate them to "release angiogenic activity";

(3) they secrete substances that release angiogenic factors already stored in the extracel-
lular matrix;

(4) they release a vascular permeability factor causing leakage of fibrinogen from post-
capillary venules.[26]

In other words, a variety of substances released by tumors cause angiogenesis, acting through a variety of different pathways. A few steps in these
causal chains have been identified, while others remain unknown.

Scientists would deny that 'TAF' refers to the same thing as do the
terms for these particular factors (a position associated with one form of
metaphysical realism), but one can still say that the original proto-explanation was essentially correct, even though 'TAF' has been dropped from the
lexicon. All the pathways seem to involve substances released by the tumor
in a causal chain leading to angiogenesis. As Ian Hacking would put it,
doing the experiments convinces one that *something* from the tumor must be
releasing angiogenic activity, even though our theory regarding what it is and
how it works may be wrong or inadequate in some ways.[27] We are now
closer to offering genuine, full-fledged explanations for some cases of tumor-
induced angiogenesis, rather than merely proto-explanations.

1.5.2   How-Possibly?   (Olbers' Paradox)

Since Sylvain Bromberger directed attention to why-questions, some philosophers have made them a centerpiece of their theories of explanation.[28] But
what about the inferences to the best explanation that seem directed at how-
possibly questions? In practice, I believe that they can often be accommo-
dated by the why-question format too. Consider: "How could the greatest
battlefield commander in history (Napoleon) lose a battle to inferior forces
on familiar territory (at Waterloo)?" This sounds like a how-possibly question, but finding any answer logically consistent with everything we know

---

[26] Post-capillary venules are the smallest veins through which blood flows immediately after
having passed through the capillaries, on its way back to the heart. (At the other end of the
capillaries one has arterioles.) Fibrinogen is active in blood-clotting, attracts macrophages, and
is related to fibrin which is active in the growth of new blood vessels to repair damaged tissue.

[27] *Representing and Intervening* (Cambridge Univ. Press, 1983), pp. 254ff.; "Experimentation and Scientific Realism," in *Scientific Realism,* ed. by Leplin (Univ. of California Press,
1984), pp. 154–72.

[28] Sylvain Bromberger, "Why-Questions," in *Mind and Cosmos,* ed. by Colodny, 86–111
(Univ. of Pittsburgh Press, 1966); Alan Garfinkel, *Forms of Explanation* (Yale Univ. Press,
1981); Bas van Fraassen, *The Scientific Image,* chapter 5.

about the battle is too easy, and I doubt that we would find an implausible answer satisfying. We really want to know *why* it actually happened.

Consider Olbers' Paradox. After Newtonian cosmology replaced that of Aristotle it became customary to believe that the universe is infinite and homogeneous both in space and time. These steady-state assumptions still had currency as recently as twenty-five years ago, though their virtues were always more aesthetic and political than evidential. Once Aristotle's cosmology was discredited, it became apparent that the universe was vast by comparison to what had been previously thought. Calling it infinite served to dramatize the break with tradition, and incidentally saved one the trouble of reckoning just how big the difference was. Awareness that these assumptions were problematic dated at least to Kepler in 1610, but the German physician Wilhelm Olbers is usually credited with calling attention to the problem when he showed that these assumptions implied that the night sky should be as bright or brighter than the sky in daytime.[29] Thus the question was formulated, "Why is the sky dark at night?" Again, this might seem like a paradigm how-possibly question, but the answer on that construal is too easy: deny one of the cosmological assumptions and possibility is no

---

[29] E. R. Harrison, "The Dark Night-Sky Riddle: A Paradox that Resisted Solution," *Science* 226 (1984): 942; Stanley Jaki, *The Paradox of Olbers' Paradox* (New York: Herder & Herder, 1969). The reason for this is as follows. Neglecting for the moment any absorbing interstellar matter, one can partition the universe into concentric spherical shells centered on the earth, each having distance from the earth of r_i (its radius), and thickness of dr. The total amount of radiation received at the earth would be the sum of the contributions from these shells, $i = 1-\infty$. Radiation obeys an inverse square law, but the volume of each spherical shell will vary with the square of the radius. Hence by homogeneity the volume of its stellar material also varies with the square of the radius. The resulting quantity of radiation at the Earth's surface will be a summation ($i = 1-\infty$) of terms of the form kr^2/r^2, where k is a non-zero density constant, all of which will equal infinity. There would be an infinite amount of radiation at every point. Assuming that stars are blackbodies (i.e. they absorb all incoming radiation and their radiation profile is a function only of temperature), we would not see any radiation on any given line of sight beyond the first star, so perhaps our temperature would not be "infinite," but only that of the average stellar surface. In the daytime the sun would appear as a dark spot in the sky because its temperature is below average.

This model assumes that radiated energy is not converted into some other form such as chemical or potential energy to any significant degree. Although this is consistent with our general cosmological knowledge, it too is problematic. For example, the argument as above formulated would go through even if all the stars were replaced by candles. And how is one to maintain homogeneity across time if the universe is dominated by an irreversible conversion of nuclear potential energy into electromagnetic and kinetic energy? The steady-state solution proposed by Bondi and Hoyle continuously added nuclear potential energy, which does nothing to alleviate the gravitational paradox.

problem. What was really sought was a good reason to deny them—i.e., one that did not have the intellectually dissatisfying effect of putting man in a privileged position in the universe once again. But what could be a better reason for denying them than that they lead to a contradiction? So the question seems better interpreted as a why-question.

Nevertheless, it is very common to suppose that once one has found *any* answer that makes the phenomenon possible in an intellectually satisfying way, one can justifiably conclude that this is *the* answer, as if it were a how-possibly question after all. In practice, scientists are not always scrupulous to note that proposed answers which would be suitable for a how-possibly question are less so for the corresponding why-question. Justifying answers as inferences to the best explanation, they reason that if there is no known alternative, any explanation can qualify as "best." Thus, Olbers thought the problem to be solved by the presence of interstellar dust absorbing the excess radiation, insofar as it was the only way he could think of accounting for the phenomenon without giving up the cosmological assumptions gratuitously. With the development of thermodynamics later in the 19th century it became apparent that the absorption of radiation by interstellar dust will heat it until it reradiates at an equal rate, i.e., it becomes as hot as its surroundings. In other words, this is no solution at all. In retrospect, this should have been obvious since the radiation paradox corresponds to a gravitational paradox (gravity also obeying an inverse-square law) for which the presence of interstellar matter makes the paradox worse, not better.

With Edwin Hubble's discovery of the expanding universe during the 1920s, it once again appeared possible to answer the how-possibly question in an intellectually satisfying way, so once again it was supposed that the answer to the why-question was at hand. When an object moves away from the Earth, its light is shifted to longer wavelengths in accordance with the Doppler effect. Increased wavelengths correspond to decreased energies, so if the rate at which the objects recede is proportional to their distance from us, the total amount of light reaching the Earth's surface would seemingly again be finite. This, at any rate, is the intuitive picture; the mathematics is not so reassuring, suggesting that the dark sky would be intensely hot, and leaving the gravitational paradox unresolved.[30]

---

[30] Using the same assumptions, suppose the shells recede at a rate proportional to their radius, r_i. Then the wavelength of the light coming from the shells will increase at a rate proportional to r_i, and the total energy coming from them will be reduced, being inversely proportional to r_i. But that still yields a total incoming energy in the form of a power series that diverges—it is just red-shifted out of the visible wavelengths.

With the advent of Einsteinian relativity and the Big Bang theory, the universe is now seen as finite in both space and time. Also, no cosmic scale has yet been found at which the universe appears homogeneous in density. Not only are the stars bunched into galaxies, the galaxies into clusters, and these into super-clusters, but homogeneity has never been found in the wake of stellar or other cosmic explosions. None of the assumptions that motivated Olbers' Paradox in the first place turns out to be true, barring some discovery that invalidates the current theories, so how much virtue is there in having inferred the "best" explanation by treating a why-question as a how-possibly question? Some might be tempted here to follow W. V. Quine's holism and say that ontology always outruns epistemology, hence theories are always "gratuitous" to a greater or lesser degree. The scientist chooses what to give up among his theories and data that together form an inconsistent whole, and his choice may not be the only one that could be made rationally. In such a situation, the "best" explanation that is "inferred" may be best in the sense that no other explanation supersedes it, even if it does not supersede all competitors. Ironically, those familiar with the science do not take such a sanguine view. Shockingly, the belief still persists in astronomical circles that the expansion of the universe, and not its density and finitude, is the primary explanatory factor—the "best" explanation—for why the sky is dark at night. Yet at best, the expansion of the universe can only reduce the level of incident extragalactic radiation at the Earth by about half, making it explanatorily irrelevant. Paul Wesson concludes, "The present level of understanding on these subjects is scandalous: only a small fraction of textbooks that treat it have a satisfactory account of Olbers' Paradox."[31]

When inferring the best explanation is allowed to cover for the investigator's ignorance, it is such an easy game to play that one should not find the frequency of abuse surprising. While I would think that the reality underlying religious experiences or the sightings of UFOs is at least a matter of controversy, Rom Harré blithely concludes regarding sightings of the Angel of Mons and flying saucers, "The plausibility control, operating through the recognitive criterion, would demand that we assert rather that there was a cloud over Mons, and that a meteorite had fallen [near] the ship."[32] 'Recognitive criterion' marks Harré's distinction between knowledge *that* something exists, which those near the mountain and aboard the ship had, and

---

[31] Paul Wesson, K. Valle, and R. Stabell, "The Extragalactic Background Light and a Definitive Resolution of Olbers' Paradox," *Astrophysical Journal* 317 (June 15, 1987): 601–6.

[32] *The Principles of Scientific Thinking* (Univ. of Chicago Press, 1970), p. 71.

knowledge of *what* exists, which Harré is claiming that he and other scientists have with respect to the same phenomena. I, too, doubt that the people near the mountain or aboard the ship knew precisely what they were seeing, and grant that scientific knowledge sometimes puts one in a better position to explain what is seen without seeing it oneself. But to move from what is *sometimes* or *could* be the case to the inference that it now *is* the case requires justification, which is precisely what Harré does not bother to give. Note also that his hypothesis goes far beyond the "proto-" variety discussed above—it is not a working hypothesis at all.

No discussion of scientific rationality is complete that does not take note of scientific irrationality, and some of the ways it occurs. I believe inferences to the best explanation are particularly vulnerable to abuse, and a common locus of scientific irrationality. Perhaps realists are right in saying that the existence of electrons should be accepted as the best explanation for the functioning of cathode ray tubes and a host of other phenomena. I do not advocate throwing out all inferences to the best explanation—one might as well infer the *best* explanation if one is to infer any. As for distinguishing spurious from legitimate uses, I defer the question until 5.4.

1.6   RELIGIOUS EXPLANATION ACCORDING TO SCHOEN

Edward Schoen has adopted one of the stronger among recently held positions on religious explanations. He claims that "there is at least one important kind of religious affirmation that can . . . meet . . . the most rigid scientific tests for theoretical adequacy." Staying away from areas of science whose explanatory value is controversial, such as biology and psychology, he follows Harré's idea of using well-understood processes as analogs for phenomena that are not well-understood, as is done in macrophysics.[33] Analogical reasoning is indeed important in science, but not all analogical models are theoretical, nor are all theoretical models analogical (1.3). How important does analogy turn out to be here?

Schoen models God's behavior as relevantly analogous to that of a father, so that his love can be understood as analogous to the love which rich parents show their children, except that God's love is not "restricted" by the

---

[33] *Religious Explanations* (Duke Univ. Press, 1985), pp. viii, 54-5, 61; Harré, *ibid.* Page references in the following discussion are to *Religious Explanations*.

"interference" of ordinary limitations of "human personality."[34] To say that God is *relevantly* analogous to one thing presumably is to deny that God is relevantly analogous to other things, and this becomes a problem. God is not a rock or a threatening cloud, says Schoen (86–7), which is certainly true insofar as God is not a material entity, but then God is not a father either. Shall we say that God is not relevantly analogous to a rock or a threatening cloud? That would require opposing a lot of historical textual evidence to the contrary (see 7.1). But the rock and cloud analogies are not relevant to what Schoen is invoking God to explain. Schoen evades questions such as, "Why did God act in this instance like a father rather than like a rock or threatening cloud?" by invoking the principle of complementarity, the standard example of which is the particle/wave duality of light in physics. Light behaves like a particle under certain circumstances and like a wave under others. In particular, diffraction phenomena "bring out" the wave behavior of light, whereas the photoelectric effect exhibits its particle nature. While we know what kind of behavior to expect in certain domains, there appears to be no general rule applicable to all.[35] Similarly, God behaves like a father sometimes, though not always, and it is hard to specify precisely when he will behave in which way.

Granting the analogy, what does it help explain? Schoen's phenomenon is that a little known theologian, Fred, finds his needs always supplied, despite circumstances in which they likely would not be (84). Calling this phenomenon X, 'God' is defined as "that [theoretical] entity which is to account for X." Defining 'God' this way is problematic, since we have prior conceptual constraints on the kinds of entities that can qualify as God (see Preface). At the minimum, they must be worthy of worship. Logically speaking, existentially instantiating a constant to which one has prior commitments is fallacious. That is, reasoning from "There exists an entity such that p" to "Let that entity be called 'God'" is fallacious, given that God may not be the entity such that p. Schoen regards being worthy of worship as a nontheoretical role for God and so not explanatorily efficacious in itself (99).

---

[34] His exact words are "love that is not restricted by the interference of other facets of human personality or blocked by the exigencies of social and economic life" (96). I am not sure of his meaning here. Recalling the woman who put two mites into the treasury, as told by Luke, the exigencies of social and economic life seem to provide an opportunity for true love to manifest itself, rather than restricting it.

[35] See Ian Barbour, *Myths, Models, and Paradigms* (New York: Harper & Row, 1974), pp. 71ff.; *Religious Explanations*, p. 107.

But the way the problem is posed I don't see how this *constraint* can be interpreted merely as a *desideratum* that can be optimized, or "satisficed." If Fred were unworthy of support then it seems quite possible that the intersection of the set of all entities worthy of worship and the set of entities accounting for X may be empty. Would the entity still be worthy of *Fred's* worship, insofar as it supplied Fred's needs? It would be idolatry to worship the local welfare department.

Suppose we grant that our conceptual constraints on God are consistent with God's being responsible for X. X is not a phenomenon in the sense that "seeing red now" is, but rather it is a pattern of phenomena, each of which may already have an explanation of its own. Hume asked why, if one has already given an explanation of every instance that is part of a whole or overall pattern, one can't be said to have explained the pattern as well. In modern terms, this question can be formulated as whether the pattern is just an *accidental regularity*—in which case it is not a genuine phenomenon at all—or is *projectible*. Is it robust? What kinds of counterfactuals can it support? This is where we turn to our religious model for answers. If the pattern is accidental, then there will be no interesting explanation of it over-and-above the explanations of its component parts. If it is robust, then an additional explanation may be appropriate.

Showing that X is not pure happenstance is nontrivial. There are many academics in America today, and it could probably be said of all of them that their needs have been supplied up to one level or another—even if not all ultimately "made it" in academia. So we would have to require that the needs be supplied at a fairly high level, call it L, or the pattern wouldn't even merit being called a coincidence—we would merely expect it on the basis of our background knowledge. We also must ask what is special about Fred, or the relation between Fred and God, that God should supply *his* needs to level L, whereas all of these other people are not getting their needs supplied. Is it because they are nonreligious? That would not be credible. Schoen is silent on this subject. Suppose we acted to deprive Fred of his needs—would they still be supplied? If God let his own son be crucified, then quite possibly not. If Fred were a Chinese academic in China, would his needs still be supplied to level L? In order to know that X is a genuine phenomenon, it would be necessary to specify some interesting ways in which the system could be perturbed and Fred's needs still supplied to level L. What interesting counterfactuals does X support? Not only does Schoen offer none, he seems only marginally aware that there is a problem here. The phenomenon, he says, occurred too frequently to be purely coincidental.

There can come a point at which a phenomenon occurs frequently enough to justify suspicion that some causal agent is at work. It does relatively little harm to pursue such hypotheses, and if *something* might have caused it, why not God? In chapter 3 we will discuss some reasons for hesitating to invoke God as an explanation. For the present I still maintain that the most we could get from Schoen's account would be a proto-explanation. We would know virtually nothing about the explanatory entity except that it is consistent with our conceptual constraints on God-like entities. The explanation would be nearly irrefutable as a bare posit—"that which explains *X*." This could not count as a full explanation, let alone an explanation passing "the most stringent scientific tests for theoretical adequacy," until the nature of this entity becomes "fleshed out" in more detail. Schoen admits (97) that an attempt to flesh it out may fail. That is understandable, since one has no clear idea where to look for additional evidence regarding the nature of God. This is where the father analogy is supposed to serve as a heuristic. I for one am not sure that most fathers really love their children, as opposed to merely expressing their "selfish genes," but further discussion must wait till chapter 7.

CHAPTER 2

TWO MAJOR SCIENTIFIC VALUES

Acquisition of Information and Avoidance of Error

2.1 INTRODUCTION: INFORMATION VS. MISINFORMATION

In 1.4 we distinguished confirmational and informational virtues of a theory. Recall that the value of the former is primarily epistemic, pertaining to the theory's evidential support, or the likelihood that it is true; while the latter is primarily of pragmatic value, contributing to the theory's informative content, putting that content into usable form, and its ability to solve problems. The principal value of explanations, like that of problem solving in general, was seen to be informative and pragmatic. Thus, I illustrated with Newton's theory a point that Larry Laudan has been at pains to emphasize: it does not take a true theory to solve a problem or give a useful explanation.[36] Indeed, the process of formulating and giving explanations is itself inherently unreliable, especially in the short run.

How can we distinguish information from misinformation if truth is not criterial? Something needs to take up the normative slack. First, I do not deny that truth is an important consideration—I merely deny that it is the *only* consideration. Since informational virtues are pragmatically oriented, explicating 'misinformation' requires taking pragmatic factors into account as well. More is at stake than simply the risk of error or falsity, since the degree of risk affects what we count as misinformation. Criteria of fit are

---

[36] *Progress and Its Problems*, pp. 123ff.

also important: Does the statement generally lead one to draw the right conclusions? Misleading statements can misinform as easily as false ones. Suppose, e.g., I reported on the performance of a guest lecturer that "he hemmed
and hawed around a lot and then we went home." Even if the statement is
not literally true, I most likely have conveyed correct and useful information
if one concludes that the subject matter was not adequately covered in class
today, that a profitable discussion did not develop, that I regarded the class
to be boring and a waste of time, and that if the same guest lecturer were
announced for a future session, fewer students would attend. One does not
need criteria of metaphorical truth to classify the statement as informative,
because on the basis of fitness or appropriateness to the circumstances it may
already be so classifiable.

Now consider psychoanalytic theory as originally formulated by Sig-
mund Freud. Karl Popper criticized psychoanalysis as pseudoscientific, yet
contemporary philosophers argue that (i) Freud's theory was not originally
formulated or defended in such a way as to make it unfalsifiable, and (ii) the
style of explanation and theory construction employed by Freud conform
with prevailing scientific practice, or at least are not counternormative.[37]
But whether a theory amounts to information or misinformation is a matter
of substance, or what the theory says, while its being above board methodologically is a matter of how it was arrived at—a different question. In retrospect, Freud's theories lead to a number of incorrect inferences. For example, from his theory that the infantile Oedipal complex is at the root of much
human behavior, it now appears more correct to infer that Freud himself experienced such a complex as a child, than that it is a universal element of
human psychology.[38] The pragmatic value of therapy based on Oedipal
theory remains unproven after many decades.[39] As for his theory in *Totem
and Taboo* that religious beliefs originated in repressed patricide, it was

---

[37] Karl Popper, *Conjectures and Refutations* (New York: Basic, 1962), pp. 34ff.; see also
Terence Hines, *Pseudoscience and the Paranormal* (Buffalo: Prometheus, 1988), pp. 109ff. On
(i), see Adolf Grünbaum, "Is Freudian Theory Pseudo-Scientific by Karl Popper's Criterion of
Demarcation?" *American Philosophical Quarterly* 16 (1979): 131–41. On (ii), Robert Cummins,
The Nature of Psychological Explanation (MIT Press, 1983), chapter 4. Clark Glymour's *Theo-
ry and Evidence* (Princeton Univ. Press, 1980), pp. 263–77, addresses both (i) and (ii).

[38] Hans Küng, *Freud and the Problem of God* (Yale Univ. Press, 1979), pp. 10, 103–10.

[39] Adolf Grünbaum, "Epistemological Liabilities of the Clinical Appraisal of Psychoanalytic
Theory," *Noûs* 14 (1980): 307–85; "Retrospective and Prospective Testing of Aetiological Hypotheses in Freudian Theory," in *Testing Scientific Theories,* ed. by Earman, 315–47.

anthropologically naive by the standards of his own time, since totemism does not occur in all cultures, and of hundreds of totemic tribes surveyed, only four have any rite approximating the killing and eating of the "totem-god."[40] On the other hand, Freud called attention to subconscious causes of human action whose existence had not been recognized previously. Thus, Freud's theories contain genuine informational value, even though leading to a number of erroneous inferences—a typical result of scientific theorizing.

In this chapter I will refer to the above two desiderata as 'acquisition of information' and 'avoidance of error', and the constraint on balancing them 'rationality'. These are among the most important values governing science as an enterprise. Unfortunately, confirmational and informational virtues tend to pull in opposite directions, as we saw in chapter 1, and the same applies to these two desiderata: usually one can be enhanced only by sacrificing some of the other. This threatens us with a dilemma. Increasing the standard of acceptability for the likelihood that an explanation is true, or increasing the ratio of information to misinformation that it must contain, would greatly diminish the number of explanations that qualify, and hence the informative output of our epistemic enterprise. Given how many scientific theories have turned out false in the past, setting a high standard of probability could nearly eliminate the explanatory power of inquiry. But achieving greater informational output means courting a greater risk of error as well. How would a rational person proceed when two of her primary values are diametrically opposed? Here the commonsensical response also seems to be the correct one: concede that there is no uniquely rational way to proceed. As Alvin Goldman says, we must learn to live "with an irreducible multiplicity of standards."[41] W. V. Quine apparently agrees, insofar as he classifies evidential value and systematic value (another pragmatic or informational value) as incommensurable: "Scientists of different philosophical temper will differ in how much dilution of evidence they are prepared to accept for a given systematic benefit, and vice versa."[42] Arguing for this pluralistic position is one of the primary burdens of this chapter and the next.

---

[40] Mircea Eliade, "Cultural Fashions and the History of Religion," in *The History of Religions,* ed. by Kitagawa (Univ. of Chicago Press, 1967), pp. 23–4; *Freud and the Problem of God,* pp. 35–40, 67–74.

[41] *Epistemology and Cognition* (Harvard Univ. Press, 1986), p. 125.

[42] *Theories and Things* (Harvard Univ. Press, 1981), p. 31.

2.2   WILLIAM JAMES AND "THE WILL TO BELIEVE"

My argument starts with the position presented by William James in his notorious paper, "The Will to Believe."[43] Perhaps the paper would have been
more famous and less notorious if it had been correctly understood as advan-
cing an epistemological argument in which religion figures only incidentally
as one area in which the argument could be applied. I begin by updating
and elaborating the argument; in subsequent sections I apply it to some common scientistic objections to religious explanation.

In barest form the argument starts by assuming that not all rationally
held beliefs are forced upon us by evidence. This claim goes beyond the
Quine-Duhem thesis that theory is underdetermined by evidence. The fact
that one could hold an alternative theory *consistently* does not make holding
it *rational.* Yet given that many competing theories are often under consideration at any time, and much evidence is needed to reject any one theory
conclusively, the existence of rational alternatives is probably more the norm
than the exception—especially when evidence is scarce or equivocal, or the
theories are vague or speculative. Specifically, James denies that evidence
forces upon us belief or disbelief in the existence of God.

The argument then runs that when one confronts several belief options
among which one is forced to choose, and when each of these options involves substantial risks and rewards, whose exact size and probability are
uncertain, a person cannot be rationally faulted no matter which option he
chooses. Forced choices occur when the alternatives are described so as to
exclude one another and jointly exhaust the logical possibilities. For example, one is forced with respect to any claim either to believe it or not believe
it—one cannot do both or neither. Suspending judgment may avoid commit-
ting oneself to believing it, but still constitutes not believing. The alternatives may be expanded, however, by redescribing the situation—say, by introducing degrees of belief. If one's degree of belief were 50% it might
appear arbitrary whether one is classified as believing or not believing, but
any person willing to draw the line would still be entitled to say that people
are forced to choose one way or the other.

James restricts his claim to certain options which he calls momentous.
What he says of momentous beliefs is also true of trivial beliefs—one may
not be able to postpone acting on them long enough for adequate evidence

---

[43]   Originally a lecture, "The Will to Believe" has been widely reprinted—see entries under
Burkhardt, Wilshire, McDermott, and Brody in the references at the end of this book.

to be gathered—but only in the case of momentous beliefs is this fact consequential. The trivial/momentous evaluative dimension has further implications. A traditional requirement of rationality is that one believe all of the logical consequences of everything in one's belief set, so that all contradictions must be expunged from one's belief system. This is unrealistic given the huge number of beliefs people customarily hold, and the impossibility of determining all of their logical consequences. A more realistic theory of rationality might require one to explore the consequences of momentous beliefs and beliefs closely related to them, expunging any contradictions one finds, while being more lenient in the treatment of trivial beliefs.

Greater momentousness involves greater risk, a factor often omitted from simplistic contrasts between the scientific preference for suspending judgment and the religious preference for belief. Suspending judgment works best when commitment offers few rewards and entails major risks. Successful research programs, on the other hand, offer great rewards. To be successful they must be timely, and to be timely they must often be undertaken when substantial uncertainty regarding underlying theoretical assumptions still exists. Suspending judgment thus implicates risks associated with avoiding commitment. In this respect, scientists arguably have opportunities for exercising faith comparable to the those found in religious contexts. Folkman was accused by fellow scientists of engaging in an irrational "act of faith," persevering when evidence of TAF was slow to materialize (1.5.1). I do not know whether he was acting rationally or not, but the outcome of the affair illustrates how faith sometimes pays off even in science.

James refers to belief options as "dead" rather than "live" when they have negligible subjective probability, and excludes them from consideration. Although James rejects Pascal's Wager as representing the morality of the casino, the point of the rest of his argument seems remarkably similar. Given the very large risks and rewards associated with belief and disbelief in God, the subjective probability that God actually exists need not be very high for action based on that possibility to become rational.[44] James runs into trouble with his implicit assumption that subjective probabilities are *always* rational, however. He states that the person who assumes the substantial risks associated with his choice of belief should not be subject to opprobrium, whichever way she chooses. Put crudely, it is easy enough for the rest of us to pronounce certain choices to be rational or irrational so long as it is somebody else's life we are gambling with, but it is less likely that we

---

[44] Cf. Richard Swinburne, "The Christian Wager," *Religious Studies* 4 (1969): 217–28.

will investigate the matter more thoroughly or more conscientiously than the person whose life is at stake. But this ad hominem defense simply won't wash. The gambler's fallacy is a fallacy and is often committed by gamblers, and one need not gamble to point that out. Hence, James cannot be correct in exempting everyone forced to choose among live, momentous options from charges of irrationality. What can be said for his position is that it is very difficult to show subjective probabilities and valuations associated with religious beliefs to be irrational, and unlikely that a general claim of irrationality can be substantiated on that basis regarding religious belief.

One common criticism of both the Jamesian and Pascalian arguments is their commitment to belief voluntarism, the view that we exercise control over what we believe, or that belief is a matter of choice. Theories of rationality for belief systems also assume belief voluntarism. Suppose people cannot help but believe that God does or does not exist as a result of enculturation, evidence, or argument. If one accepts the principle that 'ought' implies 'can', such people could not be faulted as irrational. Belief *in*voluntarism makes it easier to defend religious belief as rational, but also makes it easier to defend religious unbelief as rational.

It is easy to adduce compelling examples of beliefs that are not voluntarily acquired or held. That I am seeing red, here, now, or that the sky is grey today, are transparent examples of beliefs that would most likely be held involuntarily. Belief based on the testimony of others whom we trust, when we have no opportunity to look into it the matter further, may also be involuntary, especially for children. Perhaps many people believe or do not believe in God for this kind of reason. But mightn't rationality require that we investigate momentous beliefs over which there is strong or widespread disagreement among people whose testimony otherwise appears reliable, even if we have never seriously questioned these beliefs previously? A deeper issue is lurking here. If the residual effects of voluntary actions include involuntary changes in one's belief set, then are those changes voluntary? For example, perhaps I have no belief currently regarding whether it is raining, but I know I can find out by going to the window. Assume it is a voluntary matter whether I go to the window, but once I look out I have no choice whether to believe it is raining. Is any resulting belief voluntary or not? If not, belief in God might also be involuntary, yet the entire Jamesian argument would still apply to the decision whether to investigate momentous beliefs further, once we become aware that they are epistemically problematic. If we say that such collateral beliefs *are* voluntary, however, the argument that God-beliefs are involuntary becomes much less plausible. So this objection does not seem fatal to the Jamesian type of argument.

2.3 PERMISSIVE VS. OBLIGATORY RATIONALITY

Many discussions of rationality conflate issues regarding what a person *ought* to do or is *obliged* to believe, with standards governing what a person is *permitted* to do or is *allowed* to believe.[45] In his earlier work Wittgenstein said of mathematics that what is permitted is also required, a position typical of classical foundationalism dating to Descartes's Fourth Meditation. On Descartes's view, mere pursuit of truth apparently obliges one to believe what one perceives clearly and distinctly, since all of those beliefs are guaranteed to be true; but one should suspend judgment on everything else, since it cannot be secured to sure foundations and is therefore uncertain. Yet it seems inevitable that what rationality permits will be considerably broader than what it requires, given the difficulty of trading off information acquisition and error avoidance. In 2.6 I argue that even where these values agree we are not assured that they issue in the correct prescription, in which case rationality still may not oblige us to follow them.

This distinction is crucial to the viability of religious explanations. Philosophers since Hobbes have pointed out that nothing can prove the existence of God, nor oblige one to accept the testimony of a religious experience or text as evidence for a religious hypothesis.[46] I am not disputing this claim but only defending the rational *permissibility* of endorsing religious explanations or positing religious entities to account for some matters of fact. Permission and obligation are intimately related, of course. What rationality permits me to do I am not obliged not to do, and vice versa. My thesis is that rational standards for acceptable explanations will not be sufficient to prohibit all nontrivial religious explanations. But let us stick with the immediate sphere of application for this distinction: the issue of how to balance the values of information acquisition and error avoidance.

A similar distinction appears in American jurisprudence in the standards of proof used to decide criminal cases as compared to civil cases. Guilt must be established *beyond a reasonable doubt* in criminal cases, to provide

---

[45] Even Goldman, who recognizes the distinction (60–1), still conflates it. His intentional version of scientific realism equivocates on whether the aim of scientists *should* be to produce true theories, or whether this aim is only *permitted* (156). I worry that the former violates the 'ought' implies 'can' dictum—see 2.7 and my "A Limited Defense of the Pessimistic Induction," forthcoming in *British Journal for the Philosophy of Science*—while the latter is consistent with anti-realistic claims, such as that truth is merely a means to a more important goal.

[46] *Leviathan,* chapter 32; see also Antony Flew, *God and Philosophy* (London: Hutchinson, 1966), p. 126.

a measure of assurance that no innocent person will be punished, even if criminals occasionally go unpunished; but one need only establish that the *preponderance of evidence* is in one's favor in civil cases. One can have a reasonable doubt about whether the defendant was negligent and make him pay in a civil case, even if one could not send him to prison for the same injury if tried as a criminal. Presumably one is obliged to believe what it is not reasonable to doubt, and conversely, so this half of the distinction seems roughly congruent. But the preponderance of evidence can favor at most one point of view, whereas pluralism may function optimally if rationality sometimes permits different beliefs for different people. Hence, preponderance of evidence is at least as restrictive as rational permissibility.

Plantinga suggests that we call a person epistemically *justified* in believing *P* if she violates no epistemic obligation in believing *P*—i.e., she is rationally permitted to believe it. A person is rationally obliged to believe *P* if she is not justified in believing ¬*P*. Gettier problems and other difficulties show that being justified is not the same as having adequate truth-conducive grounds for the proposition, or for satisfying whatever necessary and sufficient conditions make true beliefs into knowledge. For the latter condition, Plantinga proposes the term *warrant*, so that deontological questions of what a person ought to believe may be disentangled from the theoretical problem of giving criteria for the possession of knowledge.[47]

2.3.1 Treatment of Angina

Ultimately, the evidential/informational dilemma is a watershed that separates science from religion. By-and-large, scientists have a tendency not shared by religious people to emphasize evidential values at the expense of lost informational content. This conservatism is sensible within scientific contexts in that it strikes a balance, or is in a tension with, the very ambitious goal of achieving maximal generality for theoretical statements. But when one's goals are less ambitious, such conservatism may also be less needed or appropriate. An old saw in philosophical circles runs something like, "I don't care if there are more things in heaven and earth than are conceived of in my philosophy, so long as nothing conceived in my philosophy isn't in heaven or earth!" This line of argumentation might play well with some scientists, but it flaunts a one-sided preoccupation with avoiding error that is not rationally sustainable given legitimate interest in acquiring information.

---

[47] Alvin Plantinga, "Justification in the 20th Century," *Philosophy and Phenomenological Research* 50 Supp. (Fall 1990): 45–71; Edmund Gettier, "Is Justified True Belief Knowledge?" *Analysis* 23 (1963): 121–3.

To illustrate this conservatism, consider the history of treatment for angina, or chest pain—a common symptom of heart disease and a frequent precursor to heart attacks—as summarized in a recent article by Herbert Benson and David McCallie:[48]

> Many types of therapy for angina pectoris have been advocated, only to be abandoned later. A partial list would include heart-muscle extract, pancreatic extract, various hormones, x-irradiation, anticoagulants, monoamine oxidase inhibitors, thyroidectomies, radioactive iodine, sympathectomies, various vitamins, choline, meprobamate, ligation of the internal mammary artery, epicardial abrasions and cobra venom.
>
> Few carefully controlled trials of these approaches were performed before the 1960s. Failure to rule out experimenter bias renders these investigations incapable of providing accurate evaluation of the procedure. However, this very weakness provides an opportunity to quantify the degree to which the placebo effect may have operated. Since most of these earlier forms of therapy are now known to have no specific physiologic effect in the treatment of angina pectoris, we can analyze the benefits reported and assess the degree of influence of the placebo effect.
>
> A recurrent pattern is present in the history of various treatments for angina pectoris. When a drug or surgical procedure is first introduced, there is general enthusiasm and hope for its effectiveness. In early studies and in anecdotal evidence, proponents of the new therapy, or, as Beecher called them, "enthusiasts," report remarkable benefits, with therapeutic effectiveness seen in the vast majority of patients. These nonblind or single-blind trials fail to control for the strong placebo effect evoked by the investigators' expectations of success. Other promising reports with similar results follow. Only later do more adequately controlled studies appear, performed by investigators who are, as Beecher described them, "skeptics." These skeptical investigators, who operate under circumstances that minimize the placebo effect, find the therapy "no better than" inert, control placebo pills. As the number of skeptical reports increases or when another new therapy appears, the original therapy is abandoned and soon disappears from the medical literature. Quantitatively, the pattern is consistent: the initial 70 to 90 per cent effectiveness in the enthusiasts' reports decreases to 30 to 40 per cent "base-line" placebo effectiveness in the skeptics' reports. This pattern was recognized by the 19th-century French physician, Armand Trousseau, who allegedly stated, "You should treat as many patients as possible with the new drugs while they still have the power to heal."

The point is not that only evidence procured through double-blind experiments is scientifically acceptable. Rather, increased concern over ethical considerations such as informed consent has made it virtually impossible to perform double-blind trials with the currently popular surgical treatment for angina, coronary bypass, a procedure whose efficacy therefore is in a sense unproved and virtually unprovable. One reason people would not consent

---

[48] "Angina Pectoris and the Placebo Effect," *New England Journal of Medicine* 300, 25 (1979): 1424-9. The mention of Beecher refers to his landmark paper "Surgery as Placebo: A Quantitative Study of Bias," *Journal of the American Medical Association* 176 (1961): 1102–7.

to participate in such a trial *is the high level of belief in the efficacy of coronary bypass surgery itself.* Apparently we can do no more than make an inference to the best explanation—but which explanation is it? That bypass surgery is an effective therapy for angina? Or that its effectiveness is most likely as a placebo? Even scientists must entertain degrees of belief at times, and the notion of "best explanation" should not mislead us that accepting explanations is necessarily an all-or-nothing affair. Hume made it a hallmark of rationality that one's degree of belief be proportioned to the likelihood that the hypothesis is true, given the evidence.

Seeking controversial treatments, such as laetrile was at one time and some AIDS treatments are now, may be rational even if the treatment is unproven scientifically. The methodological risk for science is seen in terms of falling into error when making general statements, but the individual sees his risk in terms of dying unnecessarily. When the risks posed by the possibility of error differ, then the point at which they balance the corresponding informational values will obviously differ as well. Science seeks a non-perspectival truth, whereas individuals must make decision based on their limited perspective. Individual values are not rendered nugatory by proclaiming that scientific values are universal; nor does placing a value on universality thereby give one a universal value. Under this kind of scenario, it seems that what rationality permits will be far broader than anything it can claim to require of all participants.

2.3.2   The Value of Skepticism

If the ideal of rational belief is that it mirror the evidence, what becomes of rationality in a context where there are no mirrors? The placebo effect reveals that one determinant of whether a given procedure works is what people believe regarding whether it works. Epistemologists might prefer the causal relationship to go the other way, but beliefs have causal power to change the facts just as much as facts can change our beliefs about them. Can a belief be rational that causes facts corresponding to it—a self-fulfilling prophecy, as it were—if the preexisting facts were otherwise insufficient to justify it? Visions of wishful thinking, or positive thinking that fails to exhibit the "power" advertised, may prompt a knee-jerk negative response. None of us wants to lose touch with reality. But the situation with coronary bypass surgery illustrates that the issue is not cut-and-dried. While chuckling at Trousseau's provincialism we may be forgetting that the placebo effect really heals people.

I am not claiming that skepticism is generally a bad strategy. Part of my confidence in the theoretical proclamations of scientists by-and-large, and my comparative lack of confidence in many religious proclamations, stems from the fact that science at least pays lip service to a practice of welcoming skeptics with open arms, whereas religious people typically hesitate to make even this gesture. If a skeptic proves a phenomenon to her satisfaction, that is better evidence for it than the proof of an enthusiast. But the confidence engendered by scientific conservatism in balancing the need for information against the risk of error has a downside. My confidence in the relative security of positive scientific theories is part and parcel with my doubt that science is telling or can tell the whole story about what goes on in the world. So while I don't claim that skepticism is a bad strategy, I am not ready to concede that it is the *only* rational strategy—it may need supplementation.

Richard Nisbett and Lee Ross report a psychological study supporting a conclusion similar to what the angina story suggests: the skeptical charge against believers that their "evidence" constitutes a self-fulfilling prophecy can be turned on its head—i.e., the skeptic's disbelief may be similarly misleading. The subjects were placed in prisoner's dilemma-type situations after being given an opportunity to consider what the best strategy for such a situation would be. Those adopting a competitive stance quickly forced their partners to do the same in self-defense, whereas those adopting a cooperative posture experienced strings of successful cooperations in some cases, while being forced to play more guardedly in others. They concluded,[49]

> The intriguing point of the Kelley and Stahelski demonstration is that cooperators will learn, correctly, that the world contains both cooperators and competitors. Competitors, on the other hand, will learn, incorrectly, that everyone out there is a competitor. This is because competitors' own view of correct strategy will bias the behavior of others so as to produce evidence indicating that everyone shares their own strategy.

That is, the behavior of skeptics may prevent them from seeing the evidence they claim to need in order to believe. Of course, religious people have been saying for years that if skeptics would only be more cooperative, they would find ample evidence for the existence of God. Skeptics have responded that this whole argument is question-begging. My point is that the religious argument need not be false or question-begging per se, although without criteria of what counts as cooperative it is difficult to test and hence vulnerable to ideological abuse. But if skepticism is sacrosanct in scientific contexts, it

---

[49] *Human Inference* (Prentice-Hall, 1980), p. 188. The study was performed by H. H. Kelley and A. J. Stahelski, "Social Interaction Basis of Cooperators' and Competitors' Belief about Others," *Journal of Personality and Social Psychology* 16 (1970): 66–91.

too is not without risks within general contexts, *both from the standpoints of acquiring information and avoiding error.* I say this because in practice skepticism often means not merely suspending judgment, but denying as untrue knowledge claims made on evidence that the skeptic regards as inadequate.[50] Such a policy can lead directly to false beliefs, aside from foregoing informational advantages. Hence one cannot say from the standpoint of general rationality that skepticism is always justified until the existence of a given phenomenon is proven, even though this may be practiced in some scientific contexts. This point has been much emphasized by Kuhn, Lakatos, and Laudan. I do not deny the utility of skepticism within science, but I deny that this utility is simply a matter of rationality (see chapter 4).

If the efficacy of religious practice is only on an epistemic par with that of the placebo effect, how much comfort can the religious community garner from that? Isn't that the import of Marx's charge that religion is "the opiate of the masses?" This is a serious question, but one that must await developments in later chapters. Here let me just say that lack of conclusive proof that the effectiveness of *X* is *not* solely as a placebo does not constitute proof that its effectiveness *is* solely as a placebo.

2.4   WHERE DOES THE JAMESIAN ARGUMENT GET US?

The intended conclusion of "The Will to Believe" is that religious belief is rationally permissible, however I find this conclusion somewhat dissatisfying because of the unargued assumption that belief in God is of momentous importance. Since many religious people cannot seriously question this assumption, let me approach it by way of inversion.[51] It seems to me that if I wanted to perpetrate some kind of fraud, the ideal way to do it would be to promise those who perform some crucial act that they would receive great rewards for doing so—the higher the better—whereas those who did not perform that act would suffer greatly. When people ask for evidence of this, I would add that taking what has been said in faith is part of the crucial act

---

[50] Note the positions and arguments advanced by Hines, Siegel, and Alcock in 6.2. Of course, Pyrrhonian skepticism is immune to this charge, but it still pays insufficient tribute to the value of information acquisition.

[51] That is, I will suggest how what people take to be part of the real furniture of the world may be just a human construct, and how human constructs may be part of the real furniture of the world—see Steve Woolgar, *Science: The Very Idea* (Chichester: Ellis Horwood, 1988).

that receives the reward. The crucial act would then be the act that the con artist actually gains from rather than the person on whom the fraud is being perpetrated. For example, chain letters usually suggest that if the recipient sends just a few dollars—such a small amount considering the potential—he will be rewarded by receiving perhaps a million dollars from other people on down the chain. But if he breaks the chain, he will suffer a grave calamity similar to what the letter claims has happened to previous chain breakers. Yet we know that the sap who believes this will probably receive nothing for his trouble unless he gets prosecuted for mail fraud, whereas the person who does not believe suffers no ill effect.

Christianity and Islam both promise practitioners the very highest reward possible for belief, and the greatest possible punishment for disbelief, and also insist that this cannot be proven but must be taken on faith. Suppose one *does* believe—the costs that were said to be trifling will be felt certainly and immediately, but if one slips up subsequently one's reward may turn out far less certain than originally claimed. In such circumstances, one needn't be crazy to wonder if religious people aren't perpetrating the world's greatest fraud. "But God is great and wonderful and a chain letter writer is nobody!" However, from the standpoint of potential converts, both alike are strangers. "But I have nothing to gain from another person's belief in the gospel." This is not obviously so, either. Belief is typically followed by contributions and moral support, and these go to the same people who urged belief in the first place. Now this may just be one of those things in which what looks like fraud really is not—just a "pure coincidence" as they say. My point is that at the very least, religious people owe us an account of what makes this one act so important that it merits changing a person's destiny from eternal suffering to eternal life in the eyes of a righteous God. Ironically, some religious people go on to deny that anything in the act of believing merits any kind of reward whatsoever—it is all a free gift and merit has nothing to do with it. This makes matters worse, compounding the previous difficulties with a God now portrayed as arbitrary and capricious.

In raising these issues I have no particular theory of eternal life or eternal suffering in mind. Perhaps hell is eternal separation from God, or living in heaven is dwelling eternally in the presence of God. Perhaps our eternal destiny is nothing more than a natural outcome of choices made on earth—that is, the beings we choose to share our companionship with here are the beings we spend eternity with. The question still remains: what makes the presence of God more desirable than anything else? And if it is, what makes belief in God the kind of thing that merits this highest of rewards? Suppose an omnipotent being exists—why would it be especially beneficial to dwell in its presence? Or answer the question for omniscient or immutable beings. Augustine says that if you don't believe, you will never understand, but the chain letter writer might have said this too. Do we believe only because God commands it? Why don't we obey the commands of the chain letter writer? My personal inclination is to think that Christianity cannot maintain a doctrine of eternal life or eternal suffering without having a commensurate conception of merit. To conceive God as righteous and just, rather than arbitrary and capricious, requires no less. I realize that many Christians disagree in this assessment, but the weakness in the chain letter writer's argument is that the she cannot explain why performing this little act is the kind of thing that ought to give a person a million dollars, or why failing to perform it should result in dire consequences—it's all just gratuitous. Hence our protection against unfounded faith-demanding claims is insisting that there be an articulated and intelligible theory of value or obligation that backs them up. Religious people cannot expect to be credible if they fail to come clean on this point.

I conclude that the Jamesian argument leads us not simply to religious belief, but to religious explanation. If God is a morally perfect being, and therefore rewards and punishes his creatures only on morally legitimate grounds, then we need an *explanation* of what makes belief in God so praiseworthy that it deserves greater rewards than any other type of human action. Then the Jamesian and Pascalian arguments will not reduce to the morality of the casino. While this is not religious explanation in the strict sense of explanation of events, it is similar: an explanation of what makes the event of choosing to believe in God exceedingly valuable or morally important. One cannot answer such a question without clarifying what it means to believe or place trust in God. My point is that the rationality of religious belief is not a self-contained subject—it implicates religious explanation as well. Perhaps the stakes involved in most religious explanations are less than heaven or hell, or eternal reward vs. eternal shame. But when the stakes do reach transcendental proportions, explanation of those proportions is required.

In the argument that follows, the importance of knowing God plays a critical role, so let me sketch briefly here where I imagine this importance to come from. Nothing in my sketch is particularly original. From the above argument I doubt that the value of knowing God can be cast purely or primarily in terms of an after-life. I imagine that the value of knowing God resides in, among other things, God's superior cognitive and moral attributes in which are solved the riddles of meaningful and moral existence that prove persistently recalcitrant to secular, intellectual inquiry. Jesus was a teacher, after all, and people do need to learn what meaningful and moral life is and how to live it. Approaching these questions exclusively by traditional philosophical analysis and argumentation leads to endless wrangling without significant progress. Most any subject is difficult to learn without a teacher, but with many subjects we have the slight assistance of letting the natural world be our teacher. If the natural world, as epitomized by evolution and natural selection, were the ultimate authority on questions of worthwhile and moral existence as well, then many of us would throw up our hands and concede these question as unanswerable. So if they have answers, we must seek them elsewhere. This gives us a very real and almost tangible need for knowledge of any God that exists.

2.5 AREN'T RELIGIOUS EXPLANATIONS PSEUDOSCIENTIFIC?

Since I am purporting to offer religious explanations for putative matters of fact, which is generally recognized as the business of science, doesn't that show that I am engaging in pseudoscience, and therefore am departing from sound canons of rationality? This question deserves attention if only because the philosophical quality of the literature on these issues is so low. Here are some of the points worth watching.

Rarely is the issue raised whether science is to be identified descriptively as what scientists do or normatively in terms of a particular methodology. The difficulty of keeping rational reconstructions free of non-normative idealizations also gets overlooked. Authors are frequently oblivious to the possibility that once the extensions of terms such as 'scientific', 'rational' 'pseudo-' are circumscribed so as to get the facts in line, the values typically associated with these terms may no longer follow. If their positions are reworked to make the connotations (values) fit, then the denotations (facts) may no longer be accurate. It is ironic if not self-referentially absurd to charge religious people with engaging in pseudoscience when no adequate definition of 'pseudoscience' has ever been offered. Another argument faults pseudoscience for intruding into the *function* of science. Yet the fact that S performs function E well in context C does not preclude R from performing the same function equally well, or even better. Given differences in design between S and R, it may be likely that a context D exists in which this is precisely what happens.

Another line of argumentation takes the form: "These people claim to be engaged in science. They are not. Hence what they are doing is wrong." But what makes it wrong? The strongest evidence for the second premise is usually that the activity in question is not recognized by the scientific community, but how can we decide what 'the scientific community' is short of begging the question? When methodological concerns are broached, it is usually assumed that science has a unique methodology which pervades all of its branches, and to exclude pseudoscience that methodology is so tightly circumscribed that it would exclude much of current scientific practice as well. The question is rarely raised what criteria of rationality, if any, are implicated. Even more rarely does anyone ask whether scientific methodology is *forced* by the minimal rationality of knowledge acquisition, as opposed to representing mere *desiderata* to be optimized. Only if it were forced would a methodological shortfall constitute a departure from rationality.[52]

The literature on pseudoscience repeated emphasizes the possibility of fraud, the existence of fraud, instances of mistaken identity, the dangers associated with "top-down" processing in perception and memory, human gullibility, and virtually any means by which error can creep in. In fact, some critics of pseudoscience perpetrate fraud disguised as the activity they are attacking, in hopes of tainting all such activity with suspicion.[53] But avoiding error is only one of the values which scientific inquiry attempts to optimize. If it were to be the only consideration, the most prudent course of action would be never to propose theories or offer explanations of matters of fact. One cannot give credence to methodological discussions that emphasize only one of these desiderata while ignoring the other. These authors never mention risks associated with overlooking evidence for the existence or nature of God, or missing out on the possibility of knowing God, or other informational values lost by overconcern for the risk that an erroneous belief might thereby be entertained. If religious people haven't adequately clarified these values, that does not prove them trivial. Religion (qua source of explanations regarding matters of fact) and parapsychology are two areas that are diametrically opposed ideologically but have a lot in common epistemologically, and are sometimes lumped together with UFOs and other miscellany under the rubric 'pseudoscience'. Because these areas represent the interests of broad segments of society and are epistemologically problematic, they abound with sensational claims, bad intentions, and fraud, especially in the popular literature. In defending the possibility of religious explanations, I

---

[52] Paul Kurtz exemplifies some of these argumentational shortcomings in "Is Parapsychology a Science," in *Paranormal Borderlands of Science,* ed. by Frazier (Buffalo: Prometheus, 1981), 5–23.

[53] Cf. James Randi's "The Project Alpha Experiment," in *Science Confronts the Paranormal,* ed. by Frazier (Buffalo: Prometheus, 1986), pp. 158–65.

am engaging in rational reconstruction rather than defending popular practice, so I do not deny that fraud is a concern, but deny that it is the *only* concern.

My concern has a flip side, however. Philosophers such as Quine and Kuhn have stressed that no theory-neutral observations, sense-data, incorrigible given, or epistemically privileged representations exist.[54] This has led some to jump to the conclusion that science enjoys no epistemological advantage over religion at all. The psychological phenomenon responsible for this theoretical tainting of perception is called "top-down" processing. Some epistemologists assume that because it is unavoidable and contributes to information acquisition, it is also normatively innocuous—an irreducible fact against which attempts to arrive at rational norms must founder. But I have yet to see an argument that the effects of top-down processing are not a matter of degree, or that measures taken to minimize them have no epistemological benefit.[55] If they are matters of degree, then the 'ought' implies 'can' principle has no force against norms mandating that they be minimized.

My general claim is that a rationally reconstructed science does not exhaust rationality when it comes to global epistemological concerns. A reconstruction cannot be independent of all values and goals, nor will they necessarily be universal values with regard to information acquisition (see chapter 3). If I am correct, then demarcating science from pseudoscience will be insufficient to dismiss all pseudoscience as ipso facto irrational. I do not question the value of science or the normative force of rationality, nor am I advocating methodological anarchy within science. There are cogent reasons for many precepts of scientific method, but their rationality is in part relative to the goals which the institution of science seeks to realize. Their authority cannot be taken for granted, given a different set of goals.

2.6 "HILL CLIMBING" STRATEGIES

The opposition previously developed between information acquisition and error avoidance is not perfect; these values do not simply represent competing sides in a zero-sum game. Sometimes a change of theories can enhance both

---

[54] Nisbett and Ross call the intrusion of preconceptions into the interpretation of (esp. ambiguous) data or stimuli "one of the better demonstrated findings of 20th century psychology," see *Human Inference*, p. 67.

[55] *Epistemology and Cognition*, pp. 187ff.; Daniel Gilman, *Lines of Sight* (Ph.D. Dissertation: Univ. of Chicago, 1988).

values at the same time. Not all scientific values fall neatly into one category or the other. The problem of old evidence was mentioned explicitly in 1.4, but replication by skeptical investigators (2.3.2) is another hybrid value, and there are others. One might limit pluralism by insisting that any change which can increase both overarching values simultaneously is rationally mandatory. This would give us more normative direction, even if not applicable to every situation. This suggestion has a lot to recommend it, and has been advocated by William Newton-Smith as what makes science distinctively rational,[56] but it is still inadequate as a general rule of rationality.

Frequently one has a theory that explains a phenomenon under a broad range of circumstances, only to discover some particular situation in which it does not work or requires reformulation to make it work. A standard move is to introduce an ad hoc modification to the theory to cover that circumstance, or simply delete that circumstance from the theory's range of application. Such a move obviously enhances the theory's evidential standing, but it also serves to articulate the theory further, giving it increased informational content. Indeed, science rightly uses an abundance of ad hoc hypotheses, yet adding too many does not promote the best interest of science, but indicates that one's research program is bogging down.[57] Why is this so? The method of introducing ad hoc hypotheses is just one kind of move illustrating a general strategy known as *hill climbing*. Taking horizontal coordinates to represent one's theoretical position in a landscape of possible theoretical structures, and taking the vertical coordinate to indicate the amount of epistemic and pragmatic value which each theory realizes, under this strategy one always seeks to move monotonically upward from one's current location through neighboring theories, so long as this is possible. When it is no longer possible, one has reached the top of the hill. The problem with this strategy is that it does not differentiate between small hills and large hills, and can easily leave one stranded on a smaller one when it would be much more desirable to attain a peak value inaccessible from one's starting point by any monotonically increasing path. Sometimes it is better to jettison the entire theoretical mass as an encumbrance, "cutting one's losses" in both values, and try a fresh approach.

This is not to say that the hill climbing strategy is generally a poor one. Imre Lakatos, Larry Laudan, and other historians of science have docu-

---

[56] *The Rationality of Science* (London: Routledge & Kegan Paul, 1981).

[57] Imre Lakatos, "The Methodology of Scientific Research Programmes," in *Criticism and the Growth of Knowledge* (Cambridge Univ. Press, 1970), pp. 91–196.

mented a number of research programs conceived under great optimism that eventually plateaued and began to decline, but while they lasted they were better than having no strategy at all. Lacking any point of omniscience from which to survey their potential fruitfulness, one often does not know how high the hill will turn out to be until one has climbed it. My point is simply that the strategy carries with it certain risks. We may lack omniscience, but we often have some well-founded inklings regarding potential fruitfulness, and may be rationally justified in abandoning a particular program before realizing all of its values to the limit of their potential. Indeed, those who hang on to a program until the last nail is put in its coffin (such as Priestly with phlogiston, Michelson with aether, or Blondlot with N-rays) are most often cited for irrationality within the scientific community.

2.7 SCIENTISM

Scientism, the view that the only knowledge worthy of the name is scientific knowledge, still has a strong grip on the philosophical community despite the decline of logical empiricism in the last two decades. Since undercutting scientism is one of the principal aims of this entire work, I make no pretense of resolving the entire issue in this section, but only intend to fire an opening salvo or two. The meat of my argument appears in the next three chapters.

I noted above that Quine was among those who accept a pluralistic approach, but he does not do so without equivocation for, as a stalwart advocate of scientism, Quine also holds that the standards of scientific justification simply are the standards of rational justification. There is no knowledge worthy of the name except scientific knowledge.[58] If nonscientific explanations of matters of fact cannot be rationally justified, then no distinct genre of religious explanation is possible. This position does not represent the robust pluralism I had in mind, and I reject it as a form of methodological absolutism. How the word 'science' is construed obviously affects the acceptability of scientism. In the broadest sense, it can refer to any form of systematic inquiry, and Quine does use it this way in some passages: "Science, after all, differs from common sense only in degree of methodological

---

[58] See Roger Gibson, *The Philosophy of W. V. Quine* (Univ. Press of Florida, 1982), p. 94; Paul Roth, *Meaning and Method in the Social Sciences* (Cornell Univ. Press, 1987), pp. 44, 57, and esp. 83.

sophistication."[59] If this really is the *only* difference, then when we turn up our methodological sophistication a notch we should be doing science, but proponents of scientism deny this. Elsewhere Quine notes that he uses 'science' in both a broader and a narrower sense, leaving us to guess which he is employing in his statements on rationality.[60]

If there is a uniquely rational method for trading off the desiderata of information acquisition and error avoidance, then there may be a unique method that pervades all scientific inquiry, but the trend in contemporary argumentation has been in the other direction. Since a plurality of paradigms are still found in the social sciences, the unified science thesis suggests that much of this work is unscientific. Now this conclusion is not unwelcome for my argument—it only reinforces my claim that useful knowledge can be found outside science, or that rational justification encompasses more than scientific justification. Critics of the social sciences may also welcome the argument, but the claim that the social sciences do not produce knowledge is a strong one requiring vigorous argument. The most obvious motivation for such a thesis would be a highly idealized view of science, such as was argued to lack normative force in 1.2.

Without a unity of method thesis, however, why should the methods that scientists happen to use be the several and only right methods for all inquiry into matters of fact? Feyerabend criticized Lakatos' theory of research programs for effectively making whatever scientists do rational and whatever they do not do irrational. If global, ahistorical standards of rationality exist, then it seems unlikely that one particular community of humans would have a monopoly on them, or that they could be defined simply in terms of what one particular community does.

Suppose for the sake of argument that the unity of method thesis correctly characterizes science as practiced. Then Hilary Putnam's metainductive argument from the falsity of past scientific theories to the probable falsity of present ones becomes more difficult to escape. That is, Goldman avoids Putnam's argument by denying that a single scientific method exists whose past failure to arrive at the truth can be projected to present or future failure.[61] Goldman also believes Putnam's metainduction is foiled by many

[59] *Ontological Relativity and Other Essays* (Columbia Univ. Press, 1969), p. 129.

[60] *Pursuit of Truth* (Harvard Univ. Press, 1990), pp. 72, 99–102.

[61] Hilary Putnam, *Meaning and the Moral Sciences* (London: Routledge & Kegan Paul, 1978), pp. 22–5; *Epistemology and Cognition,* pp. 158–9.

low level truths generated by science over the years which have survived paradigm shifts and other changes in higher level theory. These are not what generally interest scientists, nor are they what interest philosophers about science, and some would question whether the "butterfly catching" aspects of science are properly called scientific at all. But waiving that issue, I still question whether, or at least in what form, these low level observations or generalizations truly survive. Not only is TAF gone from the lexicon, about which we once had a low level "truth," but more commonplace terms such as 'tumor' and 'white blood cell' are rapidly giving ground to more precise terminology regarding neoplasms and macrophages, etc. If the lexicon of one generation does not even survive to the next, what can be said about its theories and statements of fact? If TAF is cashed out as a definite description, existence claims for it are false. Most of Goldman's low level truths have been abandoned by science, discarded upon the trash heap of antiquated ways of thinking, even when they have not been explicitly falsified. The upshot is that if neither of Goldman's arguments can stave off Putnam's metainduction, then saving the unity of method thesis leads one to anti-realism, which suggests in turn that nothing is normatively salvageable in it. The unity of method thesis gives us neither a basis for denying that truth is attainable, nor for denying that truth should be sought, nor for asserting that the scientific method is the best means for seeking it. Its normative content, if it has any, apparently would be best put in terms of recommendation or permission rather than in terms of obligation.

Another way of trying to salvage a unified science might be to cash out 'avoidance of error' in different terms from 'avoidance of falsity'. Science certainly has going for it a tremendous record of successes—the kind of which legends are made—even if these are not simply successes at generating true statements. This intuition is sometimes formulated in terms of the question, "What alternative to science is there?" If advocating an alternative to scientific methods were to take us back to the non-empirical methods by which medieval theologians sought to acquire information and avoid error, then it might be open to serious objections. Descartes is often criticized because his hyperbolic doubt is not rationally necessary, yet few philosophers note that given the state of philosophy at the time, it might have been impossible to prescribe a better medicine. While I grant that these are important points, let's also bear in mind that scientific success has been somewhat uneven, perhaps spectacular in the natural sciences but not so impressive in the social sciences. A lack of success with one set of methods may sometimes be remedied by trying others.

CHAPTER 3

COMPARING SYSTEMS OF COGNITIVE VALUES

In the last chapter we discussed two values that should be central to any epistemological enterprise, arguing that how one balances them is an issue over which "reasonable men may differ," in the words of Oliver Wendell Holmes. Western religions may place a lower value on theoretical and explanatory knowledge than does science, given their emphasis on faith, charity, commitment and obedience, yet it would be a sad religion that is uninterested in acquiring information about its god, or avoiding error in the process. Given the legitimacy of pursuing knowledge and explanation in religious contexts, auxiliary values can be brought into play that facilitate or are essential for acquiring information and avoiding error. These auxiliary values are the primary focus of this chapter.

The burden of the present chapter is largely deflationary. That is, for the most part I argue against some well-known theses or presuppositions about cognitive value systems employed in religious and scientific contexts, or about the rationality of these systems. Some philosophers make deflationary points by saying "nothing philosophically interesting can be said about" the subject. I hope to present the reader with something interesting in this chapter, despite its deflationary tone.

3.1 WHAT IS A COGNITIVE VALUE?

What the reader normally associates with the term 'value' is probably far afield from the values she will encounter in the following discussion. For example, 'science' and 'value' are often mentioned in the same breath when moral or ethical values are at stake, given the well-publicized and profound ethical questions raised by scientific research. Religious and moral values are often mentioned in the same breath as well. These, in addition to economic, monetary and personal values (pleasure, happiness, health), and other values ancillary to the particular goals they function to promote, play no part in the present inquiry. My focus is on peculiarly *cognitive* values specific to the activities of acquiring knowledge and giving explanations. Past discussants of scientific rationality sometimes wrote as if no such values exist, imagining that the acceptance and rejection of explanations were systematizable into a hierarchy of rules. But socio-historical work since Kuhn has revealed what many good positivists already knew, that there is no algorithm or decision procedure for accepting or rejecting theories. If no algorithm or decisive set of rules exists, then what can be doing the evaluative work other than various values that scientists attempt to optimize? These are what I call cognitive values. Let me hasten to add that I am not suggesting a noncognitive view of morality by contrasting moral and cognitive values. I call these values 'cognitive' *faute de mieux,* since standard terminology for them is lacking, the information processing tasks to which they apply are prototypically cognitive tasks, and calling them values without qualification would mislead people into thinking the discussion pertains to morality.

What is a value? The picture which I find comfortable is that values (or norms) are behavioral dispositions; when we say that someone "has" or "holds" a certain value, we mean that the person is disposed to behave in a certain way. Dispositions are the kinds of things that become manifest in appropriate eliciting circumstances, but not otherwise. For example, sugar's disposition to dissolve, or *solubility* in water manifests itself when sugar is put in water that is not already a saturated sugar solution, but not otherwise. No adequate philosophical analysis of dispositional language exists, but such language is standardly assumed to be descriptive rather than normative, telling us how the world is rather than how it ought to be. A person who holds certain values therefore can be *described* as believing that the world ought to be a certain way or develop in a certain direction. In calling some values global, as I do in the next section, I mean that all people hold or ought to hold such values in epistemic contexts, or that they are *correct.* The origin of this nondispositional, nondescriptive *ought* is not something I can analyze here; I merely presume it exists.

Ease of philosophical analysis requires that we bracket this "comfortable" picture, and talk about values in abstraction from the people who hold them, in much the same way that chemists talk of solubility independently of any compound's disposition to dissolve. Regrettably, this gives the following discussion an air of platonizing, as if I were uncritically reifying linguistic entities. I assume that some cognitive "ought" claims are objective or true, since the only alternative seems to be Feyerabend's methodological anarchy. I do not assume, however, that these truths are easily grasped, that our language for conveying them is perspicuous, or that because we employ a value laden term, therefore some corresponding value has objective existence in an abstract platonic heaven. So I beg the reader's indulgence in understanding that when I refer to, say, *importance* as a value, I should be interpreted as referring elliptically to what people take to be important. It is hard to generalize about what people take to be important, of course, even when the reference classes are limited to 'religious people' or 'scientists'. The most I can do is call attention to general trends or tendencies among religious people or among scientists which I believe are robust enough to be recognizable by most readers.

One would think that the occupational disease of philosophers who write on values must be love of vagueness. Almost every word in the english language has value connotations, or an evaluative dimension, and not only are no two the same, but even for a single word the connotations vary with context. For example, I have been assuming that the value of rationality is positive, but it may be negative when attending a party or if romance is in the offing. One also may not be able to determine univocally that a value is positive or negative when there can be "too much of a good thing."

Criteria of identity or individuation for cognitive values are a pipe dream. Value terms such as 'important' and 'significant' overlap so closely as to be virtually indistinguishable. But is the leading epistemic value of error avoidance the same value as falsity avoidance, or the desire for truth? When one avoids falsity one usually avoids error as well, yet the nuances of meaning that distinguish these are important enough to make certain formulations distinctly preferable. Falsity and truth do not admit of degrees, for example, whereas error can be more or less serious. In pragmatically oriented disciplines, the amount of damage that could result from an error affects the amount of effort one takes to avoid it, so 'error avoidance' is more apt than 'falsity avoidance'. But pure mathematics is different; 'falsity avoidance' might be the more appropriate value term there.

As mentioned, nearly every value laden term denotes a different value. To bring our discussion to heel, we cannot focus on this proliferation of values, but must consider selectively values that are both highly significant in themselves, while aptly representing the diversity found in scientific and religious contexts. Hence, if I mention 'error' and 'control' more than 'falsity' or 'manipulation' in the following sections, it is not from any desire to slight the latter, but from the assumption that sketching prominent features of the lay of the land will enable the reader to fill in the unmentioned details.

3.2 A TYPOLOGY OF COGNITIVE VALUES

Before beginning a detailed discussion encompassing specific values (3.3), it will be worthwhile to map out the kinds of cognitive values that exist, identifying the differences in their logical structure and function that are crucial in the ensuing discussion.

3.2.1 Global and Parochial Values

I call cognitive values *global* when they apply to any knowledge gathering or explanatory enterprise worthy of the name. Failure to instantiate global values in epistemic contexts is irrational.[62] This does not make a religious or scientific practice irrational every time these values are not instantiated, because values are dispositional. Even global values may not be evident in rational undertakings, if appropriate eliciting circumstances are absent. If they are *never* instantiated, or if they are not instantiated in appropriate circumstances, however, then the resulting practice is irrational. Global values contrast with *parochial* values, or those that cannot claim universality. Since my focus is on religion and science rather than any possible theoretical or explanatory enterprise, I will show that values are parochial by arguing that they are not found in one or the other of these cognitive endeavors, or are found only in a greatly diminished or attenuated form, and noting that no requirement of rationality mandates otherwise.

The unruliness of value talk rears its ugly head again in the distinction between global and parochial values, insofar as the same value term can have both a global dimension and a parochial one. Consider *prediction,* for example. Predictions have pragmatic value in helping one anticipate and therefore cope with the future, but also epistemic value in confirming theories and culling erroneous beliefs. In its pragmatic function, prediction facilitates control and manipulation of natural objects and living organisms. Predicting how an organism will react in specific situations enables one to devise effective strategies for eliciting desirable behavior or avoiding undesirable behavior.

---

[62] In calling a context "epistemic" I do not mean that only epistemic virtues are relevant in it. I assume that all cognitive values are relevant in determining what counts as knowledge, including both pragmatic and epistemic virtues.

But manipulating organisms also raises sticky ethical questions, so religious people and the populace at large might not view such a value positively. Absent compelling arguments that one side of the debate is irrational, I conclude that the pragmatic aspect of prediction is significantly parochial to science. The argument here is not that prediction has *no* value in religious contexts as a facilitator of manipulation and control. The point is that if a difference in emphasis becomes great enough, and is not irrational, then the value in question must be regarded as parochial. The distinction between global and parochial values would be worthless otherwise, since few values are so idiosyncratic to a culture as to be completely absent in all others. The difference between global and parochial values is often a matter of degree.

This does not make the epistemic value of prediction parochial as well. Proposed explanations cannot be tested adequately simply on the basis of consistency with the currently available evidence, because then there would be no restriction against ad hocness. First, note that the epistemic role of prediction is not merely a function of time. Retrodicting previous events has epistemic value too, although perhaps no pragmatic value. Retrodictions are predictive in the sense of anticipating that further evidence will be found that such events occurred, or at least that no evidence will be found that they did not. For example, when Edmund Halley first proposed that the great comet of 1682 was periodic, he predicted that it would reappear in 1758. With improvements in astrometry and celestial mechanics, it later became possible to retrodict its previous apparitions over many centuries. The return of Halley's Comet in 1758 was widely heralded for confirming his theory, but combing through observational records of previous civilizations, including a Chinese comet sighting of 87 B.C., yielded significant confirmation as well. Therefore I include both temporal prediction and temporal retrodiction as contained in the epistemic value of prediction.

Once broadened to include temporal retrodiction, prediction is the only effective means available of winnowing theories. Without some epistemic use of predictions, religious explanations would be nothing more than interpretations, and religious beliefs just "high-quality fiction," effectively emasculating religion as an authority or source of beliefs about matters of fact. While this eventuality might be acceptable to some philosophers and theologians, I suspect that most religious people would find it unacceptable, in which case rationality dictates that prediction in the epistemic sense be correspondingly valued. Note that prediction in the epistemic sense does not obviously lead to ethical difficulties similar to those associated with the manipulatory use of predictions. Not all predictions meaningfully extend one's ability to manipulate or control the world.

3.2.2   Desiderata and Constraints

Kant is usually credited with distinguishing regulative rules from constitutive rules, but Wittgenstein freshened the distinction with his concept of language games. According to the usual story, the strategic advantage in chess of controlling the center of the board is treated as a regulative rule—a good idea and an ideal to be striven for, but not a defining "rule of the game." That is, one can ignore the strategic advantage of the center of the board and still be playing chess, although one might not be playing it well. On the other hand, the rules governing castling in chess are constitutive of the game—failure to follow these rules means you simply aren't playing chess, but doing something else.

While these rules are indeed importantly different, there are really two important differences which the regulative/constitutive distinction conflates. First, there is the *functional* status of the precept in question. Some values function as ideals that are not attainable as such, but represent directions in which one attempts to move as far as possible, given other values one is attempting to realize, and other things being equal. Ideals that are thus realized by degree I call *desiderata*. Acquiring information and avoiding error are prototypical desiderata. Rules that function constitutively, on the other hand, I call *constraints*. Unlike desiderata, these can be fully realized or satisfied, and this realization is a requirement for continuing in the activity, but once they are fully realized they offer no further guidance. Some philosophers such as Wolterstorff use 'constraint' to refer to the dialectical effect of two competing desiderata, such as the values of avoiding error and acquiring information, in which neither value has veto-power over the other, but restricts or regulates its realization.[63] To avoid confusion I refer to this effect as *restraint* rather than constraint.

Noncontradiction is often thought to function as constraining scientific and philosophical contexts, although the exact content of the rule is a matter of dispute. A traditional view might allow one to violate the rule and still be doing science, but would place such a violation outside the rationally reconstructed science of interest here. But many philosophers argue that science does and ought to tolerate contradictions temporarily, in the developmental stages of a theory or discipline, or when confronting an anomaly. In Lakatos's words, every research program is "born refuted." I think the revisionists are right here, but I deny that this turns noncontradiction simply into another desideratum to be balanced or optimized along with the rest. What

---

[63] *Reason Within the Bounds of Religion*, pp. 70–7.

it shows is that the precise scope of application of the rule needs refining. Theories that are self-contradictory or contradict established facts are ipso facto unacceptable, but other kinds of inconsistencies are more problematic.

Because of the unsystematic way in which the values of science are structured, the distinction between desiderata and constraints cannot be hard and fast. For example, scientific theories require *evidential support,* yet this is neither a regulative ideal nor a constraint in any straightforward sense. Below a certain threshold, the requirement of evidential support becomes absolute—a hypothesis just is not acceptable without it. But above that level it becomes a desideratum—the more evidential support, the better. Also, some desiderata may have no governing ideal. For example, most scientists value *disinterestedness* to an extent, though they might deny that perfect disinterestedness is an ideal worth striving for.

The second distinction conflated in the regulative/constitutive dichotomy is the *centrality* of the rules to the discipline. A Kantian or Wittgensteinian analysis suggests that the most central rules for a given activity are those constitutive of it, whereas regulative rules are more like rules of thumb, or guidelines for performing the activity well. Since they don't define the activity, they seem more peripheral. Once we give up the idea that science is an activity defined by a set of rules, the centrality of those values functioning as rules can no longer be taken for granted, however. It would be more apt to categorize the values of a discipline as central when they are sought as ends in themselves, or as ends for which that kind of activity is pursued, and as peripheral when they are sought only because they are conducive to central values. For example, acquiring information is more central to science than the law of noncontradiction, which is valued primarily because it facilitates error avoidance. Yet the regulative/constitutive analysis portrays the law of noncontradiction as the kind of rule that constitutes scientific reasoning, and therefore is more definitive of it than avoiding error itself. If one had not conceived science as having a game-like structure, this confusion probably would not have arisen. The goal of acquiring information is broader than science itself, and is of such centrality to science that the "rules" of the scientific "game" are subordinate to it—they are chosen on the basis of their ability to facilitate it. So it is a mistake to think that science has defined goals only once the game context is granted, a fact that makes science less a game and more a profession than chess or rugby. The Wittgensteinian type of analysis is simplistic in reducing normative terms to descriptive terms. The "rules" of science are rules only in a metaphorical sense.

It would still be misleading to give acquiring information the place of primacy within science as that goal to which all other scientific goals are subordinate. Scientists do not seek to acquire just *any* information, after all—some kinds have more systematic value than others, or do more to facilitate control than others. Yet neither can systematicity or control be made into the premier scientific values, since systematicity and simplicity have heuristic value in facilitating the learning and understanding of scientific concepts and theories. Thus, systematicity promotes the acquisition of information, and information which promotes systematicity is especially valued. The value system governing the scientific enterprise is complex, with interrelated parts, and does not possess a single, overarching goal.[64] It is especially typical of desiderata to function in this mutually reinforcing way: theories that realize many desiderata are usually preferred to those that realize only a few. Thus, in calling *description* a scientific value, I should be read as meaning that descriptions of phenomena with *systematic importance,* leading to *testable predictions* are especially valued, whereas descriptions that lack these other features may receive only grudging recognition.

Larry Laudan calls *problem solving* the overarching goal of science,[65] but it strikes me as too vague to be useful. 'Acquiring information' is also vague, yet at least one might turn to information theory for clarification; but who can clarify 'problem' or 'solution'? Ann Landers solves problems, but she is hardly a scientist, and the same could be said for pastors, auto mechanics, and production managers. Infants think that learning to walk will solve their problems, but what light does this shed on the nature of science?

3.3 A TAXONOMY OF COGNITIVE SCIENTIFIC VALUES

What are the ultimate goals or values of science? Throwing the question open, no holds barred, invites a welter of alternative views. Traditionalists might allow that the goals of science vary from discipline to discipline, naming the betterment of the human condition, extending human life, and restoring human health in the life sciences, as well as knowledge for its own sake, achieving greater control of the environment, and improving our understanding of the world. A person sympathetic with this viewpoint might note that some of these values are not properly scientific, but societal values for which scientific activity is encouraged and supported, and to which scientists have obligingly comported themselves. True iconoclasts, however, would doubt

---

[64] Cf. Laudan's reticulated model in *Science and Values* (Univ. of California Press, 1984).

[65] *Progress and Its Problems,* pp. 12–21.

that these shibboleths represent anything more than scientific rhetoric—the values to which scientists pay lip service, but not the dispositions governing their actions. They would say that it is more realistic to think that scientists, like most of us, seek recognition, prestige, wealth, a comfortable life, or perhaps to strengthen the middle class or perpetuate third world domination. They might note further that anything scientists say about their own values, again as for most of us, is probably self-serving, politically motivated, and should be greeted with the same level of skepticism that scientists customarily level towards the members of any culture whose practices they study.

It would be a miracle if scientists were a fundamentally different breed of human from the rest of us, hence much of what these iconoclasts say is probably true, but if we can't take scientists at their word regarding their own values, the task of reconstructing from scientific practice the peculiarly cognitive values that govern it becomes much more difficult. I would be fascinated to know what the "real" values of science are—and given the rhetoric I suspect that religion-bashing is in the top echelons, under what they call "combatting superstition and intellectual darkness wherever it may be found"—but in what follows I content myself to examine the *nominal* or purported values of science. In reality these probably have more instrumental value than intrinsic value for scientists, but they are easier to get a handle on, and there is a long tradition of discussing them in philosophy of science.

3.3.1 Theoretical Desiderata

I select as the first tier of scientific value some values of *theories*, understanding that theorizing is a principal scientific activity, and fundamental to explanation. The first three, *prediction, control,* and *explanation* are uncontroversial measures by which theories are evaluated. I also provide for purely *descriptive* sciences in recognition of such specialties as histology and plant taxonomy, even though these invariably fail to fire the imaginations of philosophers. There is also a virulent movement within the social sciences taking *understanding* to be a preeminent goal of their discipline, rather than prediction or explanation. The controversies historically associated with this movement should not blind us to the fact that gaining understanding of the basic workings of nature is also an important goal of natural science.

In the next tier I include *clarity, simplicity, systematicity,* and *generality,* among others, without making any attempt to determine an order of importance for them. They are secondary relative to the first tier in the sense of representing the typical means by which the first group are realized. One can contrast them by noting that the first tier has more to do with the *content* or *substance* of scientific theories—what they *do* or *say*—whereas the second

A TAXONOMY OF SCIENTIFIC VALUES

Desiderata		
Qua Product		Qua Process
Substantive Ends	Formal	Institutional

Prediction*
Control*
   Manipulation*
Explanation
Description
Understanding
 	
Substantive Means
 	
Fruitfulness
   Promise
Interest(i)
Importance(i)
	Clarity
	   Precision*
	Generality
	Simplicity
	Systematicity
	     Economy
	
	Truth?
	Accuracy?
		Disinterestedness
		Impartiality
		   Skepticism*
		   Suspension of Judgment
		Equal Standing/Access
		Disregard for Persons/Authority
		Group Loyalty
		   Prohibition of Secrecy*
		   Giving Credit where Due
		Intellectual Freedom
		Faith in Rationality

Constraints		
Evidential Support Replicability* Corrigibility Testability	Consistency	Rationality

* Indicates values that are parochial to science to a significant degree.

Figure 1

tier addresses their *form* or how they are *expressed*. There are also subordinate values pertaining to the content or substance of scientific theories. Imre Lakatos, for example, incorporates *fruitfulness* or *promise* (potential fruitfulness) into his notion of a heuristic. Unlike generality, fruitfulness relates not to the structure of the theory or how it is formulated, but to the pragmatics of its relation to other theories, background information, and outstanding problems. *Interest* and *importance* also pertain to this pragmatic dimension of theory content.

Another scientific value sometimes invoked to discredit religious explanations is *economy,* and its career parallels that of importance and interest (see 3.7). Recall Laplace's famous statement when asked why he had not included God in his system: "I have no need of that hypothesis." He wasn't referring to a personal need, but invoking a principle of economy commonly known as "Occam's Razor," by which all posited entities without a clear explanatory function are eliminated. If the basis for economizing is simply the other values in one's value system, the existence of parochial values within that system would vitiate one's ability to give global rational status to one's economizing move. Thus, if the hypothesis of God were unnecessary only because it doesn't enhance one's ability to manipulate the environment—a value previously identified as parochial to science—that would be insufficient to mandate global rejection. If God performed a theoretical or explanatory purpose that enhanced values that are not themselves irrational, invoking God's existence in such contexts could be rational on that basis alone.

3.3.2 Institutional Values

So far the values discussed all apply directly to scientific products—theories, discoveries, research programs, etc. Sociologists such as Robert Merton and his followers have culled a contrasting set of values applicable primarily to scientific processes or practice. I call these *institutional* values insofar as they typically pertain to the relationship of the practicing scientist to her work, peers, and institutional context. They include disinterestedness, disregard for persons and authority, "equal access" to experimentation and forums for defending one's results (i.e., discrimination based solely on competence), intellectual freedom, and faith in rationality. Also included would be *impartiality* in the sense of skepticism or suspension of judgment, and *group loyalty,* which includes prohibition of secrecy and giving credit where due.[66]

The distinction between theoretical and institutional values also is not hard and fast. Some values, such as *objectivity,* could be interpreted either institutionally as an attitude or stance that a scientist takes toward his work, or theoretically as a feature of theories that can be confirmed and used by any investigator, making them part of the "objective furniture of the world."

3.3.3 The Unity of Method Thesis Revisited

To recapitulate, my argument so far has been that values offer us few hard and fast distinctions; the most we can hope for is to map general trends and tendencies within religious and scientific communities. We have identified four major groups of scientific values, encompassing those most frequently

---

[66] Ian Mitroff, *The Subjective Side of Science* (Amsterdam: Elsevier, 1974), p. 12; Robert Ackermann, *Data, Instruments, and Theory* (Princeton Univ. Press, 1985), p. 36; Robert Merton, *The Sociology of Science* (Univ. of Chicago Press, 1973), chapter 13.

cited as governing scientific theory selection. Note that all of these function as desiderata—none appear to be necessary conditions for the rationality of science, either individually or in simple combination. It thus appears that science is subject to many *restraints* but few *constraints*. Figure 1 depicts this structure, supplemented with a likely set of constraints.

Constraints have a major practical advantage over desiderata in that they do not require weighting relative to one another to determine their outcome. That is, one need not determine *how* internally consistent a theory must be, or how *important* consistency is, in order to use consistency evaluatively—even in nonscientific contexts. A theory that is internally inconsistent is unacceptable, and that's that. Given that desiderata dominate science, however, theory selection within science is seriously underdetermined, and not merely in the non-normative, theoretical sense of underdetermination popularized by Quine. Since one can assign any number of relative weightings to these values and still pass for a competent scientist, wouldn't it be a miracle if in practice all scientists assigned precisely the same weightings to these desiderata? The scientific community lacks an effective means either of arriving at agreement on relative weightings, or enforcing any agreement arrived at. So defending the unity of method thesis requires abstracting to the broadest and vaguest outline of a value structure, as my taxonomy attempts to do, in order to find methodological ground that is common to all science. But the unity of method thesis is nearly vacuous if it implies only that scientists share all of these values, and says nothing on the degree to which different scientists (or their disciplines) value them. How ironic that the thesis can be saved only through vagueness, given that it was originally advanced by philosophers known as sticklers for clarity!

Once one gets beyond the major substantive goals of science, such as prediction, control, and explanation, most of the remaining values do seem conducive to acquiring information and avoiding error. These are prototypically global values—norms within the broader academic community, including history, philosophy, and theology—and so broader than any peculiarly scientific method. Although other academic disciplines may not pursue organized skepticism or impartiality to the degree that science does, this is more a matter of relative weighting than an absence of the value altogether. Outside academia, skepticism may be a disvalue in legal, religious, and political contexts which eschew disinterestedness in favor of advocacy. But academic disciplines that openly repudiate these values, such as Marxist sociology, tend to be iconoclastic and have their hands full justifying their own value structure. So it is not these values themselves but contextual factors that make them scientific, further undercutting the unity of method thesis.

Isaac Levi, one of the more positivistically minded among contemporary philosophers, thinks that recent critics of traditional philosophy of science such as Kuhn and Rorty have relied too heavily on the fact that science lacks effective decision procedures, or algorithms, for making choices among theories. Nobody ever imagined that scientists had them, he argues, nor would positivism have so required.[67] From mathematical logic we know that even when an entire discipline's is governed by *nothing but constraints,* there still need be no effective decision procedure for determining which theories are true or false, or which are preferable to others. The fewer constraints one has, the greater the underdetermination. Once one gets to only a handful of constraints and a predominance of desiderata, the amount of underdetermination becomes enormous relative to the mere lack of a decision procedure. Thus, Levi is correct that the decision procedure issue is a red herring, but I fail to see how this fact confers any benefit on logical empiricism or the methodological theses associated with it.

3.4 TRUTH

The status of truth is perhaps more disputed than any other value appearing in the taxonomy. If at one time one could divide theories of truth into three major groups—correspondence, coherence, and pragmatic—now one must contend with any number of hybrid theories. Many philosophers associate truth with realism, so it should be no surprise that dictionaries of philosophy must now contend with internal, convergent, metaphysical, and intentional realists, and the time is long past when one could assume a univocal sense for 'scientific realism'. Discussions of values already suffer from enough vagueness without adding the indeterminacy of truth, so discussing truth *as a value* invites a veritable orgy of obscurity. I cannot vanquish all obscurity, but I put as sharp a point as I can on the following comments, to help them emerge from the nebulosity.

My first claim is that if people with a diversity of personal value structures can plausibly pass as scientists, then people with a diversity of attitudes toward truth probably can too. Why must there be a uniquely correct reconstruction of the role of truth in scientific practice, or a single value

---

[67] Isaac Levi, "Escape from Boredom: Edification According to Rorty," *Canadian Journal of Philosophy* 11, 4 (1981): 595. There does seem to be some justice in this criticism given the way that Kuhn and Rorty have written on the subject (see, e.g., Kuhn, *The Essential Tension* (Univ. of Chicago Press, 1977), p. 331.

of truth with enough normative force to resist being typecast as merely another idealization? It would be implausible to suppose that truth functions as a constraint on scientific theorizing, given that theories known to be false are often retained by scientists, as discussed in chapter 1. As Cartwright says, "The truth doesn't explain much." But then why should the status of truth be any more determinate than the status of other scientific desiderata, which we saw may be treated differently by different practitioners? In chapter 2 we noted how easily desire for the truth may be sacrificed, or a heightened risk of falsity accepted, in the name of acquiring information, especially when risk-averseness stands in the way of arriving at useful predictions or explanations for natural phenomena. A principle of economy is at work here; values are not sacrificed gratuitously. Entertaining a greater risk of falsity for the sake of achieving a better explanation or greater systematicity may be justified, whereas taking on a greater risk of falsity by allowing "wanton" advocacy to replace disinterestedness would not be, insofar as it would not advance any recognized epistemic goal. Nevertheless, the result is that all of the vagaries of the entire value structure now contribute to indeterminacy in the value of truth.

For another example, consider Ian Hacking's claim that experimentalists can't help being realists about unobservables, following the slogan "if you can spray it, then it's real."[68] On his view experimentalists have good reason to believe that their unobservable entities exist, even though their theories about these objects may be false or mistaken in many ways, by virtue of their ability to manipulate them, or use them to create observable effects. Bas van Fraassen, on the other hand, argues that virtually all scientific values can be realized merely for the sake of empirical adequacy without one caring a whit about truth, at least with respect to unobservables.[69] While a van Fraassen-style experimentalist might see less point or value in her work, and might be less motivated to pursue a career in science, it is not clear that any theoretical or institutional requirement of science would force out one type of experimentalist, or discriminate between them.

3.4.1 Different Theories of Truth
Philosophical interest in the truth of religious claims generally revolves around the correspondence conception of truth. This is because it is fairly evident that one *can* hold coherently (whether rationally is another question)

---

[68] *Representing and Intervening*, p. 262.

[69] *The Scientific Image*, pp. 9–12; "Empiricism in the Philosophy of Science," p. 255.

that God exists, along with most of the rest of what educated people in the 20th century are likely to believe. Likewise, although it would be nontrivial to establish that religious practices really have pragmatic value, we want to say that they have such value independently of their truth. Indeed, the acknowledgement of such a value is regularly incorporated as an assumption within functionalist anthropology. In other words, anthropologists assume that religions perform some valuable function for the societies practicing them, or they wouldn't be there, yet they still view themselves as being neutral on, or at least as making no concessions to, the truth of religious claims. So these amount to nonissues in comparison to whether there is anything in reality corresponding to the contents of religious beliefs or religiously interpreted perceptions.

The correspondence theory itself has come under vigorous attack in recent years, and the viability of even a modified correspondence theory cannot be taken for granted. It is a mystical theory insofar as it determines the truth of statements by referring to a nonlinguistic and therefore essentially ineffable reality. It is also metaphysical or transcendental, pertaining to the way things are independently of any possible knowledge or relation to them. I think it is significant that alternative theories of truth have been motivated less by fidelity to the original concept than by the 20th century desire to flee or reduce metaphysics to epistemology, pragmatics, or philosophy of language. Given that efforts to operationalize truth have failed, and given that correspondence to reality is simply what we *mean* by 'true'—however obscure the concept may be—and given finally that correspondence is what is at stake in philosophy of religion anyway, I suggest that we think in terms of the correspondence theory in the following discussion and leave its semantic and epistemological difficulties for another time. Although it is difficult to give a useful, positive characterization of truth as correspondence, we can say negatively that (1) the coherence or lack of contradiction in a system of beliefs is at best a necessary condition for their truth, and is not a good reason for thinking they are true; (2) mere usefulness or pragmatic value for beliefs, or the fact that they contribute to an organism's fitness, also are not good reasons for believing that they are true.

With this much said, let's proceed cautiously. The fact that our concern with religious explanations is not primarily pragmatic also does not mean that pragmatic values or informational virtues previously described (1.4) are not applicable in religious explanatory contexts. For example, I argue in coming sections that clarity and simplicity are primarily of pragmatic or informational value, but they are global cognitive values nonetheless. Because humans are incapable of grasping "knowledge" that is excessively complex or unclear, these values must be instantiated to a significant extent in any epistemic context in order to generate statements whose correspondence to reality can be recognized and tested. Let's take a moment to look at other pragmatic values that are not easily disentangled from truth as correspondence. It is sometimes said that the function of science is only to give us a "map" of reality—it is not required "to *give* the taste of the soup."[70] A map cannot reproduce everything that exists in its area of coverage; even if it could, doing so would sacrifice its utility as a map. Perhaps science aims to give us a map of the world in terms of preeminent scientific values such as prediction and control. If the religious person does not find this the most useful or important kind of map to draw, an alternative map would not automatically be more attuned to correspondence. Even if one *could* reproduce the very taste of the soup, what religious value or significance would this have? The mapping function ultimately pays off in terms of informational or pragmatic value, yet its value is still global insofar as not everything true can be said or is worth saying. In other words, the religious person's cognitive options are to offer an alternative kind of map or give up religious epistemology altogether. If the scientist's choice of features to map is transparently parochial, that does not make the mapping, schematizing, or abstracting function of theories and explanations also parochial.

With these caveats in mind, I still believe that emphasizing truth as correspondence should affect cognitive practices in philosophy of religion profoundly, because the pragmatic values that are in tension with epistemic values often have less of a purchase on a correspondence theory of truth. Recall that epistemic virtues are valued specifically because of their conduciveness to truth, while Newton's and other scientific theories are valued primarily for their pragmatic virtues, despite their lack of truth. Accepting a correspondence theory will normally shift the optimal balance between acquiring information and avoiding error toward avoiding more error at the expense of acquiring less information. This might affect even one's conception of God, since terms such as 'omnipotent', 'omniscient', 'immutable', and 'morally perfect' imply so much more than other terms that might be used, thereby courting a much greater risk of failing to correspond to reality, however useful they may be in motivating religious observance. A more guarded characterization of God would be more likely to be true, simply as a matter of logic.

---

[70] Richard Rudner, *Philosophy of Social Science* (Prentice-Hall, 1966), pp. 4, 68ff., 80ff.; Stephen Toulmin, *The Philosophy of Science* (London: Hutchinson, 1967), pp. 105ff.

Emphasizing truth as correspondence also affects the standards of evidence appropriate in evaluating religious as compared to nonreligious claims. For example, William Alston analogizes religious experience to sensory experience, arguing that the former constitutes evidence for the existence and nature of God in a sense very similar to how ordinary perception constitutes evidence for the existence and nature of concrete objects.[71] Responding to objections, he criticizes what he calls a "double standard" in the level of justification required of religious beliefs as compared to beliefs deriving from sense perception. In other words, if both were held to the same evidential standard, then experience-based religious beliefs would be accepted much more readily. However, if what I have said is correct, it may be proper to hold religious beliefs to a higher, or at least a different standard of justification than other perceptually-based beliefs, even if Alston is otherwise correct that religious experience is analogous to sensory experience.

The big picture that I am suggesting is this. In chapter 2 I illustrated the conservatism of science, suggesting respects in which scientists stick closer to evidential or epistemic values than religious people find necessary, while here I am call attention to the plethora of pragmatic values that scientists employ which unduly compromise truth as correspondence from the religious point of view. Both scientists and religious people must use some pragmatic values, but the ones which they are willing to trade epistemic values for differ. Religious people do not follow scientists in valuing manipulation and control, and consequently do not have the pragmatic need for replication that scientists do. Economy, simplicity, scope and skepticism are not usually driving forces in religion either, but religious people are driven by a sense of interest or importance which I will describe later in this chapter. They are willing to incur epistemic risks for the sake of these values which they would not incur for other pragmatic values.

Strictly speaking, religion and science are not simply aiming for different points of balance on the same continuum between acquiring information and avoiding error, because the kinds of information they are trying to acquire and the means or methods they accept for acquiring them differ. Each strives for an optimal balance of its own pragmatic values with truth as correspondence. The effect is that science's pragmatic values lead it not to safeguard truth as correspondence adequately, as seen from a religious point of view; while scientists would maintain that religion's pragmatic values

---

[71] "Perceiving God," *Journal of Philosophy* 83 (1986): 655–65; see also his *Perceiving God* (Cornell Univ. Press, 1991). He does not take a stand on the controversies regarding just how sensory experience functions evidentially, however.

result in truth as correspondence not being adequately safeguarded from their point of view. There is a formal symmetry here. Neither side believes the other is getting enough pragmatic value for the epistemic risks it incurs; each side believes the other is too conservative in not countenancing the tradeoffs it freely makes. Nevertheless, since the religious context of explanation is my primary concern, the focus of what follows will be on the religious way of looking at the issue, according to which science's pragmatic orientation does not adequately safeguard truth as correspondence.

How religious explanations fare in religious contexts will depend in part on the religion involved. Explanation is a paradigmatically informational or pragmatic value, and not all religions value it equally. If religious explanations can be produced by practices that adequately safeguard truth as correspondence, then their integrity and viability within a religious system of values may be preserved.

Before moving on to alternative general approaches to truth, let us examine one more concrete illustration of how this religious emphasis on truth as correspondence can require adjustments in explanatory practice.

3.4.2 Truth and Replication

One traditional scientific constraint on accepting any claim is that the evidence be replicable by independent (particularly by skeptical) investigators. Replication has both pragmatic and epistemic value, yet making replication a constraint does incur certain risks. Perhaps truths about the world will never be falsified (3.4.3), but they may never be replicated either—that may be just the way the world is. While one may hope that any truths lost by requiring replicability are not important, this may be wishful thinking.

Strictly speaking, no observation is replicable or repeatable, but most garden-variety observations are replicable in the sense that something very similar in content to the original observation may be obtained at will by any investigator. You may not perceive the tree in exactly the same way that I do, but we will probably be hard pressed to find significant differences in our perceptions. The replicability of observations cannot be taken for granted, however, especially when they occur under circumstances that are unstable or hard to reproduce. Most post-positivistic philosophers grant that some states of affairs or forms of theoretical evidence count against observation statements. Even so, they are not easily falsified. My contention is that failure to replicate is usually fatal to scientific interest in a phenomenon, but not generally sufficient to conclude that the original event didn't occur.

As for the signs, wonder, or miracles recorded in historical texts such as the Bible, nobody knows precisely how much of what is recorded is fact and how much fiction, but we can be confident that for the most part, the events that occurred never happened again. What is recorded as happening repeatedly is that God visited each new generation, but always in a different way. If a God exists at all like the God found in scripture, there is no reason to believe that events associated with his activity are normally replicable. Therefore, making a methodological rule such as "The astronomer's rule of thumb: if you don't write it down, it didn't happen,"[72] or "If it cannot be replicated it didn't happen," would not adequately safeguard the value of truth as correspondence from a religious viewpoint.

In a sense, replicability is nothing more than the societal equivalent of constancy of perception. We label collections of percepts 'objects' because they possess a certain complex constancy in our perception that can be abstracted from differences in illumination, perspective, context, and other factors that make their appearances vary. Percepts from which no such constancy can be abstracted we call unreal, including dreams, hallucinations, and perhaps religious experiences. Consequently, reference to religious "objects" or entities such as God requires a level of replication in perception, or they would also be considered illusory. Thus, replication is not irrelevant to religious epistemological contexts. The point is that for humans to have dealings with God and regard God as real, there may always be one sense in which God is doing a new thing, and another sense in which the works of God continually manifest the same (i.e., replicable) eternal truths. Replication thus has a place as a check on reality, but cannot be universalized as a hurdle that every phenomenon must jump over to be counted as real. Universal replication, like its parent, classical foundationalism, is too austere and impractical as a general epistemological requirement, and cannot be more than a desideratum in religious contexts.

Science's striving for generality or breadth of scope carries with it both informational virtues and epistemic risks. Maintaining stringent standards of confirmation, such as requiring replication, may be sensible in order to reduce those risks, but the standard actually serves to compound the risks for certain kinds of phenomena. To look at the problem from a falsificationist rather than verificationist point of view, once a general theory has proven its usefulness and become well-established, most scientists will not reject it when only a few isolated, disconfirming observations have surfaced for

---

[72] Clifford Stoll, *The Cuckoo's Egg* (New York: Doubleday, 1989); quoted by Daniel Dennett, *Consciousness Explained* (Little Brown, 1991), p. 126.

which conditions of replication cannot be given.[73] But treating such observations as insignificant in the face of the theory's demonstrated pragmatic
value does not justify regarding them as untrue.

The analogy of science to mapmaking is illuminating. Just because
there is no particular phenomenon or observation that is identical in every
respect with a given one does not preclude replication, so long as it can be
replicated in certain important respects—that is all science ever attempts or
can accomplish. If one disregards enough details about a particular phenomenon, one can strip it down to a description that is reinstantiated any number
of times or in any number of circumstances. One may then proceed to identify necessary or sufficient conditions for these occurrences, or causal relations into which they enter. Thus, 'There is a brick house on Elm Street'
may be a replicable observation, but 'There is a brick house at 111 Elm
Street this 15th day of November, 1993, at 12:00 noon' will not be replicable. Empirically based statements about the activity of God may fall into the
latter category when they contain specific details, but may be replicable in
a sense when confined only to generalities. To know what can be abstracted
from a statement to make it replicable without altering it beyond recognition
requires, in part, being able to distinguish what is important from what is
inessential in a particular phenomenon, and what seems essential about religious experiences from a scientific point of view may not be so from a religious point of view. Put crudely, you have to know which part of the reported experience is baby and which is bathwater. My point is that what one
finds important about a particular phenomenon may not be replicable under
controlled conditions which one is capable of discovering.

This seems especially likely when the phenomenon involves the actions of intelligent entities, such as a God. The problem goes beyond the
fact that God has no particular interest or desire in being experimented upon,
or in performing on command for the sake of achieving experimental results.
Even human subjects normally are not willing to be experimented upon unless sick or compensated. Daniel Dennett describes the difficulty in terms
of "the vexing problem of anecdotal evidence," a problem I discuss in more
detail in chapter 4:[74]

> a good scientist . . . knows how misleading and, officially, unusable anecdotes are, and
> yet on the other hand they are often so telling! The trouble with the canons of scientific

---

[73] *Data, Instruments, and Theory,* p. 26.

[74] *The Intentional Stance* (MIT Press, 1987), p. 250.

evidence here is that they virtually rule out the description of anything but the oft-repeat-ed, oft-observed, stereotypic behavior of species, and this is just the sort of behavior that reveals no particular intelligence at all—all this behavior can be more or less plausibly explained as the effects of some humdrum combination of "instinct" or tropism and con-ditioned response. It is the *novel* bits of behavior, the acts that couldn't plausibly be accounted for in terms of prior conditioning or training or habit, that speak eloquently of intelligence; but if their novelty and unrepeatability make them anecdotal and hence inadmissible evidence, how can one proceed to develop the cognitive case for the intelli-gence of one's target species?

Imagining that God is the "target species," and the problem is not only to demonstrate his intelligence, but also to determine his other properties on the basis of empirical evidence, one will encounter the same problem writ large. There are alternatives to abandoning the canons of scientific evidence, of course, at least in the case of biological species. Dennett proposes stricter controls on the situations under which anecdotes are elicited, but admits that formidable obstacles exist to implementing such a strategy outside the lab-oratory (271–5).

In the remainder of this section I look at the motivation behind two religious value structures that are often regarded as irrational, and differ rad-ically from the scientific one just adumbrated, arguing that their differences stem at least in part from differences in outlook regarding truth. By the end of this chapter these differences will develop into a general contrast between religious and scientific systems of cognitive value.

3.4.3 Truth as One Among Many Competing Values

Karl Popper proposed falsifiability as a methodology underlying and demar-cating all science from nonscientific or pseudoscientific intellectual activity. His position is inflexible, self-referentially absurd, and grossly oversimplifies scientific practice, but it does have in its favor the following intuition: if "the truth" exists—whatever it may be—it will never be falsified. That is, if we can be so lucky as to propose a true hypothesis at some time or other, and if only falsified hypotheses are eliminated, then over time true hypothe-ses should emerge above the competition.

A more realistic but less reassuring model pertaining to theory change has been advanced recently under the rubric 'evolutionary epistemology'.[75]

---

[75] See Gerard Radnitzky and W. W. Bartley, eds., *Evolutionary Epistemology, Theory of Rationality, and the Sociology of Knowledge* (La Salle, IL: Open Court, 1987); Franz Wuketits, ed., *Concepts and Approaches in Evolutionary Epistemology* (Dordrecht: Reidel, 1984); Kai Hahlweg and C. A. Hooker, eds., *Issues in Evolutionary Epistemology* (Albany: SUNY Press,

On this view, theories are transmitted to succeeding generations by the people who hold them and/or their writings. They compete against one another in the intellectual marketplace, with those judged fit tending to survive while others do not. Under this scenario, something like a process of natural selection can be expected to occur, so that theories naturally evolve, adapt, drift, and go extinct, although the analogy is imperfect. For example, organisms have relatively determinate, finite periods during which they are fertile, but books need not, although in scientific practice the 20-year limit comes close to it. Also, most theories are reproduced in the next generation only in their most recently acquired form. Hence the analogy may not apply to the units of selection, or some kind of Lamarckian evolution may occur. Finally, fitness (survival value) is not the same thing as judgments of fitness.

If the evolutionary model of theory development is apt, it offers no grounds for believing that the true theories will be the survivors.[76] Truth may contribute to fitness, but it is still only one among many values selected for. In particular, *no* species has much likelihood of surviving if subjected to intense competition in its ecological niche—i.e., if there are many competing theories treating the same subject matter, any theory is likely to get lost in the shuffle, regardless of its truth. Factors external to a theory's truth, such as competition, thus directly affect its fitness. Now some philosophers may take this conclusion as a matter of course, but for the religiously inclined it might serve as a rationale for according special protective status to theories known in advance to be true. That is, because of the desire to enhance truth as correspondence, or a different view of what it can be traded for, what might seem a worthwhile risk in another context may no longer be worthwhile. Something like this rationale operates in religious value systems prohibiting skepticism, intellectual freedom, corrigibility, impartiality, etc. These religious value structures aim to *preserve* an already found truth rather than facilitate *inquiry*. Consider, for example, cognitive value structures employed by organizations such as the Roman Catholic Church. Here we no longer have faith in rationality per se, and intellectual freedom within religious institutions is the exception, not the rule. Corrigibility, disregard for

---

1989); Michael Bradie, "Assessing Evolutionary Epistemology," *Biology and Philosophy* 1 (1986): 401–59. Here I focus on what Bradie calls the evolution of theories (EET).

[76] Stephen Stich, "Could Man be an Irrational Animal?" *Synthese* 64 (1985): 115–35; Ruth Millikan, "Truth-Rules, Hoverflies, and the Kripke-Wittgenstein Paradox," *Philosophical Review* 99 (1990): 323–53; Alvin Plantinga, "An Evolutionary Argument Against Naturalism," in *Faith in Theory and Practice,* ed. by Radcliffe and White (La Salle, IL: Open Court, 1993).

persons, and equal standing and access are also attenuated, as are disinterestedness and skepticism.

Given our experience with the undemocratic value systems associated with 20th century Nazism and Communism, there is an empirical case to be made that systems that give up the above "democratic" values thereby render themselves vulnerable to ideological abuse. Even religious people ought to recognize this, given that scientific pronouncements on matters of fact are publicly respected much more than the pronouncements of religious authority figures. Even in the ideal case of the original truths being sound and those charged with preserving them well-intentioned, a significant likelihood exists that they are not correct in the same way or for the same reasons as originally thought, so that matters of interpretation remain open. No matter how perfect God is, humans are prone to error in all that they do. Also, of all species of evidence, evidence for religious claims seems often to be the most vulnerable to multiple interpretations.[77] Furthermore, the dynamics of large institutions works against the likelihood that the preservers are well-intentioned, since people who understand the institutional structure and know how to milk it may have an institutional advantage over people who best understand the truth being preserved and its implications. In this respect, religious institutions are similar to scientific ones, where it stands to reason that many practitioners are more interested in personal gain and economic well-being than the putative intrinsic values of the discipline.

So there seems to be a conundrum here between the praiseworthy end of preserving hard-won truths from erosion by human incompetence, neglect, and "evolution"; and the means that might be employed to do this. The context of inquiry instantiates a much different set of values than the context of an archive, but once the context of inquiry is given up, it is more difficult to discover and eliminate errors that creep in. The notion of elevating the value of truth, or keeping it from being corroded by science's pragmatic rendering of the subject, seems essential to many religious contexts. At present I do not see an adequate solution to this conundrum.

3.4.4 Religious Fundamentalism and the Vanishing Middle
The growth of religious fundamentalism is sometimes referred to as the triumph of irrationalism. I do not necessarily disagree with this assessment, but whenever human irrationality on an enormous scale is being posited,

---

[77] Indeed, John Hick suggests that all evidence is in principle religiously ambiguous—see *Faith and Knowledge* (Cornell Univ. Press, 1957), pp. 150–1.

principles of charity suggest that we look for possible reconstructions of the practice that circumscribe the irrationality more narrowly than initially supposed. Such reconstructions can facilitate understanding, and understanding a phenomenon, in turn, makes it easier to cope with. In the case of fundamentalism, I believe that such a reconstruction is at hand.

First, note that words have different uses, and that they are not always or even most commonly used to make assertions for which the primary normative criterion is truth. Philosophers study this phenomenon in *speech act* theory—the theory of the kinds of actions one can perform with words. For example, philosophers and other academics are notorious for writing hyperbolic letters of recommendation for their colleagues and students. While many lament the lack of truth or integrity in the practice, this lack exists because the purposes of the letters are to assist people to whom one has personal or professional commitments, as they attempt to jump through various institutional hoops. There is little institutional incentive for strict adherence to the truth in this practice, since the potential damage to a professor's reputation can be discounted as both improbable and distant in time, whereas the harm realized by being less hyperbolic or more truthful is more immediate and more likely to occur. Indeed, those readers who recognize this as an instance of a generalized prisoner's dilemma will realize that standard rationality theory indicates that each professor should shade the truth in favor of his colleague or student as much as he thinks he can get away with, knowing that if they are successful, they will have any number of professional opportunities to return the favor, but if they fail they will not. That is, it may be rational to lie if the expected benefits of lying outweigh the expected risks. When this happens in the context of supporting or showing solidarity with someone, I will say that not telling the truth serves a *political* purpose. I am not examining the question whether this political purpose justifies not telling the truth; I am only noting that this practice is ubiquitous, and certainly not confined to religious communities. We are accustomed to discounting governmental and corporate assertions that appear politically motivated.

Christian fundamentalists are a diverse group in one crucial respect: they have many different reasons for believing that God exists, or that God is immanent and active in the world. For some it is a matter of personal experience—perhaps an experience of conviction, inspiration, enlightenment, or something more transcendental. For others, it may be from hearing the testimony of others whom they have reason to trust. Some religious people may have acquired their beliefs by patently irrational means, but many probably have not, given the weight of philosophical argumentation adduced in recent years that these may be rational ways to acquire beliefs in certain contexts. Fundamentalists would not define 'God' simply as 'one's ultimate concern', nevertheless God is and should be a being of ultimate concern to them. Now imagine believing that God exists—a being of all-surpassing value—and confronting skeptical academic literature such as the works cited herein by Harré, Persinger, Proudfoot, Reed, Siegel, Sheaffer, Argyle, Hines, Alcock, Flew, Nielsen, Freud, and others. Add also the fact that many highly regarded philosophers such as Quine, Dennett and Patricia Churchland pepper their works with anti-religious barbs. It stands to reason that this wouldn't be happening if there weren't an academic climate that is unfriendly toward religious claims and practices; when the barbs are especially gratuitous, one can't help but assume that an institutional reward structure exists or they wouldn't be there. If academia is not giving religious beliefs a fair shake, any putative academic criterion of rationality which labels them irrational may also be culturally biased.

This climate has so thoroughly infused biblical studies, that the prevailing view of God therein comes much closer to defunct 18th century deism than to modern theism. That is, while it might be allowed that God inspired some authors of some historical religious texts at some point in history, and that God might have acted at one time to alter the course of human events, perhaps in the incarnation of Jesus, it is very common to assume that any alterations or emendations to the texts or to the story of Jesus that were made since then were purely the handiwork of man and were not inspired or influenced by God, so that they are all seen as corruptions or as "noise" that obscures the original and only true message. Furthermore, there has been so much noise during the centuries of transmission, that little or nothing of the original message is left. Yet there is little in the way of argument to make this point of view preferable. Unlike most academic disciplines, the intellectual frameworks that underwrite biblical and religious studies are determined less by rational argumentation than by how much religiosity a practitioner can stomach—or the amount of scientism she can stomach—and the limits to which she is willing to depart from the norms and attitudes of her colleagues or peer group. In such a scenario, a fundamentalist might reasonably respond that the ultimately irrational act is to neglect or dishonor a being of surpassing value when such a being exists. If such a being appears to have associated himself with a particular text or religious tradition, the most rational thing to do is to take that text or tradition as seriously as one can. This is the attitude that I take literalism as an indicator for, and although these texts undoubtedly are not literally true, calling them literal truths is a speech act that keeps one from sliding down the slippery slope toward an intellectually respectable attitude with virtually no place left in it for worship of God. Fundamentalists deny that intellectual respectability is a sufficient condition for rationality, but in an academic institutional setting, challenging this assumption is a thankless and unrewarding task.

What I am suggesting is that intellectuals and academics have forced the hand of religious people into "irrational" action through the intolerance of some, and the laxity of the rest in maintaining a climate that is as tolerant or "supportive" of religious belief, as the pervasive espousal of multicultural-ism formally requires. Fundamentalism is not simply an irrationalism living alongside a highly rational academic and scientific community. Rather, the vanishing middle ground is probably the only rational ground there is.

3.5   CLARITY

Truth may not be the primary value leading science to eschew God or enti-ties like God from its explanatory scheme. If replication is one such value, it is perhaps no more important than clarity, which presents enough of an im-pediment in itself to give one pause before endorsing religious explanations. It will be helpful to illustrate this with of a less exotic theory than most reli-gious theories—one which was considered scientific at one time, but is now more commonly associated with religious viewpoints—substance dualism.

3.5.1   The Issue of Unclarity for Substance Dualism

Substance dualism, referred to sometimes as Cartesian dualism after its best known champion, is a mind/body dualism that goes significantly beyond the property dualism that is commonly discussed in contemporary philosophy. Property dualists believe that irreducibly mental properties exist—ones that cannot be defined or translated into purely material or physical terms—in addition to the irreducibly physical properties we are all familiar with. This kind of dualism is compatible with garden variety materialisms following the Quinian dictum, "to be is to be the value of a bound variable." That is, so long as one is not quantifying over properties, one is not committed to their existence in the same sense that substances exist—they may be *abstracta* but not *concreta*. In substance dualism the mind and body are thought to be two completely different substances, each with a unique set of attributes. The mind, *consciousness,* or awareness, is not merely an abstract object. It is as concrete as any immaterial entity can be, supposedly capable of existing in-dependently of the body. One almost has to endorse substance dualism to have a religious doctrine of resurrection or reincarnation, since the material body clearly does not survive death.

Mind/body dualism is virtually without supporters among contemporary psychologists, neurologists, and philosophers of mind. It is not that the theory is without evidence. Kenneth Ring and Michael Sabom have pointed out that such a dualism is the easiest and most intuitive way of making sense of near-death experiences—that is, of explaining how such experiences are possible. It has also been noted that paranormal phenomena such as out-of-body experiences are more easily explained using the substance dualist paradigm than reductively, although evidence for paranormal phenomena is rather weak.[78] And if it is a consequence of a common religious viewpoint, then any evidence for that viewpoint thereby becomes evidence for substance dualism. But scientists do not take substance dualism seriously.

Patricia Churchland believes that significant evidence against substance dualism exists, and presents the following arguments.[79]

(1) Dualists argue that the mind or self has an intrinsic unity owed to the nature of mental substance, and that this is a crucial consideration if the self is to survive brain death. But split-brain, blindsight, and other neurological research casts doubt on the notion of a unified self (182).

> In the absence of a psychological and neuroscientific theory concerning cognition . . . counting centers of consciousness . . . is essentially a guess-and-by-golly affair. Until we know *what* we are counting, we cannot begin to count.

(2) Descartes's reason for positing substance dualism was the impressive human capacity for reasoning and language, which he could not imagine being done by the clockwork machines with which he was familiar (318).

(3) The nature of the interaction between the two substances is mysterious, and Churchland questions whether there are any functions that the mind or self can perform independently of the brain, since many of the traditional tasks of reasoning and awareness are known to be affected by drugs and lesions. Yet there are many functions of the brain that are impenetrable to the mental stuff (319). Perhaps the question could be phrased as, "Why suppose that independent substances exist if their interaction is as extensive and intimate as empirical evidence indicates, and if the evidence that mental stuff

---

[78] For NDEs see Michael Sabom, *Recollections of Death* (New York: Harper & Row, 1982), pp. 184–5; Kenneth Ring, *Life at Death* (New York: Quill, 1982), p. 221. For OBEs see Stephen Braude, *The Limits of Influence* (Routledge & Kegan Paul, 1986), p. 237, although Braude is not himself a dualist.

[79] *Neurophilosophy* (MIT Press, 1986), pp. 180–2; 317–23. Page references herein are to this work.

is affected by physical stuff is so much better than evidence for causation in the opposite direction?"

(4) How could substance dualism have evolved in humans? Do other animals have selves and consciousness as well? (320).

(5) What phenomena are explained by the existence of distinct mental substances? (321–2).

Before proceeding, let me suggest how a religious person might respond to these assertions and questions.

On (1), Quine at one time insisted that there can be "no entity without identity"—i.e., without criteria of individuation—but even he has softened this position in more recent writings, leaving it with few defenders. In chapter 7 I suggest a sense in which the self may be two rather than one, so I do not see the unity of the self as crucial in defending mind/body dualism. It is not the substance dualist's job to provide criteria for counting centers of consciousness any more than it is any other philosopher's job, so I take the import of the criticism to be that only neurophysiology holds out the reasonable promise of providing such criteria in the future. Substance dualism leaves us at a theoretical dead end. Since Churchland's book appeared, clinical psychologists have called attention to a new type of ailment—Multiple Personality Disorder, or MPD—and now claim to be able to count the number of personalities that patients have (see 7.4). It is particularly interesting that they do not employ any physical or neurological criteria to make such a count, nor do they assume any particular theory of brain anatomy or physiology. Perhaps Churchland is right that they are engaging in a "guess-and-by-golly" affair, but what prospect does neurophysiology have of improving on it in the near future?

In (2), Churchland resorts to a genetic fallacy. Perhaps she has Descartes's rationale right, but we can imagine far more than Descartes. Indeed, philosophers such as John Searle still question whether the *meaningfulness* of human language can be accounted for in purely mechanistic terms, even with advanced computational devices, although Searle disavows substance dualism as a solution to the problem. I am in a similar position in having no commitment to substance dualism; I simply wonder whether its rejection is a matter of evidence or of something else.

The remaining three questions are difficult and penetrating, but questions by themselves do not constitute contrary evidence. Unlike Eccles and other neurologists who have attempted to defend dualism within a naturalistic framework, a religious person operates under no such necessity and can admit, quite frankly, that the reason for positing an independent substance is to satisfy constraints or conditions of adequacy on the development of his religious understanding of the world—not any necessity arising from empirical neurological data. Given that coherence is a necessary condition for truth, if substance dualism is necessary to make one's religious belief system coherent, then any evidence from any quarter that supports that belief system thereby becomes evidence for substance dualism, even if it has little or nothing to do with contemporary neuroscientific research. Similarly, any substantial neurological evidence against substance dualism becomes evidence against all such religious commitments. Substance dualism may be primarily a defensive tactic—an "empirically degenerating" move, in Lakatos's terms. It is more a liability to religion than an asset, but it could be justified if the system has enough other assets to stave off bankruptcy.

The question of evolution might be appropriate for a substance dualism formulated in a naturalistic framework, but is a red herring in a religious context. Since God is not a material substance, any religious person that ontologizes God has already committed herself to a second kind of substance that has existed since creation. Perhaps humans have some of that substance, being made in God's image, although for all anyone knows other created entities might have some of it too. At any rate, there is no need to believe that it is a product of evolution, or is incompatible with evolution, or that it has any naturalistic explanation.

In sum, Churchland correctly finds significant evidence against dualism *considered purely as a scientific hypothesis*. Scientists may not be remiss in rejecting dualism: Descartes's theory had its day, so far as acceptance is concerned, and proved less fruitful than alternative views. The issue is less clear for rationality in general, however. In the remainder of this section I examine substance dualism from this extra-scientific perspective.

The major problem with dualism is its lack of clarity or intelligibility. A dualist can hardly deny that the body's influence on the mind is both pervasive and profound, yet adequate sense has never been made of how two completely different substances can interact with one another. How is it possible? The attraction of monism is that it leaves so much less to explain. If Plato had posited two Goods instead of one, or if certain eastern mystics had said "All is two" instead of "All is one," they would have invited unwanted conceptual difficulties upon themselves. By the same token, modern physicists are bent on expunging from physics any hint of duality or plurality—the four forces must be shown to emanate from a single force, and the dualities of matter and fields, or of matter and spacetime, are also slated for elimination as soon as someone can figure out how. I can't help wondering, however, whether the imperative for the elimination of all dualisms is driven by the disinterested pursuit of truth, or the passionate desire not to look into the abyss. Perhaps the natural world is not wholly explicable in the way we would like it to be.

Descartes suggested the pineal gland as the locus of mind/body inter-action, leaving unanswered what could happen there to accomplish it. The conceptual nature of this problem makes it especially intractable. Yet this unclarity, and the attendant lack of fruitfulness, have no direct bearing on whether the substance dualist's thesis is *true*, because the problem is more methodological than substantive. For example, one can draw a standard dis-tinction between knowing *how* and knowing *that,* such that a child or pet can know *that* dinner is being served without knowing *how,* or knowing where it came from or what made it possible. We all know that a man landed on the moon, but virtually none of us has any clear idea of how it was done. Even if we could *never* know how, this would not affect our knowledge that it happened. Similarly, we need not have the slightest idea how it is possible for the mind and body to have independent existence for us to possess evi-dence that they do. Methodologically, however, nobody wants to be commit-ted to a theory that leaves the "how" question an irreducible and untouchable enigma, but truth is a separate issue from methodological nicety.

What could it mean to say that consciousness exists independently of a person's body? How could this be known? Some neo-Wittgensteinians suggest that these conceptual problems are insurmountable, in which case it makes no sense to talk of "evidence" in favor of substance dualism, or the possibility that it is true "in spite of" its lack of clarity. But here the sub-stance dualist may reply, following Descartes, that it is imaginable that I be a thinking being, and therefore exist, with or without my body. Reports of near-death and out-of-body experiences present us at least with *possible* sce-narios under which consciousness and perception exist and function without apparent benefit of the body, as seen from a first person perspective. Verify-ing that this appearance is not illusory is nontrivial, but the mere fact that things can appear this way means that the view is not wholly unintelligible.

Scientists do not reject out-of-hand any thesis which lacks perfect clar-ity or intelligibility, so one must probe deeper to understand the rejection of substance dualism. Indeed, one of the most celebrated scientific theories of all time—Newton's theory of universal gravitation—suffered from similar difficulties. Newton postulated the notorious concept of action at a distance which seems impossible from our impingement conception of causation—not to mention our entire experience with causal phenomena and explanations. Even in contemporary physics, it is essentially an article of faith that a low energy *graviton* will be discovered to rescue the mechanism of gravitation from being this paragon of unintelligibility. So why was Newton's theory universally praised when Descartes's is ridiculed? Or consider quantum mechanics, another widely accepted theory in which not all causation occurs via impingement. These theories illustrate that the values of clarity, intelligibility, etc., may be sacrificed for the sake of significant gains in other scientific values, since both theories resulted in gains in prediction, control, explanation, systematicity, economy, simplicity, and fruitfulness. This is why Newton's theory could be immensely successful for three hundred years in spite of postulating a metaphysically otiose form of causation. The problem with substance dualism is that it has neither promised nor delivered any similar windfall of scientific benefits to compensate for its unclarity. Hence, its unpopularity is to be expected. Still, some of the values for which scientists willingly sacrifice clarity are parochial to science. Nothing in this procedure constitutes clear evidence that hypotheses lacking such values are *untrue*.

3.5.2 The Explanatory Value of God

Turning now to considering God as an explanatory entity, we find the same problem of unclarity, only writ large. Assuming God is immaterial, the notion that God can influence or affect anything in the material world raises the same problem of understanding how one kind of substance can influence or interact with a different kind. If an immaterial entity which is commonly thought to be omnipresent is capable of affecting the material universe, then presumably it could affect it at any time, in any location, and in any way. If so, any phenomenon whatsoever could be the effect of God. Yet such a belief contributes nothing to our understanding of natural phenomena, or our ability to predict or control them. Even as an explanation, it furnishes little useful information or understanding regarding either the phenomena themselves, how they were brought about, or the God that caused them. Perhaps the causal dependence of all things on God is a formal truth similar to the formal status of noncontradiction as a law of logic: its informational value manifests itself only in roundabout ways.

Aside from the metaphysical problem created by God's immateriality, we also have the intelligent nature of God. In the case of the natural world, the more intelligent the creature, the more unpredictable its actions, at least from a human perspective. That is, predicting an action seems to require at least as much intelligence as performing it. A posteriori considerations bear this out, for the social and biological sciences have made the least headway toward predicting the behavior of their objects of study, whereas physics and chemistry have made the most, dealing with a substrate with the lowest degree of intelligence. Since God's intelligence far surpasses that of man, his actions should often be unpredictable. Positing God as an explanatory or theoretical entity thus effectively forecloses the possibility of predicting or controlling whatever phenomena he is enlisted to explain, while also foreclosing the possibility of achieving clarity or understanding regarding the production of those phenomena. Such explanations represent a net disvalue to science—a step backward, if you will. So great is the disvalue, in fact, that God could aptly be called the explanatory equivalent of a black hole. Most scientists would sooner give up explanation altogether or treat the phenomenon as an outstanding problem than accept a God-based explanation of it. Even for the broadest questions, such as why there is something rather than nothing, the problems of unclarity and the lack of informative value constitute serious drawbacks to religious explanation. Once again, clarity is a global value to the extent that exceedingly unclear or obscure claims cannot be comprehended well enough to inquire meaningfully after their truth. Hence, unclarity poses a serious threat to the adequacy of religious explanations, though no direct evidence of their untruth.

3.6 SIMPLICITY: SWINBURNE'S EXPLANATORY KEY

Another attempt at a religious explanatory scheme has been offered recently by Richard Swinburne.[80] Like Schoen, Swinburne assumes that there is a unique legitimate value system governing all explanatory practice, and that it is epitomized by the value structure employed by science. Schoen explicitly acknowledges this assumption in arguing that religious explanations (i) fit scientific models of explanation rigorously; and (ii) constitute a potentially competing research program alongside scientific ones, one that would stand or fall according to its relative progressiveness. Thus, he applies one standard of evaluation across the entire explanatory spectrum. Swinburne is less clear on this point, so let me explain why I construe him this way.

First, he calls explanations that cite a person's intentions or reasons *personal* explanations, distinguishing them from *scientific* explanations. He does not base this distinction on any difference in values, however, but apparently on the basis of beliefs regarding matters of fact, viz., Swinburne's dualism. The distinction has the odd consequence of construing social scientific explanations, which typically employ intentional idioms, as personal and therefore *not* scientific—a move probably inspired by Swinburne's assumption of the outdated D-N model as a scientific standard.

---

[80] Page references herein are to *The Existence of God* (Oxford: Clarendon Press, 1979).

Second, he does not cite a difference in the weight of values as creating the possibility of religious explanations. Rather, he seems to believe that scientific values, if carried through to their logical conclusion, would lead one to endorse religious explanations. I have argued in 3.4 for the propriety of elevating the value of truth relative to some pragmatic values parochial to science when in religious contexts, and argue similarly in 3.7 for *importance* and *interest*. Without these changes, it seems unlikely that religious explanations could ever be legitimated. It is not an accidental oversight that God was left out of science's explanatory scheme, nor is it just because scientists are irrational or stubborn, even if, like everyone else, they sometimes are. Religious explanations do not harmonize well with the scientific value structure, since God is on the one hand supernatural, but scientific values embody the desideratum that explanations be given in naturalistic terms.

Failure to recognize this partly reflects the fact that Swinburne's taxonomy of values is less fine-grained than the one presented in this chapter. This makes it possible for him to overlook many parochial scientific values other than overtly reductionistic ones. Indeed, he recognizes only four cognitive values: scope, simplicity, agreement with background knowledge (i.e., knowledge outside the theory's scope), and explanatory power (52, 78ff.). Noting correctly that the greater the scope or generality of a theory, the less likely it is to be true, he discounts this as a consideration because greater scope is usually accompanied by greater simplicity, and he believes simplicity counts more in favor of a theory's truth than scope counts against it. So heavily does he weigh simplicity, in fact, that he proclaims "the simple is the sign of the true" to be the dominant theme of his book (56).

This error is fatal to his whole program. As noted in 1.4, simplicity is primarily a pragmatic or informational virtue, not an epistemic or confirmational one. Thus, in his book on simplicity, Elliott Sober equates it with informativeness and contrasts it with probability (likelihood).[81] We choose simple theories because they are easier to learn, understand, and use, not because they are more likely to be true. Simplicity is a criterion in curve-fitting not because it is a rosetta stone for truth or likelihood, but because it produces more useful results. As pragmatic virtues go, simplicity has an aesthetic dimension similar to the aesthetic dimension of *elegance* in mathematics. Aesthetic values may have legitimate cognitive functions in religious

---

[81] *Simplicity*, pp. 1–37, 166. However, Sober ultimately adopts a pragmatic theory of truth in which truth and simplicity are positively correlated. This leaves one uncertain what probability he is talking about. See also Nelson Goodman, *Problems and Projects* (Indianapolis: Bobbs-Merrill, 1972), pp. 346, 351–2.

contexts, but they are as much in tension with truth as any pragmatic value. Those who note the tendency of modern physicists to employ aesthetic values as criteria for theory selection (e.g., with respect to quarks or the unified field theory) have done so specifically to suggest that truth as correspondence is thereby put at risk. The fact that simplicity usually increases with scope should have tipped Swinburne off to its inimical proclivities vis-à-vis truth. The upshot is that Swinburne's coarse-grained value system effectively lumps systematicity, economy, and generality—pragmatic virtues all—under 'simplicity', smuggling everything that normally works against avoiding error through the back door into the camp of supposedly epistemic virtues.

A Bayesian, Swinburne takes simplicity and agreement with background knowledge to inform our prior probabilities, and only explanatory power to inform our posterior probabilities. This means that on the basis of the first two we supposedly form a judgment of the likelihood that a theory is true antecedent to performing any tests on it or gathering any evidence. By conflating pragmatic and epistemic virtues, the most his Bayesian program can offer is a mechanism for justifying theory acceptance, but the term 'probability' employed has a prior association with truth. Thus, Swinburne's program employs a hidden assumption that a pragmatic theory of truth is adequate in this context. Once it is clear that the pragmatically oriented conception of truth we usually find in science is not appropriate for the philosophical evaluation of religious questions, it should be evident that the same Bayesian "black box" cannot work for both.

There is a deeper problem with the Bayesian approach. If there is no agreed upon method for fixing one's prior probabilities, the Bayesian system is incapable of producing any determinate or meaningful results. What basis is there for estimating the prior probability that a Christian God exists, given the way the world is? Fundamental disagreement on this issue appears unavoidable within a purely Bayesian framework. Thus Robert Prevost remarks of two Bayesians, "Richard Swinburne believes in the existence of God; Mr. John Mackie does not. Their disagreement ends there."[82]

I have no quibble with the global credentials of simplicity as a precondition for the possibility of knowledge, but this cannot justify the reification of simplicity that takes place when it is assumed correlated with truth *tout court*. Swinburne calls upon simplicity to argue that his version of theism, which is allegedly simpler than any other, is therefore a priori the most likely

---

[82] "Swinburne, Mackie and Bayes' Theorem," *International Journal for Philosophy of Religion* 17 (1985): 175.

theism to be true. In fact, it is *so* simple that it has significant antecedent likelihood overall. But to think that a theory's truth qua correspondence can be pulled out of a hat like a rabbit, strikes me not as a virtue of simplicity, but as a vice of simple-mindedness.

As for the important global value of clarity, Swinburne makes no mention of it. He cites the purposes and intentions of God as being a natural stopping place for explanations, beyond which there is nothing to be gained by inquiring further. Picking up on my previous analogy, one could indeed say that black holes are a natural stopping place for matter, and there is little point in inquiring what happens to matter after entering one, since its form and identity are irretrievably lost and only its mass "survives." Yet that does not lead us to believe that we have arrived at clarity regarding what black holes are like, what goes on in them, or what happens to the matter "afterward," nor that such question are not worth asking. To preserve useful explanatory content and advance the goal of understanding, one should avoid explanatory black holes, not embrace them gladly. Thus, not only is there some justification for making God an explanation of last resort, but it is incumbent on anyone offering such an explanation to determine to the extent possible the nature of this God and the reasons for his action.

3.7 INTEREST AND IMPORTANCE

By themselves, interest and importance are vague enough to represent significant evaluative factors in any kind of theoretical system, and so qualify as global values. Yet nothing could be more variable or parochial than the particular concepts, theories, or evidence considered interesting or important in different contexts. To be sure, some of this variability can be accounted for as variation in the rest of the value structure. If one values control, then theories which help clarify and facilitate control will seem more important than they would to someone who does not value control. 'Importance relative to the rest of one's value structure' may be a global value, even if the value structure at issue is parochial.

3.7.1 Parochial Aspects of Interest and Importance
Beyond this, however, finding global aspects of the values of interest or importance is difficult. For example, it would be pure fantasy to suppose that the personal interests of researchers do not help determine which problems they work on or which theories they propose. It is only natural to work on problems which one finds interesting. One consequence is that scientists,

tending as they do not to believe in an after-life, have more of an interest in seeing the present life prolonged, and consequently take a greater interest in solving the riddle of aging, than do religious people who expect to be better off in an after-life. Here the difference in interest or importance stems not from differences in the value structures of science and religion, but from different substantive beliefs regarding matters of fact. If rationality alone cannot show that one of these beliefs is irrational, the resulting evaluations of interest or importance will be parochial to that degree.

Can anyone claim that what she finds interesting is therefore important in some objective sense? If so, the charge that these values are parochial could be overturned. Scientists attempt to achieve as much universality or as broad a scope in their theoretical undertakings as possible; hence they might claim that what they regard as important or interesting has a universal claim to be so valued. But placing a value on universality does not automatically give one a universal value—the former is a matter of purpose or intent, while the latter requires that the purpose be accomplished or the intent fulfilled. Religious people might argue in a similar vein that religion deals with questions of life and death; of the wonderful, sacred, and beautiful; and of what is worthwhile, meaningful, or fulfilling in life. These cannot help but be ultimate concerns for all people; hence they have a universal claim to importance. The rub here is that importance and interest have a pragmatic dimension: once it is determined that an otherwise important question is impossible or nearly impossible to answer objectively, the objective importance of seeking answers becomes greatly diminished. How important must it be "to dream the impossible dream; to beat the unbeatable foe"? Won't this vary with a person's predilections, rather than being fixed by some objective state of affairs?

Indeed, there is a recognizable tendency among scientists to apply their technical tools on problems that these tools offer some prospect of solving. That is, science seeks explanations wherever they can be found, rather than pursuing a preset agenda, as is typically done in religious inquiry. Pragmatic considerations favor such a policy. For example, it could be viewed as a "maximin" solution to the allocation of intellectual resources in the face of uncertainty, on the rationale that it is less risky to work on a small but soluble problem, where at least some progress appears guaranteed, than on a bigger problem where it is possible to devote considerable effort without making any headway. This *modus operandi* is also implicit in Laudan's theory which marks the solved problem as the unit of scientific progress. Contemporary analytic philosophers also tend to pass up traditionally insoluble riddles in favor of narrower, more tractable problems.

By contrast, the phenomena inviting religious explanation typically have great importance, at least subjectively for the people involved, and their importance sets the agenda of seeking explanations, not the apparent solubility of the problem. This is arguably rational too, though decidedly less practical. For example, the failed arguments for Pascal's Wager or James's Will to Believe might be reconstructed as "maximax" solutions to decision problems under uncertainty. A religious person could say that focusing on picayune questions while ignoring ultimate existential issues of right and wrong, life and death, the beautiful and the wonderful, heaven and earth, has all the rationality of rearranging deck chairs on the Titanic. If one can't find a way to save the ship or the lives on board, one might as well play backgammon.

Within religious explanatory schemes I envision importance being promoted to one of the places of primacy—it becomes one of the ultimate defining values on the basis of which religious explanations are sought. It is not just that religious beliefs center around questions of life and death, or existence and nonexistence—this could also be said of science. It is important but impractical qualities generally ignored by science, such as *wonderful, worthwhile,* or *meaningful* existence, which cast the former concerns in a different light. Religious belief is involved with a preset agenda which is inalienable to it, and properly so. Its problems are of ultimate importance to a great many people; they cannot be ducked just because they are difficult to solve. To "table" or shunt such questions to a list of outstanding problems would be to take a more scientific and less religious attitude toward them.

Considerations from previous sections suggested that some infirmities of religious explanations (e.g., lack of clarity and prediction) do not merely reflect the parochial viewpoint of science, even if others do. Given such global disvalues, compensating positive values may be needed to make religious explanations viable. Two positive values have already been mentioned: (1) If there is a Supreme Being, it seems that information about who he is, what he is like, and what he does, would be important information to have; (2) Explanations involving God may be legitimately withheld from straight-up competition with explanations derived from a system in which truth is not adequately safeguarded. The pragmatic values that predominate in science compromise its ability to evaluate religious claims, whereas a re-structured system of values that promotes importance and truth as correspondence appears essential to the rationality of the religious agenda.

3.7.2 Interest vs. Disinterestedness

Like importance, *interest* is largely subjective, but its ambiguity is compounded by the "objective" economic and/or political interests people have in the outcome of a particular line of inquiry, and its status is further complicated by a prima facie conflict with another global value, *disinterestedness.*

Not all judgments of personal interest are sacrosanct, yet they are difficult to fault. If Husserl did not find anthropology interesting, that is not chargeable to the subject matter. On the other hand, it also does not reflect poorly on Husserl. As a value, interest tends to be more personal than normative, yet it still influences academic disciplines. For example, what dooms many discussions of religious positions is not disinterestedness per se, but simply disinterest. Widespread indifference within the academic community to discussions of the rationality, truth, or evidence for religious claims seems attributable to the fact that the parties to the debate tend to be partial, or speak from the perspective of their own entrenched economic, political, or religious interests. In such an atmosphere one does not expect discussion to produce anything new or valuable. Thus, when the parties to a debate are not *disinterested,* we sometimes lose *interest* in what they have to say. Let us take a moment to disentangle these values.

Kuhn made a point of tying incommensurability to interest, claiming that the problem of incommensurability between paradigms is no more intractable than that of translation, but persists because scientists do not seem interested in overcoming the language barrier. Their tendency—perhaps their preference—is to speak at cross-purposes, rather than take care to explicate their conceptual differences. Kuhnians do not always use 'interest' to refer to this phenomenon, but often describe it as a difference in the perceived importance of outstanding problems.[83] The problem of incommensurability, and of the tunnel vision of interest, is not limited to interdisciplinary contexts. Even at the intradisciplinary level, especially within the social sciences and religious studies, where a multiplicity of paradigms are in force, people operating within different paradigms find the sets of assumptions employed by others so unpalatable that they can hardly sustain interest in one another's work. For example, behaviorists and clinicians are both psychologists, but often have little tolerance for one another's work. Perhaps paradigms could be defined in terms of divisions among shared interests. The point is that here we have a value with very weak normative credentials playing a major role in setting the agenda for scientific research. It is not that we are in a position to overrule individual interests, or deny people their

---

[83] "Reflections on My Critics," pp. 232–3, 267–8, and esp. 276–7. See also *The Structure of Scientific Revolutions,* 2nd ed. (Univ. of Chicago Press, 1970), pp. 109–12, 148–9; Gerald Doppelt, "Kuhn's Epistemological Relativism: An Interpretation and Defense," in *Relativism,* ed. by Krausz and Meiland (Univ. of Notre Dame Press, 1982), pp. 118–23.

preferences, yet at the same time these preferences, though strongly held, have little to recommend them "objectively." It would be nice to have a value structure without such a glaring weakness.

Now consider the value of disinterestedness. It is ostensibly conducive to arriving at the truth through the rejection of advocacy, partiality, prejudice, and bias—traditional sources of erroneous belief. But where does that leave phenomena in which people are inherently interested—those involving attributes that are widely regarded as personally important, such as the religious phenomena mentioned above? If one's primary interest is to see the truth come out, that should not be counternormative, but it is quite possible that one cannot help having an "objective" interest in a particular outcome no matter which side of the question one defends. Either one is religious or one is not, and a great many people develop deep personal stakes in their positions on religious questions. When this happens, it seems inappropriate to declare the issues off-limits to inquiry so that a disinterested posture may always be maintained. All scientists advance some theories and criticize others, thereby developing interests in seeing one or another position prevail.

In sum, inherent interest in a phenomenon or issue can be a liability, but the religious program by which interest is elevated to a central place in the value system is not irrational, if the only alternative is to give up on the subject matter altogether. Interest in what makes for meaningful or worthwhile existence is not merely pursuing a personal interest or hobby, but an interest that most everyone can appreciate. Once interest is acknowledged as a legitimate consideration in setting one's explanatory agenda, it would also seems to militate in favor of pursuing religious issues. If qua methodologist or qua pedagogue one has little interest in pursuing religious explanations, it still seems difficult qua human being not to be interested in the wonderful, in love, or worthwhile existence, if such there be.

3.7.3 Is Disinterestedness Out of Place in Religion?

Swinburne makes no mention of institutional scientific values such as *disinterestedness*. If one believes God to be real and to have the power to give or deny people ultimate rewards and punishments, then one will have the greatest possible "objective" interest in currying God's favor, an interest that conceivably could lead one to praise God in reckless disregard for the value of truth as correspondence. Thus, it sometimes seems to me that religious people are worshipping not God the Father, but the Godfather. In particular, Swinburne's apparent willingness to ascribe to God every conceivable perfection "sight unseen" (90ff.), seems illustrative of a common tendency uninformed by the value of disinterestedness.

At first blush, disinterestedness seems inappropriate for religious contexts, even epistemic ones. This is because much of religious "knowledge," at least from the standpoint of revealed theology, is knowledge in the sense of *connaître* rather than of *savoir*. It is not knowledge of facts or about a subject so much as it is knowledge of a person through acquaintance or intimate contact. One does not acquire such knowledge through disinterestedness, nor does it seem to be the proper posture to take when renewing one's acquaintance. Disinterestedness involves *distancing* oneself from the object of knowledge, but few religious people see distancing themselves from God as a positive value. Put another way, perhaps the scientist can afford to be hardnosed about his subject-matter, being mere atoms and compounds and rocks and trees, but most religious people cannot in good conscience maintain a similarly hardnosed attitude toward God.

My recommendation is not that disinterestedness be made into a standard operating procedure or policy in religious contexts. It would not be viable as a rule or norm for religious behavior, even limited to epistemic contexts. But there is some value in providing for the occasional exercise of disinterestedness in order to let some fresh air into what often become stale and tedious discussions of God's many perfections. There is no harm in forming one's conception or knowledge of God out of both intimate and distant perspectives, and a plurality of perspectives may aid one in framing a more balanced picture. Furthermore, disinterestedness could be valuable even for attaining *connaissance* of God. My suspicion is that God may have every conceivable perfection, but cannot be known (*connaître*) as such. Theists maintain that God has a personality and made man in his own image, yet nobody would presume that he could know what any particular man or personality is like by reasoning a priori about the nature of man in general, or of personality in general, as opposed to meeting the fellow face to face, or living with him. Now imagine living for a while with someone who never admits to any wrongdoing, never apologizes, thinks he is the greatest on earth, takes liberties in telling others what to do, and basically wants nothing other than to be worshipped constantly by everybody. Suppose further that he reproves those who (inevitably) fail to endorse him in all of this. How long would you then maintain the same opinion of him? Yet are any of these traits not truly ascribed of Jesus of Nazareth? Perhaps there *is* a downside to God's nature worth taking account of, after all! None of these personality traits are inconsistent with God's perfection—my claim is only that they may make that perfection a little hard to appreciate from our vantage point, which is necessarily the only vantage point we have. Thus, one apologist for Beethoven argued that he was not egotistical even though he thought himself the greatest composer on earth, because it was true. I doubt that this was much consolation to the people whose lot was to live with him.

I know this sounds wonderfully blasphemous, but the point is this: if we disregard the value of truth here, which to a degree disinterestedness functions to advance, what other peculiarly *cognitive* values will thereby be promoted to justify its dismissal? Perhaps knowledge of God is dangerous, but there may be little alternative for the religious person who refuses to identify "true religion" with worshipping the equivalent of Locke's "something, I know not what."

3.9 CONCLUSION

My suggested alternative value structure, as adumbrated during the course of this chapter, is presented below in Figure 2. For ease of presentation, the positive values emphasized within this structure appear in the top tier of desiderata, while the formal values have been retained in the same column, although this does some violence to the formal/substantive distinction. Importance, interest, and truth as correspondence are the major values being elevated. The democratic institutional values have generally been retained, because I assume that the context of religious explanation is a context of inquiry rather than of an archive. Most scientific constraints have also been preserved. While some parochial scientific values are specifically downgraded, I do not believe this is necessary for skepticism and suspension of judgment. Once they are brought into harmony with the enhanced values of importance, interest, and anecdotal evidence (chapter 4), they may function well, although their customary scientific valuation cannot be carried over to religious contexts without modification. The same could be said for anecdotal evidence: it is promoted only to a point of balance appropriate for the dearth in quantity and quality of other evidence on those questions that are of greatest religious concern. However, I omitted it from the group to be harmonized because this group's other members generally share a common pragmatic orientation that would suffer somewhat under the proposed emphasis on truth as correspondence.

Although the epistemically important values of prediction and control have been downgraded, they are still perhaps the best means of ensuring testability, whose status as a constraint still seems incontrovertible. It seems incumbent on religious people who abjure prediction and control to articulate an adequate alternative means of testing theories, in order not to shortchange the value of error avoidance.

A PROPOSED RELIGIOUS REVALUATION OF COGNITIVE VALUES

Desiderata		
To Retain the Same Value or be Upgraded		
Substantive Ends	Substantive Means	Institutional
Truth (emphasizing correspondence) Importance Interest Explanation Description Understanding	Fruitfulness Promise Anecdotal Evidence (used cautiously)	Intellectual Freedom Equal Standing/Access Disregard for Person/Authority Giving Credit where Due
	Revalue to Harmonize with the rest of the Structure	
	Replicability	Disinterestedness Skepticism Suspension of Judgment
To be Downgraded	Formal	To be Downgraded
Control Manipulation Prediction	Clarity Generality Simplicity Systematicity Economy	Prohibition of Secrecy Faith in Rationality
Constraints		
Evidential Support Corrigibility Testability	Consistency	Rationality

Figure 2

CHAPTER 4

ANECDOTAL EVIDENCE

4.1 INTRODUCTION

Where can I find a good auto mechanic who doesn't charge an arm and a leg? How about a professor who really teaches well and cares about his students? What would be my chances of making a living as a free-lance photographer? On which streets are the speed limits strictly enforced? Which bars and restaurants are hot spots on Saturday night? When are the wildflowers at their best in the Colorado Rockies? What these and many questions like them have in common is that their answers may be quite important to us but not readily available. In such cases we often must rely on anecdotal evidence—testimony from people who happened to be in the right place at the right time to know something about the subject. Anecdotal evidence may take the form of reports of first-hand experiences, but also includes second- and third-hand retellings.

Something can be *evidence* only relative to one or more hypotheses, which distinguishes anecdotal evidence from mere anecdotes. It is evidential to the extent that it represents a single instance of the hypothesis in question—the smallest unit of confirmation allowed by traditional inductivism. Yet anecdotal evidence normally receives short shrift among philosophers of science compared to, say, evidence that has been systematically gathered and replicated in controlled settings by skeptical investigators. There are epistemic and pragmatic reasons why the latter lends stronger support to a hypothesis. Replication means that more instances of the hypothesis have been found; control means that at least some potentially confounding factors can be discounted; and skeptical defenders are less likely to be biased in its favor than enthusiasts. This does not prove that anecdotal evidence has no value, but explains why many scientists and philosophers of science regard it as almost worthless (recall 3.4.2).

Stereotypically, anecdotal evidence features narrative accounts that are both concrete and of human or emotional interest.[84] While often thought to be isolated observation reports of nonscientists, we saw in 2.3.1 that it need not come from nonscientific sources. Rather, the most important differentia of anecdotal evidence are (I) its stemming from situations lacking adequate *controls* and (II) the absence of *replication*. Direct observations fitting these criteria qualify as functionally anecdotal, even when they are one's own. Experimental evidence can also qualify as functionally anecdotal under the above conditions, especially in the social sciences.[85] This makes anecdotal evidence a much broader category than customarily supposed. I construe anecdotal evidence broadly here because my primary concern is to delimit an epistemic natural kind, not to provide a faithful rendition of ordinary language.

Each of these differentia is somewhat fuzzy, so let us take a moment to unpack them. Criteria for the adequacy of controls have varied over the history of science. For example, discovery of the placebo effect demonstrated that blind studies are necessary to establish the efficacy of medical treatments. Yet soon after this discovery it became evident that single-blind studies—studies that control for the influence of patient beliefs by giving some patients placebos and others treatment with therapeutic value—are also inadequately controlled, because the expectations of the health-care practitioner can also bias the results. The brief history given by Benson and McCallie of treatments for angina reflects changing scientific criteria of adequacy for experimental controls, in addition to the stock movement of scientific investigation from the hands of enthusiasts to those of skeptics. Once better-controlled studies were available, the evidential value of the former were reduced to that of "interesting stories" about what some investigator or other found under circumstances of questionable value—i.e., equivalent to anecdotal evidence. This is not to say there is universal agreement on what controls *are* better. Thomas Cook and Donald Campbell argue that randomized double-blind studies may not be preferable to studies that selectively control for factors which one has a special reason to believe might be causally active.

---

[84] Herein I take 'anecdotal' to modify 'evidence' and 'narrative' to modify 'explanation'.

[85] See Nisbett and Ross, *Human Inference*, p. 282; as well as the discussion in 2.3.1.

That is, randomized, double-blind trials take a shotgun approach to the problem of control. One might prefer careful targeting of potentially confounding factors, if one can identify them in advance.[86] Ethical or other pragmatic reasons may also necessitate a selective approach to control.

Turning to lack of replication, this may be due either to the absence of attempts to replicate, the failure of replication in the face of efforts to do so, or successful replications that are limited to uncontrolled circumstances. In the case of parapsychology, where failure of replication is often cited as grounds for skepticism, one typically finds recurrence of equally unusual phenomena under circumstances that make more routine explanations unlikely, but the occurrence usually is not of the same "kind," and does not occur when predicted or on any reliable or dependable basis. A lot depends on one's choice of kinds, or how specific the predictions are expected to be. It is consistent with all of this that the phenomenon is genuine and investigators have simply failed to identify the right group of causal factors, or *reference class*, under which it regularly arises. But almost any hypothesis can be made consistent with the evidence if one is willing to tinker enough with auxiliary assumptions.

Many reasons why a phenomenon hasn't been replicated are fairly innocuous. Here are a few:

1. flaws in experimental design
2. experimental conditions that are not easily duplicated
3. not enough time has elapsed to perform additional experiments
4. incomplete information about the original experimental setup
5. nature is not uniform in the way it is assumed to be
6. some phenomena are extremely improbable, even relative to their causes.

Not only are these considerations consistent with the phenomenon's being genuine, but most of them crop up frequently, and require little in the way of auxiliary assumptions to explain why replication failed.

Aside from the two principal features of lack of control and lack of replication, the concept of anecdotal evidence involves a number of grey areas. Any experimental result obtained for a first time will lack replication. Does that make all such results anecdotal? Epistemologically, yes: scientists tend to be cautious about initial results until other investigators have confirmed them—a policy with a transparent rationale—even if the original experiment was well-controlled otherwise. For non-experimental evidence,

---

[86] "The Causal Assumptions of Quasi-Experimental Practice," *Synthese* 68 (1986): 141–80.

some social and biological sciences employ field investigations or case studies involving unique conditions or circumstances. Such nonreplicable, minimally controlled evidence differs from what I call anecdotal evidence more in degree than in kind. Photographs and other measurements made with scientific instruments could count as anecdotal if made in uncontrolled settings and unreplicated. Yet such evidence is usually regarded more highly than most anecdotal evidence because of its immunity to the vagaries of human memory and rehearsal, and because the act of measurement effectively imposes a number of controls on the situation that would otherwise be absent.

As we will see, phenomena that are both rare and transient lend themselves to being known initially only through anecdotal accounts, and tend to be controversial when they lack other evidence. Anecdotal evidence encompasses many odds and ends of scientific and extrascientific observations, not yet assimilated into any theoretical corpus. Not all anecdotal evidence involves contested claims to reality, either. In the Ford/Rockefeller example (see 4.2.2), the facts of the matter are well-attested among medical practitioners, and only their interpretation or significance is unproven.

4.2 TWO CRITIQUES OF ANECDOTAL EVIDENCE

My overall normative position is that anecdotal evidence usually inclines without compelling acceptance of any hypothesis for which it is adduced. The parents of a biblical man born blind (4.2.1) may have compelling evidence that he was born blind but now can see, but the compellingness of this evidence falls off rapidly for people in an evidentially more remote position. Since this much seems fairly obvious, most of this chapter is devoted to defending the claim that anecdotal evidence can justify or legitimate beliefs about phenomena that would not be justified otherwise. An important preliminary question must be tackled first, however. Before considering what beliefs anecdotal evidence justifies, we need to argue that using anecdotal evidence *as* evidence is itself justified, even when other evidence is available. This is the topic of this section.

Here is the rough picture that informs my discussion of the subject. Assuming that theoretically integrated observations make up the backbone of science, anecdotal evidence may be thought of as constituting its "soft underbelly." A Nietzschean who wants to "live dangerously" might feel comfortable using anecdotal evidence, but "fools rush in gladly where angels fear to tread," or so they say. My point in repeatedly invoking the necessity of using anecdotal evidence in everyday life, and the availability of rational principles undergirding skillful use of it, can be put crudely thus: a backbone is only an organ, not an organism. In a world in which only the fittest survive, "dangerous" living may be the only kind possible. Scientists who abjure anecdotal evidence when wearing their white lab coats, may not be able to afford doing so when they go home. The lesser evil may be to seek a rational basis for one's value judgments in sifting through handfuls of anecdotal material, taking advantage of the safeguards available, rather than abjure its use altogether.

I cannot prove this, but I have a convenient illustration in a positivistically-minded colleague who told me of a time when he was playing craps in Las Vegas. With $20 on the line every time he rolled the dice, at one point he won eleven times in a row. The chances of such a run of luck are less than one in two thousand, but in the fast action at the craps table this is not unheard of. The remarkable part was his claim (made off the record) that during the run, he *knew* he was going to win with each next roll of the dice, though he did not have the courage to parlay his money into the theoretically possible $40,000. No contemporary epistemological theory sanctions such knowledge claims, however, and when he puts on his philosopher's hat he does not allow them either. Perhaps he was wrong to say that he knew he would win, and his prudence in not increasing his bets seems rational, but it is inconsistent and intellectually dishonest to claim such knowledge on the one hand and deny its possibility when changing hats. If his original knowledge claim is correct, any theory that makes such knowledge impossible must be wrong. As a philosopher, one has the option of formulating and endorsing theories that reconstruct only a well-defined or well-behaved range of human knowledge, but one cannot then pretend universal validity for one's epistemology, as if it pertained to all knowledge as such. Of course, my colleague's claim is totally unrespectable—what could have justified his belief that he would win? My point is that anecdotes are not evidentially void just because they are unreplicated, arose in uncontrolled circumstances, and lack theoretical backing. I do not claim that he knew he would win or was justified in believing so, but stand by my previous contention that knowing *how* is not a precondition for knowing *that.* You don't have to be an epistemologist to have knowledge, and you need not understand how your belief is justified for it to be so. Otherwise, we would have a vicious regress of needed justifications for our beliefs about the justifications of our beliefs, which we would need to believe and therefore to justify.

The argument of this section can be anticipated in outline by returning to the questions that began this chapter. Suppose that statistics exist on how students have rated professors in the past, or suppose one can find an expert on marketing photography and the prospects of free-lancing. Not all experts or collections of statistics are trustworthy. In fact, the old saw is that "you can prove anything with statistics," if you've got an ideological agenda or an axe to grind. Experts often have axes to grind. Statistical information may also be unhelpful when professional pedagogy or a standardized format cause the issue of immediate interest to be addressed only obliquely. For example, statistics from course evaluations probably won't directly address whether a professor "really cares," leaving one to guess this on the basis of whether her class was "well-organized" or she "stimulated thought." In such circumstances one might prefer to trust one's senses, common sense, or an anecdotal account from a trustworthy source. What should one do when statistical evidence is couched in incomprehensible technical terminology, or when experts are not ready at hand, or disagree? *Availability* of alternative evidence is not enough to make failure to use it irrational—one needs *ready availability* given one's limited resources in time and money to research every question that arises. Hence, (i) reliance on anecdotal material may be rational if there is nothing better; (ii) we have the potential for considerable adeptness, through much first-hand experience, at evaluating the comparative authenticity and usefulness of anecdotal evidence; (iii) a policy of refusing to countenance any anecdotal material whatsoever has questionable rational credentials. It is natural for people to use anecdotal evidence, and their welfare partially depends on their ability to use it wisely.

4.2.1 The Bounty and Peril of Anecdotal Evidence
The strength of anecdotal evidence depends in part on the strength of the hypothesis (call it *H*) it is being used to support. Is the claim merely that one can have experiences suggestive of *H,* or is it that *H* may be true, or that *H* typically holds in circumstances *C,* or that *H* is a universal law of nature? Anecdotal evidence might go a long way toward establishing the first of these, but virtually nowhere toward the last. Statistical evidence, expert testimony, and controlled experiment distill a much larger informational base into a few selected conclusions, a process of shrinkage that normally brings about the shrinkage and elimination of errors in one's original database. Because anecdotal evidence lacks this shrinkage or comparable safeguards, it seems to magnify errors by comparison. Verbal testimony arising from unreplicated and uncontrolled situations is vulnerable to human tendencies to lie, embroider, engage in hyperbole, recycle hearsay, and speculate or "confabulate" without forewarning one's listeners. Even when a person's testimony can be considered reliable, eyewitness accounts of the same incident are notorious for their apparent inconsistency. Drawing inferences from such

testimony is fraught with pitfalls. What a person sees is influenced by his expectations and background knowledge—a well-known source of error to which uncontrolled situations are especially vulnerable.

So there is a rationale for the scientific posture of demanding controlled studies, a conservative approach to drawing conclusions, and replicability of results, and abjuring the use of anecdotal evidence. What I deny is that anecdotal evidence has no value. Although the opposing view is rarely stated explicitly, as Dennett says, "a good scientist . . . knows how misleading and, officially, unusable anecdotes are." The problem is reconciling this intuition with the competing one that skillful use of anecdotal evidence is necessary for people to function well in a complex society. Part of my position is that scientists can afford to treat anecdotal evidence as worthless because they are used to having better evidence. If they cannot find better evidence, they tend to find more promising projects to work on. As said, religious people have less flexibility in setting their agenda—they cannot always defer questions about God when epistemological problems arise (3.7.1). Because scientists theorize from a standpoint of epistemic wealth which their religious counterparts can only envy, they can take a harder line against anecdotal evidence.

The evidential quality of anecdotes is affected by factors other than the credibility of the person making the report. Another primary determinant of quality is the person's proximity to the evidence. For example, in the case reported in *John* 9 of a man born blind, allegedly healed by Jesus—an unreplicated event occurring in an uncontrolled setting—the evidential strength of this spectacular anecdote cannot be the same for us as it was for the blind man himself. To repeat, the strength of the evidence also is relative to what one is using it as evidence for. If the claim is merely that "formerly I was blind, but now I see," the man's personal experience is conclusive; if the claim is that "Jesus is the Christ," then there is more room for different interpretations, especially given that the man could not identify the source of his healing without prompting. But for the moment, let's bracket what claim the anecdote is being adduced as evidence for, and examine how the strength of the evidence varies for different users. The blind man's parents were in nearly as good a position as he to know what happened, because of their proximity and their knowledge of his situation. If they said, "He is of age; let him speak for himself," it was not because they doubted whether he had been born blind but could now see, but because they did not know first-hand how his vision came about. The Pharisees who questioned him were in a much poorer evidential position, however, and the intellectual descendants of John who wrote the book that ultimately got handed down to us were many years, many retellings, and many acts of recollection further away from the original events than were the pharisees. We are many more transcribings and translations of the book further away from the original event, creating still more opportunities for error or misunderstanding to creep in. Perhaps God has prevented serious errors or misunderstandings from arising, but if so, this is another miracle requiring its own evidence. The point is that the evidential status of this story is far weaker for us than for the Pharisees who questioned the blind man; hence the beliefs that it justifies or rules out are also comparably fewer for us.

Pragmatically, the major task facing would-be users of anecdotal evidence is to evaluate:

> (1) the reliability of the informant,
> (2) how well-positioned she was to know the facts of the matter,
> (3) the likelihood that her experience is either
>   (a) an artifact of her expectations or ideological propensities, or
>   (b) veridical but with a different explanation or interpretation than she suggests,
> (4) the overall likelihood of the recounted occurrence given the relevant laws of nature and other background information.

While scientists are fairly comfortable evaluating (2) and (4), (1) and (3) require value judgments that tend to be much more subjective and unreliable. Since no dependable criteria exist, one must resort to heuristics or rules of thumb in one's reckoning. Critics rely on such weaknesses to make their general case against anecdotal evidence.

4.2.2 The Psychological Critique of Nisbett and Ross
Nisbett and Ross's primary worry is that people put too much credence in anecdotal evidence relative to other kinds of evidence; nevertheless, they do not officially acknowledge any inferential value on its part. Specifically, they allege that people overutilize anecdotal evidence relative to statistical evidence which, due to regression, is more reliable.[87] "Regression to the mean" is how statistical evidence avoids sampling error or the error induced by small sample size, which is endemic to anecdotal evidence. That is, anecdotal evidence is less likely than statistical evidence to represent common experience or a large population or reference class. Nisbett and Ross refer to the overutilization of anecdotal evidence as the "vividness effect" (45–51), by which they mean that information that is concrete, proximate (temporally,

---

[87] *Human Inference,* pp. 25–6, 139–66. Page references herein are to this work.

spatially, or sensorially), and/or of emotional interest exerts a disproportionate influence on the inferences one draws from it. If this effect is real, then anecdotal evidence may "poison the well" for other evidence—it makes it impossible for other evidence to "get a fair hearing" short of vigorous countermeasures. Such a phenomenon could justify denying anecdotal evidence any evidential value.

There is at least spectacular anecdotal evidence for the existence of the vividness effect. Mastectomies performed on Betty Ford and Happy Rockefeller in 1974 produced a flood of visitations to cancer detection clinics that years of dissemination of sobering statistics on breast cancer had failed to precipitate (56). This does not show that vivid evidence was being overutilized in any absolute sense—the visitations thus caused were not counternormative. But vividness still seems irrelevant to evidential value, in which case *any* distinct vividness effect would be counternormative in some sense. One experiment apparently demonstrating such an effect involved exposing two sets of subjects to information about welfare recipients. One set was[88]

> given a description of a single welfare case [painting] a vivid picture of social pathology. The central figure was an obese, friendly, emotional, and irresponsible Puerto Rican woman who had been on welfare for many years. Middle-aged now, she had lived with a succession of "husbands," typically also unemployed, and had borne children by each of them. Her home was a nightmare of dirty and dilapidated plastic furniture bought on time at outrageous prices, filthy kitchen appliances, and cockroaches walking about in the daylight. Her children showed little promise of rising above their origins. They attended school off and on and had begun to run afoul of the law in their early teens, with the older children now thoroughly enmeshed in a life of heroin [and] numbers running.
>
> [The second set was given only] statistics showing that the median stay on welfare for all middle-aged welfare recipients was two years and that only 10 percent of recipients remained on the welfare rolls for four years or longer. These statistics, which actually are correct, stood in sharp contrast to the subjects' beliefs about welfare (. . . that the average stay on welfare was about ten years).

In spite of the sharp contrast of this highly probative but dull statistical information to their previous beliefs, it "had no effect on subjects' opinions about welfare recipients . . . whereas a vivid but questionably informative case history had a substantial effect on inferences" (57–8).

Ironically, most of Nisbett and Ross's evidence for the vividness effect is anecdotal (as they acknowledge—pp. 50, 282), and a general survey of

---

[88] R. Hamill, T. D. Wilson, and R. E. Nisbett, "Insensitivity to Sample Bias: Generalizing from Atypical Cases," *Journal of Personality and Social Psychology* 39 (1980): 578–89; see *Human Inference*, p. 57.

experiments relevant to the vividness effect conducted by Shelley Taylor and Suzanne Thompson found it much more elusive than the anecdotes suggest. That is, some experiments seemed to demonstrate a vividness effect while others did not, and this in spite of the fact that, generally speaking, journal literature is biased toward the reporting of "effects" or positive results rather than negative findings. What they found instead was the better known and documented effect of salience.[89]

> *Salience* refers to the phenomenon that when one's attention is differentially directed to one portion of the environment rather than to others, the information received in that portion will receive disproportionate weighting in subsequent judgments.

In many of the vividness studies, including the one just mentioned, each set of subjects saw only one kind of evidence, and their responses were tested relative to subjects who saw only another kind, or to control subjects who saw no evidence. Such experiments cannot demonstrate a differential use of vivid information as convincingly as experiments in which both kinds are available. Taylor and Thompson found a consistent effect only in cases involving differential attention to several sources of stimuli. However, they agreed that when vivid and nonvivid information are both present, the vivid information generally competes for attention more successfully.

This still seems counternormative, but it is hard to see what lesson to draw from it. A conclusion drawn by Nisbett and Ross and emphasized by Goldman is that differential utilization of anecdotal vs. statistical information may be due in part to the latter not being well-understood. Rather than absolute overutilization of anecdotal evidence, we may have relative underutilization of statistical evidence consequent on a lack of skill in using it.[90] This seems likely given that even students who know some elementary statistics regularly fail to appreciate the impact of sample size on probability, as was found when such students were presented with the following problem:[91]

> The average height of adult males and females in the U. S. are, respectively, 5′ 10″ and 5′ 4″. Both distributions are approximately normal with a standard deviation of about

---

[89] "Stalking the Elusive 'Vividness Effect'," *Psychological Review* 89 (1982): 175.

[90] *Human Inference*, pp. 276–81; *Epistemology and Cognition*, p. 276; "Stalking the Elusive 'Vividness Effect'," pp. 162ff.

[91] Daniel Kahneman and Amos Tversky, "Subjective Probability: A Judgment of Representativeness," *Cognitive Psychology* 3 (1971): 430–54; quoted from *Human Inference*, p. 78.

2.5″. An investigator has selected one population by chance and has drawn from it a random sample. What do you think are the odds that he has selected the male population if:
       (i) The sample consists of a single person whose height is 5′ 10″?
       (ii) The sample consists of 6 persons whose average height is 5′ 8″?

That is, they will believe or assume incorrectly that the probability is higher for case (i) than for case (ii).[92] If people have much more practice and so more facility in working with anecdotal evidence than with statistical evidence, this is not necessarily counternormative for the individual. It may be another instance in which individually rational behavior occurs within the framework of an irrational social structure, where the prisoner's dilemma is the canonical example of individually rational action leading to a socially undesirable result. It may be rational for people to make the best use of the cognitive tools they have, including the anecdotal evidence available to them, even if it behooves society to educate people, equipping them to use statistical and other kinds of evidence more effectively.

4.2.3 How Superior Is Statistical Evidence?

I do not accept Nisbett and Ross's general conclusion that statistical information is far superior to anecdotal evidence, though I grant some superiority. One of Nisbett and Ross's favorite examples is a 1977 study by Borgida and Nisbett, done on introductory psychology students who planned to major in psychology.[93] Again, the students were divided into two groups, one of which received "statistical summaries" of "dozens" of student evaluations of particular upper level courses—i.e., they were informed of the mean value of those evaluations. The second group saw a panel of psychology majors face to face, two or three of whom would give their comments and rate from one to five each of the upper level courses in question. Nisbett and Ross held the statistical information to be more probative, hence from a normative standpoint it should have had greater influence on the subsequently stated preferences of the subjects. In fact, the opposite happened.

W. V. Quine writes of the "torrential output" humans produce in verbiage, or specifically in theories, on the basis of meager sensory input, but I

---

[92] The median odds given by the subjects were 8:1 and 2.5:1 respectively, whereas the correct odds are 16:1 and 29:1. Kahneman and Tversky found the absolute magnitude of the error less significant than the failure to get the probabilities in right relation to one another.

[93] "The Differential Impact of Abstract vs. Concrete Information on Decisions," *Journal of Applied Social Psychology* 7 (1977): 258–71; see *Human Inference*, p. 58.

believe that Quine's adjectives are reversed.[94]   Literally speaking, the statistical summaries were a distillation of what was itself a very meager valuational output (perhaps "Rate the course on a scale of 1 to 5 in these categories") from students who received a torrential input of information all semester long about the subject matter, the instructor, and other qualities of the course. Although the summary draws on a larger sample size than two or three students, people using it have no readily available way to determine the relation of their interests and proclivities to the mean values for the class as a whole. Never having watched what other students mark on their evaluation forms, and never having occasion to discuss it with them, one has no idea whether they tend to evaluate on the basis of criteria resembling one's own. The statistical summary is undoubtedly a better reflection of the opinions of the student body as a whole, but this still yields only a single reference point from which to estimate the suitability of the course for oneself. By watching several majors comment on their courses face to face one can at least make some cursory value judgments regarding their character, interests, and attitudes, and the degree to which one's own are similar. This includes judgments of reliability and acuity, none of which can be made for the statistical summaries. One also gets several reference points from which to triangulate, not just one. That is, statistical summaries average the evaluations of majors together with those of jocks, airheads and nerds—relevant and irrelevant reference classes are thrown together, willy-nilly. A face to face confrontation can help disentangle these. Also, people talking freely would be more likely to address the most significant issues relating to the quality of the course—such as whether the instructor really cares about his students—issues that standardized statistical formats obscure because they are not salient features of every course. In all, one receives a relative torrential amount of information from the face to face discussion, compared to the meager information in the statistical summaries.[95]

Presumably, Nisbett and Ross would reject my argument by denying that observers can assimilate this torrential input adequately. They buttress their contention by calling the common belief that a person's behavior is attributable to semi-permanent dispositions that make up her character, rather than to her immediate circumstances, the "fundamental attribution error." Given how controversial this claim is, applying the label 'fundamental' to

---

[94]   *Ontological Relativity and Other Essays*, p. 83.

[95]   See also Dretske's distinction between analog and digital forms of representation in "Precis of *Knowledge and the Flow of Information*," *Behavioral and Brain Sciences* 6 (1983): 60–1.

such an "error" seems tendentious,[96] for it goes far beyond a commitment to the primacy of nurture in the nature/nurture debate. Many elements of a person's upbringing or nurturing still causally affect her future actions by becoming incorporated into her character traits or dispositions—the very factors that the person weighing anecdotal material is trying to assess and that Nisbett and Ross are labeling "erroneous attributions." Neither nature nor nurture are part of the immediate setting or circumstances in which action takes place, so Nisbett and Ross seem to be suggesting incredibly that most behavior is caused by *neither nature nor nurture*.

They also cite as supporting evidence the phenomenon of "interviewer illusion"—that interviewers habitually overestimate their ability to predict how well an employee will perform on the job (79). Interviewers make this mistake presumably because they are relying on vivid input from meeting the subject face to face rather than relying on sober statistical information. Nisbett and Ross present no evidence for this phenomenon, but it should not be surprising that people overestimate their ability to identify character traits in others—it is a familiar theme from Plato that people tend to overestimate their own abilities in almost every respect. Nisbett and Ross also offer no evidence that this tendency is irremediable, or that it justifies banning the use of vivid or anecdotal evidence. Their argument only implies what I have been saying all along: anecdotal evidence should be used with caution.

Nisbett and Ross resort to a great deal of anecdotal evidence in their own work under the pretense that it is necessary for comprehension even if its inferential use is dubious (282). Such an explanation is factitious since, as every psychologist knows, illustrations function cognitively by helping us develop scripts, personas, and other schemas or "stereotypes" which, in turn, function inferentially. Ultimately, informational value simply *is* inferential value. There is no logical difference between anecdotes and observation reports of any kind.

In sum, most people need to become better educated and more adept at using statistical information, but this doesn't show that their handling of anecdotal evidence is counternormative in any absolute sense. Even if there were a general tendency to mishandle anecdotal evidence, that does not indict its evidential value so much as suggest a need for remedial measures.

---

[96] Nisbett and Ross's definition of the term (31) is more consistent with 'fundamental' modifying 'attribution', as in 'the error of fundamental attribution'. This definition is neutral regarding the direction in which the error is made, but their subsequent discussion does not recognize the term as applying to errors in which one mistakenly attributes the cause of behavior to setting or circumstances rather than to personality or character.

4.2.4   Do Fairies Exist?

The suspicion persists among philosophers that with anecdotal evidence one can prove just about anything, in which case its evidential value must be about nil. Robert Sheaffer wrote a satirical article with the above title recently, expressing this reservation by claiming that the evidence in favor of fairies—most of which is anecdotal—is on par with the evidence for virtually any paranormal phenomenon, including religious experience as evidence for religious claims.[97]

Being satirical, Sheaffer leaves unclear whether his comparison is directed at all anecdotal evidence, or is limited to parapsychology in particular. In any case, Sheaffer's argument reconstructed is (i) fairies do not exist; (ii) the evidence in favor of fairies is as good or better than the evidence in favor of p; hence (iii) the evidence in favor of p has no probative value. Substituting q for 'fairies', one sees that this argument is not formally valid, since even high quality inductive evidence is consistent with the falsity of its corresponding hypothesis. But if Sheaffer could make a case for (ii), it would certainly cast doubt on any p he has in mind.

To do this, he needs to make the evidence in favor of fairies look as good as possible, and this is where his satirizing gets in the way. He maintains only a casual pretense of examining the evidence for fairies. This can be humorous and telling if the reader thinks that his examination is no less thorough than the examination typically made by enthusiasts for the paranormal. Popular subjects like this always invite fraudulent operators—there is money to be made—so it is not hard to find evidentially lax parapsychologists. But not all are lax, and Sheaffer's pursuit of humor leaves this crucial part of the argument without any adequate demonstration. If the anecdotal evidence for fairies were really good, one could believe Sheaffer and be done with this messy subject. But it isn't.

Not all of the evidence for fairies is verbal. The principal additional evidence is a set of five photographs taken by children in Cottingley, England, in an uncontrolled environment. Although never replicated, they were reproduced by Sir Arthur Conan Doyle in a book devoted to discussing their authenticity.[98] At some point one must question Doyle's purpose in writing the book, a question Sheaffer never raises. Although the evidence linking

---

[97]   "Do Fairies Exist?" *The Skeptical Inquirer* 2 (1977): 45–52. Reprinted in *Paranormal Borderlands of Science,* ed. by Frazier, 68–75 (Buffalo: Prometheus, 1981).

[98]   *The Coming of the Fairies* (London, 1922). They were reprinted by the theosophist, Edward Gardner, in *A Book of Real Fairies* (London: 1945).

Doyle to the Piltdown hoax is circumstantial,[99] it raises a red flag and might lead one to wonder whether Doyle did not intend to give the rest of us a real-life opportunity to do some sleuthing, rather than merely reporting the results of disinterested scholarship. In particular, it is hard to understand why one with such a sharp eye for evidence would spend so much of the book debating whether the photographic plates were faked, or whether trick photography were involved, when it seems obvious upon inspection that the most likely explanation is that the "fairies" in the picture are two-dimensional cardboard cutouts whose conformance to the fairy stereotypes and artistic conventions then prevalent are striking. To be sure, Doyle mentions these possibilities, but each is dismissed casually—the first because enlargement of the photographs reveals no superficial cuts that one would expect scissors to make; the second because it is possible that real fairies just happen to correspond in appearance to the abilities and imaginations of contemporary artists. Doyle's preoccupation with "objective reporting" leaves it further unclear whether he concurs with those who dismissed these hypotheses casually. What is clear is that members of the local Theosophical Society took the photographs to be impressive new evidence for the existence of fairies, and disseminated them widely.

I mentioned the need to emphasize truth as correspondence in religious contexts in 3.4. Lest someone think that the person saying "fairies might just be that way" is conforming to my directive, let me point out that to get from a hypothesis of possibility (which is true but uninformative) to one of likelihood or plausibility—hypotheses with far greater informational content—one must account for the totality of counterevidence which argues against correspondence. Everyone knows the arguments—e.g., why are fairy sightings such rarities in other cultures? These questions bear on the likelihood of truth as correspondence. If determining truth as correspondence did not involve difficult and painstaking scrutiny of evidence, its existence and possibility would not have been so vigorously attacked by philosophers.

Sheaffer does recount some verbal reports of fairy sightings but, again, the weakness of the material itself seems the primary culprit, not its anecdotal form. Thus, on the fact that corroboration by a second eyewitness is considered significant, Sheaffer uses a case in which the corroboration of a fairy sighting consisted merely in the second person nodding when asked in a whisper, "Do you see them?" A person whispering outdoors could easily be

---

[99] John Winslow and Alfred Meyer, "The Perpetrator at Piltdown," *Science 83* (Sept. 1983): 32–43; Charles Blinderman, *The Piltdown Inquest* (Prometheus, 1986), pp. 155–82.

misunderstood; the word 'them' is ambiguous; and there are many possible causes of nodding other than the intention of giving assent—all of this almost goes without saying, except that Sheaffer apparently fails to realize that it undercuts his own thesis. All that remains, then, is the brute fact that there are many people who have reported fairy sightings. But I make no general claim to the value of anecdotal evidence apart from considerations of quality—e.g., the reliability of the subject involved, his acuity, how well-placed he was for observation, the nature of his expectations and ideological propensities, etc. By itself, quantity of anecdotes has trifling significance.

4.3   BALL LIGHTNING AND THE GREEN FLASH

One could give many examples of real phenomena whose existence was doubted by scientists, being supported initially only by anecdotal evidence. A recurrent pattern in the history of science is for such phenomena to become accepted later as they are (i) measured by scientific instruments, (ii) explained theoretically, and (iii) reproduced in the laboratory. Meteorites are a notorious example—scientists originally heaped ridicule on the notion that rocks could fall from the sky. But it will suffice to illustrate this tendency here with two other examples from the natural sciences—the green flash and ball lightning. My conjecture is that whenever there is anecdotal evidence for a phenomenon but (i)-(iii) are lacking, there will always be a significant number of scientists who question the phenomenon's authenticity. This suggests that no genuine science can ever be founded on anecdotal evidence alone, but my primary point is that scientists are going beyond any skeptical requirement imposed by rationality in this regard.

It should also be noted that many phenomena which some scientists believed in turned out *not* to be genuine. Cold fusion is but a recent case in a history which has brought us Piltdown man, polywater, phlogiston, aether, and N-rays.[100] In 2.3.2 I argued that a general policy of disbelief until a phenomenon is "proved" is excessively restrictive and not immune to error, but some might reply, "Look at how much worse things could have been if scientists were less skeptical!" Whether general disbelief results in the least

---

[100] Not all of these were supported primarily by anecdotal evidence—some were supported by the "evidence" of erroneous theories. For those that involved laboratory experiments, most were not shown to lack adequate controls until after the phenomena were thoroughly investigated. That is, one may not be able to say how well controlled a study is, or whether the resulting evidence is anecdotal, until one learns what factors need controlling.

amount of error and the least damage due to error is ultimately an empirical question, but any attempt to answer it must account for the existence of credible alternatives to policies of blanket belief, blanket disbelief, or blanket suspension of judgment. One can, for example, adopt a pluralistic policy, allowing significant latitude between the beliefs that evidence justifies and the beliefs that it mandates. One can also employ "working assumptions" in situations of uncertainty, in order to contain the damage that incorrect beliefs might cause. Hence, no quick argument can be made from these examples to a general claim that it is irrational to endorse a hypothesis on the basis of anecdotal evidence alone.

4.3.1 The Green Flash

The green flash is an rare atmospheric phenomenon associated with sunrise and sunset. For it to appear, one's horizon must be virtually perfect, which generally occurs only at sea or in a desert. The skies must be perfectly clear, and there must also be an air inversion—the more the better. Even if all these conditions are met the phenomenon is not dependable—unusually high atmospheric refraction is necessary, but high latitude, and even luck may contribute. When it appears, it is at the very instant that the upper limb of the sun vanishes at sunset, or first appears at sunrise, at which time there may be a momentary, brilliant green flash.[101] In so describing the phenomenon I have identified several necessary conditions for its occurrence—conditions that might have been guessed from observation alone, but could not have been ascribed with certainty. I can do this because a theoretical explanation for the phenomenon exists. Theory thus comes to inform our very description of the phenomenon.

The first published observations of the green flash did not appear until 1869, even though the heavens have been watched assiduously since ancient times, and there are extant records of an abundance of other astronomical phenomena. (Actually, the green flash is a meteorological phenomenon, but it was often treated as astronomical before it was explained.) When scientific attention first became directed toward it in the late 19th and early 20th centuries, some were understandably skeptical that the phenomenon was genuine, and many early investigators proposed explanations with a physiological or psychological basis, such as that the green flash is an afterimage from watching the red sun set. These were proposed even by some claiming to

---

[101] See D. J. K. O'Connell, *The Green Flash* (New York: Interscience, 1958), which contains photographs of the phenomenon.

have seen the flash, suggesting that they *did* see an afterimage and assumed that others reporting it had seen the same thing. As the theory behind it became clearer, as photographs of it were produced, and with laboratory replication of the phenomenon, this skepticism gave way to acceptance within the scientific community, although not as rapidly as one might hope. Indeed, skeptical explanations continued to appear in astronomical journals for years after the phenomenon was well-understood. As early as 1923 Schuster suggested including the phenomenon in standard textbooks, even though it has no systematic importance, just to stem the tide of spurious "explanatory" literature, which unfortunately persisted yet another twenty-five years.[102]

Light striking the earth's atmosphere is refracted by air, and is refracted more the more obliquely it strikes the atmosphere. This refraction is enough to increase by a few minutes the time the sun is above the horizon, both in the morning and evening. In fact, by the time the lower limb of the "apparent" or visible sun touches the horizon, the "real" sun (the sun's direction without atmospheric interference) is already entirely below it. The sun's red color at that time is due to differential scattering of optical wavelengths in the atmosphere, but wavelengths also refract differentially, with longer wavelengths refracting less than shorter ones. At sunset, the total refraction normally amounts to 35' of arc, for which the corresponding differential refraction between green and red light—called the *dispersion*—would be 10", below the threshold of human perceptibility. If we had greater visual acuity, the more refracted "green sun" would appear ever so slightly higher than the apparent red sun. Blue and ultraviolet light are entirely absorbed and/or scattered at low angles of incidence and normal elevations, and yellow and orange light are more strongly absorbed by the atmosphere, so most of the visible light remaining at sunset is green and red. This is why one sees a sudden flash of green rather than a continuous slide across the spectrum at the moment of disappearance.[103]

Times of unusually high refraction are necessary for the green flash to be perceptible, and atmospheric refraction can exceed 1 or even 2 degrees. At such levels the flash may last a second or two. Scintillation ("twinkling")

---

[102] *The Green Flash*, pp. 11-2. For examples of subsequent skeptical literature, see D. M. Barringer, "Note on the 'Green Flash'," *Popular Astronomy* 57 (1949): 252–3; L. J. Comrie, "The Green (?) Flash (?)," *Journal of the British Astronomical Association* 58 (1948): 280; reprinted in *Popular Astronomy* 57 (1949): 42–3.

[103] The reader may note that if it is the bottom limb of the sun that is the first to appear or the last to disappear, as from behind a cloud, one might see a red flash. In fact, this phenomenon has been observed, but is even rarer than the green flash (*The Green Flash*, p. 23).

caused by atmospheric turbulence may unpredictably heighten or dampen this effect. At high latitudes, where the sun sets very slowly, the flash can be greatly extended—even over a minute. But the primary contributor is still enhanced atmospheric refraction due to the air's density gradient. A normal temperature profile for daytime air is for warm, less dense air at the surface to be overlain by cooler air above. This actually inverts the way we normally think about air density—viz., as progressively decreasing with altitude. In saying that an inversion is necessary to see the green flash, what is meant is the customary meteorological meaning of *temperature inversion,* which actually exaggerates rather than inverts the density gradient, thereby enhancing the normal refractive effect of air and the dispersion of green and red light. Small temperature inversions are normal at sunrise and sunset when the air is clear and calm—in humid locations dew may start forming before sunset—but more than the usual amount is necessary to see the green flash.

With this much theory behind the explanation of the phenomenon, the anecdotal evidence in the phenomenon's favor is virtually immaterial in justifying belief in it. Evidence for the theory effectively becomes evidence for the phenomenon. Only if the green flash *never* occurred, or if the theory had serious problems, would the observational evidence be significant. The obstacle created by the capriciousness and brevity of the phenomenon, which initially forces reliance on anecdotal evidence to gain knowledge of it, is entirely obviated by the existence of a theoretical explanation.

4.3.2 Ball Lightning

The case of ball lightning is quite different. It cannot be described in terms of necessary or sufficient conditions for its occurrence, because there is no accepted theory for it. Singer characterized the situation as follows:[104]

> Despite the extremely limited information available on ball lightning from measurements made during its appearance in nature, its general characteristics are well-known. These have been obtained by study of approximately one thousand random observations by chance observers recorded over the past century and a half in the general scientific and meteorological literature.
>
> The glowing spheres are usually associated with ordinary lightning in severe thunderstorms. In contrast to the common flashes of lightning, however, these globes remain visible for an appreciable time while floating freely through the air in extended paths which may take them into houses. Their velocity is relatively moderate, as indicated by witnesses who have escaped being struck by the flying balls by leaping aside.

---

[104] S. Singer, "Ball Lightning," in *Lightning,* Vol. 1, ed. by R. H. Golde (London: Academic Press, 1977), p. 409. Page references in this section are to this work.

Generally speaking, the globes are spherical, about 25 cm in diameter, and last from one to ten seconds, although there is a great variation in size and some have been reported to last well over a minute. Most often they move horizontally at one to two meters per second—not necessarily in a straight line—but a large number have been observed to fall directly down only to change to a horizontal path suddenly near the ground. It is not uncommon for them to appear spinning, or making a hissing or crackling sound, and they may disappear either silently or with an ear-shattering explosion. They have been known to enter buildings through doors and windows, and entrance through chimneys is surprisingly common. Incidents of burns, destruction, and death have been attributed to ball lightning, but more commonly it disappears without a trace (409–10).

Like the green flash, ball lightning is a rare and transient phenomenon. But unlike the flash, it has never been reproduced in the laboratory nor measured with scientific instruments. It has received considerable scrutiny from theoretical physicists, and many explanations have been proposed, but all are far enough from being adequate that even bizarre theories postulating antimatter or nuclear reactions cannot be ruled out as too unlikely. About the only matter of widespread consensus is that it is probably a globe of positive charge. Singer believes that some of the theories are plausible enough to subject to laboratory study (412, 433).

A minority of scientists continue to question the reality of ball lightning, however. K. Berger gave the following synopsis:[105]

> The [a]uthor's 30 years of research in lightning phenomena on Mount San Salvatore near Lugano, Switzerland, including [scrutiny] of thousands of photographs and more than 1000 oscillograms, failed to confirm the existence of "ball lightning." On the basis of the extensive literature and his own experience, the author stresses the need to distinguish between subjective and objective observations. All published photographs of "ball lightning" have proved to have a physical explanation. To explain the numerous reported visual observations, the author recommends physiological research on "afterimages" produced by lightning flashes on the human retina. New reports of ball lightning should be examined on the spot by high-voltage engineers and physicists.

Another skeptic, Edward Argyle, suggests that ball lightning is explainable as a positive afterimage, claiming that this would account for[106]

---

[105] "Ball Lightning and Lightning Research," *Naturwissenschaften* 60 (1973): 485–92.

[106] Edward Argyle, "Ball Lightning as an Optical Illusion," *Nature* 230 (1971): 179–80.

a. the smaller reported size of indoor balls generally as compared to outdoor balls
b. reported variations in color
c. the reported tendency of balls to drift linearly (caused by futile attempts to focus on them—positive afterimages are a cone effect and usually form near the fovea)
d. apparent ability to pass through a metal screen, glass, etc.
e. normal length of duration (2-10 seconds)
f. sudden disappearance
g. appearance only in subdued light (afterimages require a sharply contrasting background)
h. although its disappearance is frequently reported to be violent or noisy, seldom does ball lightning actually damage anything
i. the most frequently reported physical effect is sound, but it is not uncommon for people to report hearing sounds with such natural phenomena as the aurora borealis, which are known not to be audible
j. the relatively fewer reports of odors correspond to fewer people having odor expectations
k. the remaining reports of energy releases would have to be considered unreliable, but are not numerous.

As mentioned, all proposed explanations of ball lightning have serious problems, and this is no exception. Difficulties with Argyle's position include:

1. reported disappearance when moving behind objects
2. reported changes in apparent (angular) size as it moves closer or farther away
3. afterimages do not disappear instantaneously, without recovery after blinking
4. potential sources of afterimages abound at all times, not just during thunderstorms
5. observations by several people at the same time, including two involving commercial aircraft. Mutual agreement would not be expected if it were merely subjective.
6. observed direct and permanent physical effects.

Resisting Argyle's conclusions, P. C. W. Davies claims the issue is more philosophical than over nuts and bolts:[107]

The appeal to physiology, then psychology, to explain embarrassing puzzles in physics epitomizes a quite general and interesting tendency in the scientific community. We are presented with two varieties of phenomena in science, which we may loosely call "laboratory" and "natural." The first variety is reproducible and can be subjected to experimental manipulation, or is at least predictable in advance. The second variety is unreproducible and unpredictable (consisting of, for example, meteorites, ball lightning, novae) and if also transient the experimenter is fortunate indeed to have his apparatus at the right place at the right time. Consequently science must rely for its information on that much mistrusted individual, the layman, to whom is attributed the property of being able to observe objectively anything that can be explained, but imagining every-

---

[107] "Ball Lightning or Spots Before the Eyes?" *Nature* 230 (1971): 576-7.

thing that can't. History is replete with examples, not least that of the meteorite . . . . The philosophy of this approach seems to be that if a naturally occurring phenomenon is hard to account for conventionally (i) decide that it has no physical reality; (ii) construct a physiological or psychological explanation; (iii) ignore the physical evidence that contradicts this explanation.

If this type of dispute is philosophical, nevertheless many epistemologists would side with Argyle. Antony Flew cites the example of Herodotus, who believed that the Phoenician sailors sent by Egyptian King Necos to circumnavigate Africa had indeed proved that Africa is a peninsula, but did not believe their report that they kept the sun on their right hand throughout the voyage.[108] Herodotus did not know that the Earth is round, or what consequences its roundness would have, but he did know that the sailors left Egypt from one direction and returned via the other. Given that the report was unsupported by other evidence and conflicted with current theory, Flew reasons, his skepticism was justified. In retrospect, their claim seems to substantiate the veridicality of the report, since the Phoenicians could not have anticipated this occurrence and their report informs us of their direction of travel. Flew points out that Herodotus had to weigh the "best astronomical and geographical information available [against] the veracity of travellers in general, and of Phoenicians in particular." But when even the best information available is not very good, this hardly forces one's conclusion. Even if Herodotus's disbelief were justified, surely the sailors were justified in their belief. First-hand observers are privy to a "torrent" of additional information that never makes it into their observation reports—information that would discount the possibility of physiological, psychological, or other explanations. Furthermore, it is hard to fault those who believed their report. Given that most physicists believe ball lightning to be a genuine phenomenon—and supposedly they are as hardnosed as scientists come—skepticism of ball lightning can hardly be obligatory.

I conclude that the extensive, high quality anecdotal evidence regarding ball lightning is sufficient to justify belief in the phenomenon, in the permissive sense of rationality discussed in 2.3. As mentioned, this is the prevailing view among physicists in spite of the lack of

(1) experimental evidence
(2) theoretical evidence
(3) measurements by scientific instruments
(4) systematic observations.

---

[108]   *God and Philosophy*, pp. 147–8.

I do not deny that each of these constitutes evidence against the reality of the phenomenon. But if it is the nature of ball lightning to be rare and transient, both of which seem likely, then (3) and (4) should not be surprising. (1) and (2) are where the problem arises, and make it permissively rational to suspend judgment regarding the phenomenon.

4.4 SOCIAL AND INDIVIDUAL CONSTRUCTIONS OF REALITY

To complete our abstract picture of what constitutes rational belief on the basis of anecdotal evidence, I must add that what constitutes rational behavior for an individual will not always be rational for an institution or social entity. In particular, the larger a structure one intends to build upon a given foundation, the more certainty one requires that the foundation is free of structural weakness and so capable of supporting it. In science, the weight of research and the number of auxiliary theories and theoretical extensions which the most fundamental structural components of scientific knowledge must bear is enormous. The lives of a great many people depend on its soundness. Hence, on a cost/benefit basis alone it behooves the scientific community to prove the soundness of each structural component *beyond a reasonable doubt* beforehand.[109] Scientific theories do change, of course, but major changes cause major dislocations and disruptions in the scientific community, and scientists associated with discredited theories often come out as losers professionally.

Recalling the distinction between criminal and civil law, note that findings of liability, which are decided on the weaker basis of the preponderance of evidence, do not become incorporated into the legal system's structure of precedents where they can dilute its evidential basis. They are findings of fact, not findings of law. Since only anecdotal evidence for ball lightning is available, and it inevitably leaves open a reasonable doubt of the phenomenon's existence, ball lightning cannot play any structural role in the development of science until its evidential status changes. Organized skepticism thus functions to keep the institutional structure of science free from commitments that might imperil it. Hence it is rational from a social viewpoint, even if unnecessarily restrictive from the standpoint of individual rationality. Skepticism may be a value parochial to science, but benign in that context.

---

[109] Proof beyond a reasonable doubt does not make one's claim incorrigible—that would require additional assurance that no new grounds for doubt will be found. Also, my mention of "foundations" here is metaphorical—not an endorsement of foundationalism.

At first blush this may seem paradoxical. How could the life of a single person be less important to herself than the life of an institution is to the people who constitute it? How then can rationality be different for individuals as opposed to institutions? The question is well-taken; the answer turns on a difference in epistemology rather than a difference in rationality. When dealing with nonreplicable evidence, it is impossible to get all of the members of an institution into the same relation to the evidence, because there is no theoretical possibility of repeating the demonstration or trial for each one. Some people will inevitably be in a better epistemological position relative to it than others, and those who are so privileged may be able to affirm more as "beyond a reasonable doubt" based on it than others can. Hence, anecdotal evidence may make belief foundationally safe for an individual, whereas it cannot do this for institutions because a canonical standpoint for the institution relative to the evidence is lacking.

In the foregoing discussion I have followed the individualistic epistemological tradition dating to Descartes and Kant. It is not an objection to Descartes's thought experiment regarding the piece of wax (Second Meditation) that not all philosophers have access to fireplaces or are familiar with the properties of wax. It is assumed that every philosopher is capable of understanding and carrying through the thought experiment on her own, so that an assertion can be made "objectively" or as a general proposition, even when people come to understand it in isolation from the rest of the community. Put another way, Descartes's thought experiment is to be understood as replicable, and each philosopher who reads the *Meditations* is replicating it, arriving at the same clear and distinct perceptions. The individual is the one who reckons evidence and possesses knowledge—at least in theory.

When it comes to incidents of ball lightning, or the healing of the man born blind, the pretense can no longer be maintained that all can replicate the findings for themselves, or arrive at the same epistemic distance from the original evidence. One person may have seen ball lightning for himself, while another did not but knows the first person well and is in a good position to estimate his reliability and acuity as an observer. Still another person would not know him from Adam. Without a reasonable expectation of reproducing what the first person saw, the question of what a rational person would believe can have no unique answer applicable to all. The independent forms of authentication that support the evidential use of anecdotal material will not be equally available to all, if for no other reason than differential proximity to its source, and without them such evidence simply cannot be assigned a determinate value. Hence, extensive use of this kind of evidence would undermine socialized attempts at constructing or reconstructing reality. If the

Cartesian experiment were truly replicable, there would be a canonical stance or understanding that a whole community could reach—a basis for achieving consensus. This is how replication functions in science. But this can only be done by refusing to countenance anecdotal evidence as a structural part of science. Insofar as religions cannot do without anecdotal evidence, they have no corresponding basis for claiming that a canonical position exists toward a piece of anecdotal evidence—i.e., a position which all members of the institution ought to adopt. Put another way, if they claim that there is such a canonical position, then they must be relying on something other than anecdotal evidence to determine what it is.

The philosophical trend away from individualistic epistemology and toward theories of social epistemology might permit these limitations to be circumvented. Through mechanisms that effect a division of labor such as *specialization,* some members of the community may be given the job of replicating results while others are expected to recognize their results as authoritative without repeating them. In this way it might be possible for the community as a whole to arrive at a canonical position relative to the evidence. In fact, the argument goes, this is really what happens in science, and the individualism described in the previous paragraphs is just a mythical idealization of scientific method. My misgivings about this argument are that I fail to see how the resulting community stance toward anecdotal evidence can claim to be canonical in the sense of peculiarly correct or legitimate, rather than merely being canonical in the sense of institutionalized. That is, I don't see how any particular institutional mechanism for dealing with anecdotal evidence, whether arrived at by mutual agreement or fiat, solves the problem of finding a uniquely rational institutional approach to the epistemological problem that anecdotal evidence poses. With individuals, one can at least imagine that a right or wrong answer exists regarding what one ought to believe given the evidence as presented, even if none of us knows quite how it was presented to her and therefore does not know the answer. But if the institution itself is made the arbiter of rationality, the result is simply relativism. And if not, how does the institutionalized judgment supersede individual judgment?

To recapitulate, my argument so far has followed a commonsensical principle articulated by Locke, that[110]

> . . . *any testimony, the further off it is from the original truth, the less force and proof it has.* The being and existence of the thing itself, is what I call the original truth. A

---

[110] *Essay Concerning Human Understanding,* book 4, ch. 16, sec. 10.

credible man vouching his knowledge of it is a good proof; but if another equally credible do witness it from his report, the testimony is weaker: and a third that attests the hearsay of an hearsay is yet less considerable. So that in traditional truths, each remove weakens the force of the proof: and the more hands the tradition has successively passed through, the less strength and evidence does it receive from them.

Yet C. A. J. Coady rejects this claim on the grounds that it implies the disappearance of history thesis, that "the evidential credentials of well-established facts will become negligible as they recede into the distant future."[111] I think the disappearance of history thesis is probably true, if only the time for the evidence to degrade be made long enough, but Coady is wrong to say that Locke's view implies it. Locke did not say how much each change of hands weakens the evidence—this undoubtedly varies with *how* it changes hands. How *often* it changes hands also affects how rapidly it degrades. For example, orally transmitted histories disappear fairly quickly, whereas written histories disappear slowly. If the way it changes hands could be made progressively more secure, or the frequency of changes progressively reduced, the overall evidence for a well-established fact could decrease asymptotically toward a non-negligible positive value rather than to zero, in which case the history of that fact would never disappear entirely.

Locke's claim does require qualification to answer one of Coady's arguments, however (212–3). A person who is more distant in time from the original truth may have better evidence for it if he can find additional corroboration not available to a more proximal person. Locke's claim implies monotonic degradation along lines of transmission taken singly, but not necessarily for the combined effect of all lines of transmission. If, as seems likely, our efforts to dig up new lines of evidence for the same event peter out over the long haul, Locke's claim could eventually be reinstated for the totality of evidence. But the rest of Coady's argument seems to ignore the fact that even memory and rehearsal of first-hand experiences constitute intermediate hands through which they are transmitted. Perhaps Locke would be impressed by modern means of preserving documentary evidence, but no original endures forever, and even originals get altered by the hands they pass through. If one makes a Xerox copy of a Xerox copy of a Xerox copy enough times, eventually all of the definition in the original will be lost. Evidence is information, the opposite of entropy. Ultimately, the disappearance of history follows from the second law of thermodynamics.

---

[111] *Testimony* (Oxford: Clarendon Press, 1992), p. 199. Page references in this subsection are to this work.

4.5 THE EXISTENCE OF GOD AND ANECDOTAL EVIDENCE

The evidential status of anecdotes regarding God's existence is not simple. First, there is a straightforward deductive proof that one of the most common conceptions of God is impossible—the argument from evil. If God is omnipotent he is capable of preventing evil. If he is perfectly good then he is willing to prevent evil. God does anything that he is both able and willing to do. Evil exists. Hence an omnipotent and morally perfect God does not. Space does not permit me to examine the many efforts at circumventing this argument—that would require a book in itself—but at best they have only brought the issue to a standoff. I can only note that a large gap exists between what I gave in the Preface as necessary conditions for godhood—that God be immaterial, intelligent, capable of action, creator of the world, and worthy of worship—and the apparently self-contradictory conception of an omnipotent, morally perfect being. However, this affects only the logical problem of evil, not the more important evidential problem that the existence of any good God seems less likely given the amount of evil in the world. It also leaves unaffected the problem of understanding why evil exists or what function it plays in creation.

Setting these problems aside, revealed theology provides two sorts of evidence regarding the existence and nature of God, one being historical textual evidence—the testimony of previous generations of believers—and the other contemporary religious experience. Both forms of evidence are almost exclusively anecdotal. If what I have said so far is correct, there can be no unique answer regarding the evidential value of this testimony, since it will vary with our proximity to the original source, our knowledge of the source and its reliability, our experience with other forms of verbal testimony, and whether we have had experiences similar to the ones being reported.

One dissimilarity between ball lightning and God is that God is not so well-defined phenomenally, and it is unclear whether experiences ostensibly of God have phenomenal uniformity comparable to experiences of ball lightning. There is also significant "negative" anecdotal evidence—evidence suggesting that God does not exist. Although this could also be said of ball lightning, the logical relation is different because ball lightning is not conceived as omnipresent. Another issue is whether it is proper to consider anecdotal material purporting to describe experiences of God as being evidential at all. To make sense of this suggestion, one needs something akin to Swinburne's deeply problematic principle of credulity.

A major problem still remains in the tendency of religious evidence to be equivocal or ambiguous, especially when one's conception of God is not agreed upon in advance of the inquiry. For example, suppose the ultimate reality regarding human psychology (were it possible to discover) contained nothing remotely similar to the religious conception of a "metaphysically" free will (5.2). Assuming that retributive justice is fair only if humans have a free will, this would still only prove that a god who is morally perfect and gives out eternal rewards to people differentially on the basis of a retributive scheme of justice does not exist. A god that is not morally perfect, or one that is but rewards all people the same, or does not reward people retributively, might still exist. Perhaps some of these alternatives could be removed by rational argumentation, but it seems to me that all are at least arguable possibilities. And then, there may still be something in human psychology resembling free will enough to remove any transparent argument that retributive justice is unacceptable. This diffuseness strikes me as a major obstacle in the path of any effort to make general evidential use of religious experiences. In 6.4 I argue that there are fewer impediments to making evidential use of near-death experiences than for religious experiences generally. Although the general problem of providing theoretical models of God is taken up in chapter 7, it should be apparent from what follows that the anecdotal evidential support upon which these models rely makes it unlikely that they can command a broad consensus based on epistemic credentials alone.

To sum up the argument to this point, rationality does not require banning the use of unreplicated evidence arising in uncontrolled environments, yet such evidence naturally leads to idiosyncratic conclusions. Given that virtually all evidence for the existence of God drawn from revealed theology is anecdotal, and given the ambiguity of all experientially-based evidence for religious claims, the problem of finding a uniquely rational approach to religious questions becomes essentially irremediable at the institutional level, although not necessarily at the individual level.

4.5.1 General Approaches

Philosophers have proposed a number of different principles as purportedly generally valid rules for handling anecdotal evidence. In this section I will briefly examine the views of William James, Richard Swinburne, Caroline Davis, C. A. J. Coady, and William Alston representing the "believers," and Daniel Dennett and Wayne Proudfoot representing the "skeptics." Although their views are complex and hard to categorize, and none are formulated specifically in terms of "the problem of anecdotal evidence," one can extract from their positions generally recommended attitudes, both toward first-hand *experience,* and toward the *testimony* of others and as evidence for claims that are otherwise unverifiable and unsupported theoretically. In particular, one can distill from these attitudes the circumstances under which they regard belief as rationally permitted or rationally obligated. Examining them briefly provides an opportunity for me to articulate why I favor neither a policy of generalized credulity nor generalized incredulity. I will start by summarizing their views, leaving more detailed analysis and argumentation for subsequent subsections.

Starting with the most senior, William James sums up his conclusions with regard to mystical experiences as follows:[112]

> (1) Mystical states, when well-developed, usually are, and have the right to be, absolutely authoritative over the individuals to whom they come.
> (2) No authority emanates from them which should make it a duty for those who stand outside of them to accept their revelations uncritically.

He goes on to suggest that a person receiving testimony of a mystical revelation would still be justified in accepting the testimony as veridical.

Richard Swinburne articulates a principle of credulity with respect to religious experience that brings him very close to the same conclusion.[113]

> . . . in the absence of special considerations, all religious experiences ought to be taken by their subjects as genuine, and hence as substantial grounds for belief in the existence of their apparent object—God, or Mary, or Ultimate Reality, or Poseidon.

After discussing at length the kinds of special considerations that might be brought to bear on religious experiences, he concludes (270):

> . . . a religious experience apparently of God ought to be taken as veridical unless it can be shown on other grounds significantly more probable than not that God does not exist.

He is unwilling, however, to extend this much credulity to other religious percepts, such as Mary or Poseidon.

Swinburne's principle of testimony is stronger than James's. Paraphrased, it is that in the absence of special considerations—i.e., positive evidence that in general or in the specific case at issue, the subject misremembers, exaggerates, or lies—the experiences of others are (probably) as they report them (272). Once again I assume that anything which is probably true

---

[112] *The Varieties of Religious Experience* (New York: Random House, 1929), p. 414.

[113] *The Existence of God*, p. 254.

has the preponderance of evidence in its favor, hence at the very least belief in it is rationally permitted.

Caroline Davis endorses both Swinburne's principle of credulity and principle of testimony as fundamental principles of rationality applicable to all "seemings." That is, unless one can justify doubting them *en bloc,* as we do dreams and hallucinations, one should extend credulity to them all *en bloc.*[114] In a display of hairsplitting, she extends a presumption of innocence to religious experiences *en bloc,* saying

> the onus is squarely on the skeptic to show that religious experiences are *not* reliable perceptual experiences.

One page later, however, she qualifies this by saying,

> It would be a complete misuse of the principle of credulity to say, 'The onus is on the skeptic to produce challenges and therefore I can completely trust all unchallenged religious experiences.'

On her view, an initial presumption of innocence does not absolve beliefs of any need for justification; indeed, the believer *should* investigate them further before making a substantial commitment to them, if the believer can anticipate as yet unarticulated challenges (103–4). The easiest way to make sense of her position is to construe it as conflating the belief/acceptance distinction (1.4). Reconstructed, she appears to hold that religious experience reports should be *accepted* initially as working hypotheses, "innocent until proven guilty," but should not really be *believed* except and to the extent justified by further investigation.

Coady's work on testimony does not specifically address religious questions, or whether one has an epistemic duty to believe first-hand experience, religious or otherwise. While he believes that Davidson takes charity to excess in interpreting the testimony of others, he agrees with Davidson for the most part, saying[115]

> . . . extensive commitment to trusting the reports of others [is] a precondition of understanding their speech at all.

---

[114] *The Evidential Force of Religious Experience* (Oxford: Clarendon Press, 1989), pp. 100ff.

[115] *Testimony,* p. 176.

He follows Swinburne in excepting "special considerations to the contrary," but apparently does not allow such considerations to invalidate a great deal of the testimony we receive. This sounds fairly strong, however he might exempt skeptics of religious experience by arguing that they really do not understand the testimony of people having such experiences, and so need not trust them. But we may sometimes understand speech in the sense of being able to explain why the person said what she did, while denying that much of what she said is true; if, for example, the statements were viewed as manifesting primarily the speaker's entrenched socio-economic interests.

William Alston, on the other hand, treats religious experience specifically but does not specifically address verbal testimony, holding that

> . . . experience of God is a source of justification for M-beliefs, somewhat in the way that sense experience is a source of justification for perceptual beliefs,

where M-beliefs are beliefs regarding how God is currently related to us, particularly that God is manifesting himself to us now more-or-less in the way we perceive.[116] Although he does not explicate 'justification' here, he makes it clear that only prima facie justification is intended. Elsewhere he repudiates deontological explications of justification, preferring to cash it out as something similar to Plantinga's conception of warrant. While deontologizing Alston's position violates it, it would be strange for him to call such beliefs justified while denying that the percipient is rationally permitted to believe them. As for the question of what beliefs are obligatory, his view has the advantage of appearing weaker than either James's or Swinburne's.

Turning now to the skeptics, Dennett says of introspection,[117]

> we are fooling ourselves . . . when we claim to be just using our powers of inner observation. [I suspect] we are always actually engaging in a sort of impromptu theorizing—and we are remarkably gullible theorizers, precisely because there is so little to "observe," and so much to pontificate about without fear of contradiction.

I presume that his view generalizes to any testimony regarding unverifiable, nonpublic experiences. His method for handling such testimony is to let the collection of reports constitute a "heterophenomenological" world much the way that a work of fiction constitutes the world that the characters live and act in. That is, the text of these reports determines the world by fiat, so that

---

[116] "Perceiving God," pp. 655–6.

[117] *Consciousness Explained*, pp. 67–8.

whatever the text does not determine remains indeterminate. Dennett suspends judgment on whether any of the events reported are real unless they can be verified independently by physical evidence, on the grounds that people tend to confabulate, or make up theories and causal stories without realizing it. Since no alternative, physical evidential pathway exists for most religious experiences, Dennett would presumably adopt blanket incredulity for such reports. In answer to the charge that this approach gives only patronizing, "mock respect" to the testifier, who wants to be believed rather than bracketed, Dennett shrugs (83),

> . . . deviation from normal interpersonal relations is the price that must be paid for the neutrality a science . . . demands.

Wayne Proudfoot writes directly on the topic of religious experience, but is more evasive in his recommendations. While acknowledging that describing an experience accurately requires mentioning the entities ostensibly experienced, he points out that explanations of such experiences are exempt from this restriction. Just because a community has no concept of 'culture' or 'economy' does not mean that such concepts are inappropriate in explaining the community's activities; the fact that they explain them by appeal to God is no reason why we must as well. He points out further that phenomena or experiences are not in themselves the kinds of things that one can explain; they can only be explained relative to how they are described. This much is clear and uncontroversial; the rest of his position is neither. Rather, he gives examples of explanations that might be acceptable for why an experience was described in a certain way, which include reference to the historical and cultural contexts in which the report was made, and the predispositions of the person giving the report, but makes no mention of a reality that exists roughly in the way that it was reportedly experienced.[118] This confuses explanation of an utterance event with explanation of the event that the utterance is about; Proudfoot leaves the reader to guess whether it goes without saying that the way the world is affects the way we experience and report it, or that in the case of religious experiences there are no legitimate explanatory factors other than physiology, psychology, history, and culture.

Before proceeding, let me say that what we find here is typical of the literature at large. Religiously inclined people often seem prejudiced in favor of belief. Given that commonality of experience is a major benchmark of

---

[118] *Religious Experience* (Univ. of California Press, 1985), pp. 218–27.

reality, it seems implausible to give equivalent evidential status to uncommon, private experiences, as to intersubjective experiences. Appeals to a principle of credulity or "proper basicality"[119] seem like special pleading. Davis's choice to draw the line between religious experiences and dreams and hallucinations seems arbitrary given that they are all private, and any truth they contain is unverifiable. It is true that religious experiences are intersubjective to the extent that a community exists to stand behind them, but these communities are very narrow compared to those that stand behind reports of trees and chairs. Neither can they vouch for specific experiences; they can only say that the report is of a kind that generally fits the reputation of God, or what he is known to do. On the other hand, one readily recognizes in Dennett's hardheaded position the misanthropic scientism attributed to Argyle earlier in the chapter. Given that some scientific values are parochial, one cannot help wondering, "What if I don't want to do science? (Why should I?) I only want to know what a reasonable person would believe!"

The above authors manifest the party line of their preferred intellectual subculture or milieu. Part of the problem stems from seeking a simple solution for a complex problem—something that can be formulated as a generally applicable rule or principle. Starting from the assumption that God either exists or doesn't exist in a way that lends itself to being experienced, it is natural to reason that either most of these experiences are veridical, or none of them are. But given the amount of disagreement among religious people, and the amount of impromptu theorizing that may inform reports of religious experience, I think the hypothesis should be entertained that God exists, yet most of the putative experiences of him are false or misleading, or contain significant misinformation. To borrow a Cartesian metaphor, God may exist while an "evil demon" exists also, bent on deceiving us. This scenario would defeat both policies of generalized credulity and generalized incredulity. If I am on the right track, the ultimately correct posture to take toward anecdotal evidence resists straightforward formulation; its epistemology is more complex than we want it to be. In what follows I discuss specific problems with the above approaches in more detail.

4.5.2   The Credulity of Swinburne and Coady

The plausibility of Swinburne's principle of credulity and Alston's talk of perceiving God is tied to the success of the analogy between religious experience and experience in general, where some sort of prima facie credibility

---

[119]   Alvin Plantinga, "Reason and Belief in God."

is normally extended to the contents of perception. Note here that the analogy can be made in different ways. One can say that experiences of God are phenomenologically similar to experiences of physical objects, or point out semantic similarities between one kind of report and the other, or to pragmatic or functional similarities that make the term 'experience' appropriate in both cases. Yet the issue here cannot be any of these, but the similarity in evidential or epistemological status of the two kinds of experience.

Some argue that experience of the presence of an omnipresent being should no more be taken at face value than should experience of its absence, and this latter kind of experience seems far more common.[120] Davis notes that an absence of experience of God is not the same as experiencing God's absence. The former is reported far more frequently, but is epistemologically less significant.[121] Swinburne argues (254) by analogy that the failure to see a table in the room is not evidence that tables don't exist—it only shows that most likely there is no table in the room. Such an argument would be far more persuasive if God were not at the same time being claimed to be omnipresent. In a sense, God's omnipresence "turns the tables" against the principle of credulity, since without omnipresence the claim that God exists is an existential one that requires only a single instance to be true, but with omnipresence it becomes a universal one that requires only a single counter-instance to be false. Alston replies that there are standard theories to explain why God does not appear to everyone at all times—e.g., not all are prepared to meet the moral requirements of interaction with God, or God selectively chooses to whom he reveals himself. At best this rearguard action brings the issue to a standoff; it does not, for example, go far toward explaining why God is perceived when he is, or with the frequency that he is, let alone why anyone's stance should change from incredulity to credulity.

Another problem with Swinburne's principle of credulity is that it is hard to ascribe evidential value either to experiences of God's presence or to experiences of God's absence when one has no idea under what circumstances God can be expected to appear.[122] In the case of a given table, the question of whether it exists would be virtually unanswerable if one had no

---

[120] Michael Martin, "The Principle of Credulity and Religious Experience," *Religious Studies* 22 (1986): 79–93; J. William Forgie, "The Principle of Credulity and the Evidential Value of Religious Experience," *International Journal for Philosophy of Religion* 19 (1986): 146–59.

[121] *The Evidential Force of Religious Experience,* p. 99.

[122] "The Principle of Credulity and Religious Experience," pp. 85–6.

idea where to look for it, or the circumstances under which one could expect to find it. Since no such specification can be given for religious experiences, this becomes a major obstacle to assigning them evidential value. William Rowe takes this point a step further, arguing that one must also be able to tell under what conditions perceptions of God are illusory or delusional, or else one has no basis for an experience/reality distinction.[123] Rowe thus puts his finger on perhaps the biggest disanalogy between religious experiences and the contents of ordinary perception, since the circumstances under which the latter can be expected not to be veridical are well-known. This does not preclude developing such a criterion, but if one uses received traditions to winnow delusional experiences, the plurality of traditions will lead to a plurality of experience/reality distinctions. Perhaps we can tolerate the balkanization of belief systems in a pluralistic world, but not the balkanization of metaphysics. They cannot all be correct, in which case some of them are giving only an appearance where they are purporting to deliver a reality. If anything, balkanization argues for incredulity rather than credulity.

Treating religious experience without benefit of an interpretive tradition, one would confront something comparable to what Quine calls "radical translation" of native utterances, having to start from scratch. Worse, one would lack a source of evidence normally available to the radical translator: the shared reality or *stimulus conditions* on the basis of which to translate observable terms. On the positive side, one would at least start out knowing the "native's" terms for assent and dissent. Although it is hard to imagine how one could learn anything groping amid such utter confusion, the point is that people somehow manage to learn language under such conditions, so perhaps one could learn to make coherent sense of religious experiences as well. Initially one must rely heavily on coherence as an interpretive crutch, but eventually one may be able to formulate an appearance/reality distinction. Thus, it seems that the initial stages of inquiry constitute an important exception to Rowe's requirement.

Swinburne's original principle made no assumption about a context of inquiry, and in this respect his principle seems defective, since we normally have a prima facie basis for incredulity regarding alleged entities that are not publicly perceptible, such as those appearing in dreams and hallucinations. Moreover, Swinburne formulates his principle in terms of obligation rather than permission. That is, he says that one *ought* to take these experiences

---

[123] "Religious Experience and the Principle of Credulity," *International Journal for Philosophy of Religion* 13 (1982): 90–1.

evidentially, not that one *may* do so, leaving room for the possibility that one may not. These two factors make his claim essentially a "burden of proof" argument, *pace* Davis, and this seems unreasonable. My position is that a context of inquiry is needed to justify offering God as an explanation in the first place. Overcoming Rowe's difficulty now also seems to require such a context. One's evidential body must reach a critical mass before one will be in a position to identify delusional experiences, but it will not grow if one is not in the context of ongoing inquiry. While some religious practices may not tolerate this kind of context, the need to come to grips with religious anecdotal evidence suggests that other types of practice would be preferable.

Turning next to Coady, we already saw his strong view lead him to renounce the commonsensical principle that transmission diminishes the evidential force of testimony. It also leads to a questionable attack on modern psychology. His lead example of wrongheadedness is Robert Buckhout, whose survey of a half century of psychological evidence on the reliability of human testimony concluded that, by-and-large, it is not very reliable.[124] Coady calls this "absurd to the point of idiocy" (265), since Buckhout is relying on the testimony of other human beings as evidence that human testimony is unreliable, and has the gall to expect us to believe *his* testimony! Coady's criticism may be biographically accurate, but logical considerations favor Buckhout's conclusion rather than Coady's. First a terminological point: calling testimony reliable is calling it substantially correct; calling it unreliable merely denies this—it is *not* the same as calling it substantially incorrect. I assume that 'substantially' means 'far more than 50% of the time'. Hence the testimony of psychologists and the population at large may both be unreliable if, say, both are correct 50% of the time and incorrect the other 50%. They cannot both be reliable, however.

Now for the argument: either the testimony of these psychologists can be relied upon or it cannot be. If their testimony is reliable, then human testimony in general is not; but if not, this is only so much more evidence for the unreliability of human testimony—you can't even trust the psychologists!—not evidence that human testimony is reliable by-and-large. We do not have a zero-sum game in which the only way for the psychologists to be wrong would be for the general population to be right.

Lest this strike the reader as logical hocus-pocus, let me reiterate that Coady's mistake is a common one but the argument is a straightforward *reductio ad absurdum* of the reliability of human testimony. In a *reductio*,

---

[124] "Eyewitness Testimony," *Scientific American* 231, 6 (1974): 23–31.

if one intends to prove some claim, say, *A*, then one assumes the denial of it, ¬*A*, and shows with the aid of uncontroversial assumptions that this leads to a contradiction. It leads to a contradiction if it implies anything that contradicts one of the original assumptions, including ¬*A* itself. Any collection of premises that implies a contradiction is inconsistent—they cannot all be true. If the other premises are uncontroversial, however, then the originally assumed denial (¬*A*) is most likely at fault, in which case what one intended to prove (*A*) is vindicated. What Buckhout intends to prove is that human testimony is by-and-large unreliable, so he starts by assuming the denial— that human testimony *is* reliable—to see what this implies. Examining the available testimony, Buckhout finds a large body implying that human testimony is unreliable, in which case he arrives at the desired contradiction that human testimony is by-and-large both reliable and unreliable. The same would happen if he found collections of testimony that regularly contradict one another, as is often alleged of eyewitness testimony and of reports of religious experiences. One of our premises must be wrong, and an obvious candidate is the premise that human testimony is reliable.

If the logic of Buckhout's argument is impeccable, he may still be wrong in point of fact. That is, perhaps most human testimony *is* reliable while only the testimony of certain groups, say, psychologists, is not. Perhaps psychologists demand an unreasonably high standard of reliability, or their experiments lack ecological validity. Nothing is so gallingly obvious about this that we should suppose it "absurd to the point of idiocy" to think otherwise. It would be highly ironic for the only people to have undertaken systematic empirical study of the accuracy of human testimony to end up more mistaken or misled about it than the rest of us—but it could happen. It would not be surprising if Kahneman, Tversky, Nisbett, and Ross, have exaggerated and sensationalized their negative findings somewhat to capitalize on their shock value, so why shouldn't other psychologists have done to human testimony what they have done to human inference? But in so doing they would be following a ubiquitous pattern of human motivation—people frequently exaggerate for the sake of personal gain. Hence their testimony is probably no less reliable than the run of human testimony.

If these psychologists are at all correct, however, it dooms any sort of principle of testimony such as Coady, Swinburne, and Davis advocate. Yes, people may be entitled to *accept* the testimony of others insofar as pragmatic considerations force their hand, but this does not license any blanket generalization regarding *belief*, the reliability of human testimony, the burden of proof, or the need for special considerations before suspending judgment. One cannot both apportion credulity to the strength of the evidence and extend it to all anecdotal evidence willy-nilly. Perhaps the weasel phrase 'special considerations to the contrary' could be construed broadly enough to make the principle true, but I doubt that it would be useful in that case, or have the advertised implications for religious experience.

4.5.3   The Incredulity of Proudfoot and Dennett

Turning now to the explanatory principles of Dennett and Proudfoot, they have already had an extensive career in the sociology of scientific knowledge (SSK), in which they have been applied to the claims of other scientists rather than to the experiential claims of religious believers. The problem at the bottom of this research program is its apparent lack of reflexivity, or its self-referential absurdity. This problem manifests itself somewhat differently in the approaches of Proudfoot and Dennett, so I consider them separately.

Proudfoot's is perhaps the more straightforward, because he explicitly allows only socio-cultural causes for reports of religious experiences. Without explicitly rejecting religious explanatory entities, for ease of exposition I assume that he rejects them implicitly, in keeping with the popular assumption of naturalism. Some radical sociologists have suggested that only socio-cultural causes be countenanced for the pronouncements of scientists as well, in which case the reality of any theoretical entities that scientists postulate to explain their phenomena—entities such as pulsars, electrons, subconscious drives, chemical bonds, or tectonic plates—cannot be appealed to in explaining why scientists have postulated them.[125] We all hope that part of the reason or cause for our statements is that they are true, but such sociologists often suggest that truth lacks causal or explanatory power. Thinking of truth as correspondence, however, it seems reasonable to believe that entities "out there" have causal power which in part explains our uttering sentences that "correspond" to them. The relation between the sentence and the entities can be causal in one direction and semantic in the other. More generally, these sociologists seem to employ a strongly chauvinistic methodological principle that, of all the sciences, sociology and only sociology is able to formulate accurate explanations of its subject matter. That is, they feel that to be scientific about the scientists they are studying, they must suspend judgment regarding the accuracy of any of the theories and explanations those scientists propose, but adopting the same skeptical stance toward their own theoretical entities and explanations would lead to explanatory paralysis.

---

[125]   See, for example, Andrew Pickering, *Constructing Quarks* (Univ of Chicago Press, 1984). For discussion, see the interchange accompanying Paul Roth and Robert Barrett's "Deconstructing Quarks," *Social Studies of Science* 20 (1990): 579–631.

Most sociologists of science take the weaker position that theirs is only a partial explanation of the behavior of the scientists under study—a part that supplements rather than contradicts the causal role played by the entities (e.g., electrons) these scientists believe to have caused their phenomena, and so indirectly their beliefs about those phenomena. Put another way, the theoretical entities that other scientists postulate are not sufficient to determine their beliefs about them, since socio-cultural factors help to determine these beliefs as well, but most sociologists do not deny that both kinds of factors play a role in causing beliefs. Proudfoot's approach to religious experience appears out of step with this generally methodology. It works only if one antecedently assumes that the case of religion is unique in that such religious entities are already known not to exist. Were he merely to suspend judgment regarding them, he would then have to allow that as far as anyone knows, they may be part of the explanation for religious experience reports. Proudfoot might argue that the assumption of naturalism amply justifies treating religious experiential testimony different from scientific experiential testimony, but this assumption is transparently parochial to science (see 5.3).

Dennett's position is slightly different in that he allows that the entity mentioned in the report may exist and be part of the cause of the report, but only when there is positive, independent, physical evidence to verify it. Other first person reports of experiencing "the same thing" have no corroborating value. Roughly, his is a principle of *incredulity,* absent special considerations to the contrary. His physical chauvinism has a longer history and more respectability than sociological chauvinism, but it is more often assumed than argued for, and seems blatantly parochial to science.

Why does Dennett's stance here differ from his statement regarding anecdotal evidence of intelligence in 3.4.2? Presumably he is articulating here an "officially acceptable" scientific methodology, whereas before he was chafing under its restrictions. More importantly, his previous comments were about experiences of intelligence which are public in the sense that the intelligent entity is available for others to observe and either corroborate or dispute one's findings. Finally, not all "seemings" are born equal, contrary to a view hinted at by Davis. To me, 'special considerations to the contrary' means bent sticks in the water or lakes on the pavement on a hot day, when we justifiably expect our perceptual apparatus to mislead us. Dennett is calling attention to the fact that we receive ample feedback from the environment to educate our sense of how things seem in some cases, whereas in others our sense of seeming operates in blissful ignorance. Our sense of seeming should not be trusted when it is uneducated, or operates "without fear of contradiction," as often happens with nonpublic experiences. Here

I tend to agree with Dennett, but must add that "fear of contradiction" comes in degrees, both for anecdotal evidence generally and religious experience in particular. For example, whenever a person *bases decisions* on how things seem—as often happens in religious contexts—she creates the possibility of disappointed expectations that will educate her sense of seeming as surely as any behaviorist's schedule of reinforcement.

Once again, to think of the problem in terms of SSK, the sociologist studies and believes to be real the sociological factors which theory indicates are causally and explanatorily active. Otherwise, he could not purport to explain the actions of other scientists in terms of interests, alliances, opportunism, etc. Meanwhile, the scientists whom the sociologist studies, study and believe to be real the factors (physical, geological, astronomical, chemical, etc.) which their theory indicates are causally and explanatorily active. These are factors in which the sociologist suspends judgment as the "price" to be "paid" for the neutrality that science demands. Each operates within the methodological constraints peculiar to his intellectual subculture. But what is the rational person observing this whole affair to believe? Should she doubt the existence of both the entities postulated by the sociologist and the scientists the sociologist is studying? Or should she rather believe that all of the entities posited both by the sociologists and the other scientists are real? In practice, scientists generally respect the integrity and authority of other scientists outside their discipline, and so seem to take the latter attitude on the whole. Yet the methodology advanced as peculiarly scientific by Dennett and the SSK program is to suspend judgment on all explanatory entities other than ones that are independently verifiable by a privileged kind of evidence—usually the kind with which one has special expertise. So it appears that different construals of scientific method could have one suspending judgment on almost everything, or believing almost everything. The very concept of a "scientific" attitude toward testimony appears to manifest more clearly a cultural prejudice than a consistent methodological stance. Again, privileging a special kind of evidence seems like special pleading: it gratifies the members of a particular intellectual subculture, but not those adopting a general epistemological standpoint.

4.6   THE BALANCE OF EVIDENCE

There are a number of serious problems with Pascal's famed wager, but it highlights an important truth: we may not have the luxury of proving the existence of God beyond a reasonable doubt before acting on the basis of it.

Given the importance of knowing about the nature of any God that exists, when the balance of evidence favors the existence of God over alternative explanations, it becomes prudent to pursue that hypothesis further. In fact, if any concessions are to be made to the fecundity of pluralism, the hypothesis of God would be worth pursuing well *before* it attains the status of having a balance of evidence in its favor.

Even if anecdotal evidence lacked sufficient probative value to establish any facts beyond a reasonable doubt, it still could tip the balance of evidence in favor of one hypothesis or another, as in the case of ball lightning, especially in the absence of other kinds of relevant evidence. The existence of enough evidence to tip the balance in favor of God's existence may be sufficient to justify or even behoove individual people to seek more evidence on the subject. Of course, one should seek any evidence that has a bearing on claims regarding the nature and existence of God, not just anecdotal evidence. The more evidence one seeks, and the more of a commitment one is called on to make, the more certain one must be of one's presuppositions. The more of one's life that becomes affected by belief in the existence of God, the more necessary it is to verify this belief beyond a reasonable doubt, and not simply on the basis of being on balance the most likely explanation. The burden of proof is always on everybody—it does not cease when the first "on balance" judgment is made.

CHAPTER 5

IDEOLOGICAL ASPECTS OF SCIENCE

5.1 THREE SENSES OF 'IDEOLOGY'

In this chapter I offer several examples of ideological positions and arguments which are responsible for the repudiation, unwarranted on the basis of rationality alone, of the possibility of religious explanation. I will start by introducing several senses of 'ideology' that have attained philosophical currency, but all draw on an underlying theme of

(1) relative immunity from falsification,
(2) orientation around a practice or aim which the ideology functions to perpetuate,
(3) widespread adoption within a community or social group,
(4) the suggestion of some kind of cognitive impropriety.

The last of these must be emphasized because, with the decline of Marxist polemics in recent years, it has become more commonplace to see some ideological positions as relatively innocuous. Although reasons for this are suggested below, one usually does not label a position ideological unless one intends to call it into question. When this happens, the charge that it has been going unquestioned when it is open to question is equivalent to calling it insidious. Thus, even the law of noncontradiction could be regarded as ideological if its cognitive impropriety could be argued. Indeed, some charge that it *is* ideological, but usually in the context of questioning its status as an a priori principle of rationality, rather than impugning its truth.

The root of the possibility of ideology lies in the Kantian principle that the structure of one's cognitive apparatus, whether in the form of language or concrete perceptual systems, places a limit on what one can verbalize, making it difficult or impossible to articulate opposing viewpoints.[126] In other words, an ideological claim functions as if it were system-analytic. The differentia of the three senses of ideology discussed herein are their sources of immunity from falsification. As will become apparent, it is the second sense—the ideological implications of methodology—that figures most prominently in this chapter.

5.1.1 Value-Laden Language and False Consciousness

Historically, our concept of ideology came from Karl Marx and Friedrich Engels, who tied it pejoratively to false consciousness. The notions prevalent in capitalistic societies of freedom and equality regarding the right to enter into contracts—labor contracts in particular—are paradigmatic examples. Marxists see these notions as ideological because there is a lack of real freedom for the working class—they must work in order to live—whereas the capitalist's investment comes from his surplus wealth. The appearance of equality in contractual situations is also illusory—a constant surplus of labor and shortage of work ensures that capitalists will be able to dictate for the most part the terms of labor agreements. Yet the concepts of freedom and equality, although falsely applied, still support the belief that the system is for the most part equitable and deserving of our participation and support. Just as he who controls the airwaves controls what people know, and hence what they believe and opine, even so anyone who controls the words we use has considerable power over what we can use them to mean or say.

This sense of ideology arises in scientific contexts with the value-ladenness of terms associated with scientific discourse. The very words 'scientific' and 'unscientific' are like 'freedom' and 'equality' in being heavily value-laden, and yet are ostensibly descriptive terms with objective truth conditions. We noted this phenomenon in 2.5 with the word 'pseudoscience', and in chapter 3 with words that have both descriptive and evaluative dimensions, not least of which is 'rational'. It also arises in 6.2.1 with 'hallucination'. Despite my concessions to rationality, people who exemplify perfect rationality are probably inhuman and possibly immoral. Why shouldn't contexts arise in which acting irrationally is best, given that rationality, in the sense of the best means to a given end, is often faulted for its amorality? Undoubtedly these words have acquired their value connotations through

---

[126] See W. V. Quine, "Ontology and Ideology," *Philosophical Studies* 2 (1951): 14–5; "Ontology and Ideology Revisited," *Journal of Philosophy* 80 (1983): 501.

natural historical processes, and many deserve the connotations they have acquired, but value-ladenness can easily lull one into thinking uncritically when applying them. Like our "freedom" and "equality" of contract, some objective state of affairs always nominally warrants use of the term, but it may not deserve the value baggage that customarily goes with it. We are all familiar with the use of euphemisms and literary devices to give value connotations to states of affairs that otherwise would not have them. The sticker price of a new car may contain an item described in apparently legitimate, value-neutral terms as 'ADP', but probably will not mention that this stands for 'additional dealer profit'. 'Domestic engineer' has different value connotations from 'homemaker', but probably the same truth conditions.

In 5.4 we will consider a particularly subtle manifestation of this kind of ideology, but more typically it does not cut very deep, due to the difficulty of establishing that some person or class really has significant control over our language. If not, one person's choice of value-laden expressions can be counteracted by an opposing choice of language. What the scientist values as "healthy skepticism" regarding anecdotal evidence may be labeled "misanthropic" by others. What some philosophers praise for its clarity and precision is derogated by others as picayune "logic chopping." Do scientists exemplify "group loyalty," as sociologists say, or is their behavior more akin to what Friedrich Nietzsche calls "the herd"? These kinds of ascriptions can almost always be fought to a standoff.

5.1.2 Ideology as a Product of Methodology

Scientists often claim to abjure metaphysics, but some metaphysical positions are considered benign or innocuous within the scientific community because of their deep roots in methodology, and these lead to the most invidious ideological stances. Suppose a theoretical position accords so well with scientific methodology that it can be seen as a manifestation of the scientific value system itself. One's methodology would cast a substantive shadow on what becomes accepted as theory in that case. Insofar as the values prescribing that methodology are taken for granted within the scientific community, and are not typically on trial, that position will be relatively immune from falsification. The holists W. V. Quine and Larry Laudan both agree that scientific values *can* be on trial as much as scientific theories. Nevertheless, conflicts over values typify revolutionary science more than normal science.

Science is in the business of giving explanations, among other things, hence from a scientific standpoint, the prospect that a given phenomenon *cannot* be understood or explained is not a happy one. The credibility of science has been buoyed for years by a steady stream of explanatory successes, so there is pragmatic justification for the scientific program of looking for explanations wherever they can be found, no holds barred. But this scientific program may also be informed by something as overtly ideological as the principle of sufficient reason in concert with the unity of method thesis. The principle of sufficient reason is the general claim that nothing happens unless a reason or cause necessitates it. It implies determinism and is inconsistent with modern quantum mechanics. Whatever the influences, scientists do not ordinarily distinguish phenomena that *cannot* be explained from those that simply *have not* been explained to date. Both are classified as unsolved problems in practice. How might this be rationally reconstructed?

One rationale combines naturalism with reductionism, i.e., the assumption that all observable phenomena have exclusively natural or material causes, combined with the assumption that the composition and efficacy of these causes can be accounted for in exclusively physical terms. No successful, full-fledged reduction has ever been completed, but enough exist in incipient form to buoy the hopes of reductionists that they are possible in principle, and our best course of action is to await patiently their creation. Thus they maintain the goal of a completed science as a regulative ideal that informs and motivates scientific practice, whether or not it is practically realizable. Virtually *any* problem might appear soluble so long as 'in principle' means nothing more than 'logically possible'. The drawback to this approach is its grandiose and often unargued idealization regarding what science can accomplish—an idealization whose normative credentials are suspect at best.

Here is a more reasonable way to avoid distinguishing what has not and what cannot be explained. Rather than present science in an *idealized* form that is *exclusive*—it precludes other empirical methods as unscientific *and therefore irrational*—one might advance a value system as scientific and as having proven to yield many pragmatic benefits, without thereby ruling out as irrational any and all other value systems that attempt to provide empirical knowledge. It is much easier to defend a value system in terms of its permissive rationality than in terms of its obligatory rationality. If one's method does not claim to be the exclusive means to all a posteriori knowledge worthy of the name, then one may be entitled to one's method without defending it on the grounds of general rationality, but on the more limited grounds of conduciveness toward one's general purposes, and the rationality of those purposes. Thus, one might defend science as an especially efficient means of knowledge acquisition and error avoidance. If one's methodology happens to encourage or facilitate certain theories while making others virtually untenable, these become essentially assumptions or liabilities of the system, and their warrant can be judged on the same instrumental grounds.

Such a move would be away from correspondence and toward a pragmatic conception of truth, of course, but is implicit in defenses of scientific realism claiming truth for science based on its record of successful accomplishment. Some argue that it would be a remarkable coincidence that scientific theories work so well when they do not correspond to reality, but this is not obvious. The pragmatic orientation of the scientific method may not be sufficient in itself to yield theories that work well—its success also depends on nature's uniformity, for example. But with minimal cooperation from nature, it is sufficient to yield theories that work well whether they correspond to reality or not, as van Fraassen argues.[127] If one wants to investigate the correspondence to reality of results obtained under a pragmatically oriented scientific methodology, one would need to retune one's method so as to place greater emphasis on virtues associated with correspondence.

In sum, there is no necessity in identifying phenomena that have not been explained with those that cannot be explained in principle, but this identification is encouraged by a scientific methodology that recognizes no particular value in drawing the distinction. This methodology, in turn, may work well, but that is not sufficient to license it as the exclusive representative of rationality in the field of knowledge acquisition. What is innocuous methodology where science's sovereignty is uncontested may take on an ideological character when applied in disputed territories.

5.1.3 Ideology in the Modern Sense

With the rise of Kuhnian philosophy of science it has become commonplace to classify as ideological any worldview or set of framework beliefs which is held more-or-less immune from falsification, and not necessarily in the pejorative sense. This is not the Kantian position that everyone must use the same a priori framework in order to reason at all. Rather, with a plurality of paradigms to choose from, there is no one in particular that must be used, but inquiry simply cannot be undertaken without using some framework or other. Neither does this mean that such commitments cannot be evaluated, or that reasonable grounds for their rejection cannot be given. But it would be question-begging to evaluate one framework simply on the basis of a competing one, since they all stand equally in need of legitimation. There is no neutral "Archimedean point" from which to arbitrate all disputes among worldviews. Rational evaluation requires at least that they share enough common assumptions to "float" an inquiry.

---

[127] "Empiricism in the Philosophy of Science," pp. 259–98; *The Scientific Image*, p. 98.

Here I have in mind Neurath's boat, a metaphor for the sum of all scientific knowledge which, having no foundation, is supposedly rebuilt in its
entirety with each new generation, "while in the water." Even if science's
belief system contains nothing that is ultimately incorrigible, a substantial
amount of the structure must be left intact at any one time while the remaining parts are reconstructed, or the whole boat will sink. That is, one cannot
profitably question everything at once; something must be left unquestioned
in order to have material to answer the questions with. The figure is usually
formulated so that all parts of the boat are on an equal empirical footing, as
if each could be tested independently relative to the rest. This suggests comparison to Glymour's bootstrap procedure for confirming scientific theories,
by which each hypothesis contained in a theory is supposed to be independently testable relative to the rest of the theory.[128] In the real world, however, many kinds of problems cannot be fixed at sea, and some systems may
be so critical that their failure results in the whole ship's being scrapped.
Under this picture, pragmatic considerations may conspire to render some of
one's theoretical commitments immune from falsification. Such commitments are essentially ideological; there are not enough mutually agreeable
assumptions to float an inquiry into their legitimacy.

Each of the following sections exhibits a concrete case in which the
above senses of ideology rear their ugly heads. These senses tend to operate
in collusion, rather than individually; nevertheless I place emphasis on the
second sense in 5.2 and 5.3 because it is so insidious. The third sense has
received much attention recently and gets no special mention herein.

5.2   FREE WILL

A philosophical problem that often divides religiously and scientifically
oriented people is free will. Religious interest in free will stems from
various sources, one of which is a retributive view of justice, the only view
that seems consistent with eternal reward and punishment as conceived in
western religions. For example, Antony Flew asks how it can be just for
God to punish people for actions which God previously arranged that these
people do.[129] Assuming that ought implies can, eternal reward or punishment would be unjustified if humans had no power to act differently. This

---

[128]   *Theory and Evidence,* pp. 62, 122ff.

[129]   *God and Philosophy,* pp. 44–57.

notion of control, or power to act differently, is what the concept of free will is supposed to capture.

For a retributive notion of justice to be well-founded it would not be sufficient that humans have a subjective sense of being free—one that comes with experiences of deliberating and choosing—since this is consistent with such choices ultimately being determined by external causes. In other words, it does not establish responsibility to say that the person could have done otherwise if she had so chosen, and she perceived within herself the power to choose differently had she so desired, if she still had no control over her desires. In that case the causes of those desires (however far back the causal chain may go), and not the person herself, would ultimately be responsible for the action. At any rate, this principle of responsibility is widely recognized in case law. A God that retributively rewards beings who are not responsible for their actions is unjust. To salvage the justice of a retributive God, then, we need a metaphysical or *incompatibilist* notion of a free will—a notion incompatible with universal causal determinism. Let me explain. We think of most actions as having internal causes, but wouldn't be surprised if some of these internal causes could be traced to environmental, cultural, or genetic—i.e., external—factors. A necessary condition for a person having metaphysically free will would be that some of these internal causes cannot be traced back to external causes, either because they have no causes at all, or because all of their causes are internal. This description of the issue is not universally agreed upon, but its secular aspects have been defended by Peter Van Inwagen and seem substantially correct.[130]

My purpose in this section is not to solve the problem of free will, or treat it comprehensively—that would require a book in itself[131]—but to call attention to the ideological nature of the debate. If metaphysically free will exists, then scientific explanations of why certain human actions take place would be impossible *in principle*. Most events are the result of many impinging causes, but it is more common to know that these causes made the

---

[130] *An Essay on Free Will* (Oxford: Clarendon Press, 1983). This defends the incompatibilist thesis that (metaphysically) free will is intelligible and inconsistent with determinism. Dennett disagrees—see his *Elbow Room* (MIT Press, 1984); and "I Could Not Have Done Otherwise—So What?" *Journal of Philosophy* 81 (1984): 553–65. Van Inwagen replies in "Dennett on 'Could Have Done Otherwise'," *Journal of Philosophy* 81 (1984): 565–7; see also his "Ability and Responsibility," *Philosophical Review* 87 (1978): 201–24.

[131] Those seeking a more comprehensive treatment are referred to Jennifer Trusted, *Free Will and Responsibility* (Oxford Univ. Press, 1984); and Robert Kane, *Free Will and Values* (Albany: SUNY Press, 1985); in addition to the above references.

event probable than that they made it necessary. An event may be explained to the extent that causes for it can be given, but if the event were not necessary or determined by those causes, then some aspects of it cannot be explained by them. The incompatibilist conception of free will lives in these explanatory gaps, and this is what prevents it from harmonizing with scientific methodology, or the scientific value structure. The incompatibilist is supposing that some features of human action that have not been explained scientifically cannot be explained scientifically. It should be no surprise, then, that if a particular human action has at present no explanation, scientists by-and-large do not suppose that it manifested the person's free will. They keep looking until an explanation is found, and until then regard it as just another outstanding problem. Methodology thus effectively precludes the free will explanation. Once again, not all agree that this issue is ideological, but I am not unique in this attribution.[132]

If a "God of the gaps" is inadequate either as a conception of God or of religious explanation (see 1.1), why should a "free will of the gaps" be different? It is not wholly adequate, but bear in mind that free will is performing primarily a defensive function with respect to religious explanation, saving the concept of a righteous and retributive God from bankruptcy. Presumably, we have other sources for our concepts of God and religious explanation, and substantive reasons why we hope that God is not the explanation for everything that is unexplained scientifically—we hope that God *not* be the cause of evil. Whatever evidence exists for such a God is evidence for free will, hence the concept has an independent source of intellectual sustenance. Also, the above description is not really a "free will of the gaps" since we aren't supposing that free will is responsible for *everything* in the explanatory gaps of human action—only for *some* of what remains unexplained.

5.2.1 Is Free Will Impossible?

A standard argument against free will is that there is no evidence for events occurring uncaused or *ex nihilo* in nature. If nature is governed by universal causal laws, and humans are a part of nature, a metaphysically free will is impossible. This argument has three major problems. Regarding universal causal laws, Cartwright points out that at present there are not enough of these laws to explain many natural phenomena for which we think we have reasonable explanations, let alone those that are still unexplained. Thus,

---

[132] Arbib and Hesse specifically label the issue ideological, but in the third rather than the second sense given above, see *The Construction of Reality*, p. 85.

even the most exacting sciences make liberal use of ceteris paribus generalizations, idealizations, and "phenomenological" laws to fill the explanatory gap left by the paucity of legitimate universal causal laws.[133] It is an article of faith that causal laws can be found to govern all phenomena, eliminating this handwaving. Moreover, quantum mechanics yields a plethora of events which apparently occur uncaused in the sense that no previous events necessitate them or affect their probability. Indeterminacy at the atomic level does not guarantee indeterminacy at the macro level, and would not guarantee the existence of free will even then, but it is not inconsistent with the incompatibilist notion of free will the way that deterministic causation is.

Finally, regarding lack of evidence, the argument is question-begging in that the way one goes about looking for evidence puts limits on the kinds of evidence one can expect to find—i.e., the standard argument is oblivious to the very issue I am raising. If cases of free will would be treated by science as unsolved problems, then the abundance of unsolved problems in the social sciences, usually described as a relative lack of progress vis-à-vis the natural sciences, already constitutes inductive evidence that free will exists or is a nontrivial possibility. Classifying phenomena as either part of a causal pattern (i.e., determined) or random—a classification found reasonable by Dennett[134]—also begs the question against free will. Accepting the classification and assuming that free actions would appear random or patternless to an investigator, the prevalence of unpatterned actions in the best available accounts of human behavior also constitutes evidence for free will.

Alternative explanations have been proposed for the comparative lack of scientific progress in solving the causal basis of human action, or fitting actions into predictable patterns. The exceptional complexity of the subject matter and the comparative youth of psychology and neurology are not to be sneezed at, but this should not preclude free will from receiving a fair hearing as well. If the structural or methodological bias built into scientific contexts prevents scientists from giving free will a fair hearing, perhaps philosophers can serve in their place. Note that free will, the complexity of the mind, and the youth of psychology and neuroscience are mutually compatible explanatory factors—all could play a role in bringing about the dearth of explanations of human action. Why don't more philosophers suppose that all *do* play a role? The nonlinear relation between explanation and evidence

---

[133] *How the Laws of Physics Lie*, pp. 45–52. Phenomenological laws are laws whose individual terms are physically uninterpretable, or literally meaningless.

[134] *Brainstorms* (MIT Press, 1981), pp. 287ff.

created by the practice of inferring the best explanation reduces its appeal. I discuss this topic at greater length in 5.4, but sketching one aspect of it will prove instructive here.

Explanations typically compete with one another for evidence, hence any evidential factor that strengthens one explanation will effectively weaken the others, even though it is prima facie irrelevant. "Screening off" among statistical explanations illustrates how this works.[135] For example, why is coffee drinking positively correlated with heart disease in the general population? One might suppose that it causes heart disease, which would lead one to suspect that coffee drinking is positively correlated with heart disease in most subpopulations. As it turns out, coffee drinkers who smoke are no more likely to get heart disease than nondrinkers who smoke; nonsmoking drinkers also are no more likely to get heart disease than nonsmoking nondrinkers. Thus, one broad division of the population into smokers and nonsmokers makes the apparent correlation between coffee drinking and heart disease vanish. It is "screened off" by a positive correlation between smoking and heart disease, which more likely indicates a causal connection. This leaves us with a residual, unexplained correlation between coffee drinking and smoking, and if coffee drinking causes smoking then a coffee-heart disease connection would still exist even though the explanation that smoking causes heart disease is also correct. The two explanations are compatible. But the hypothesis that coffee drinking causes smoking is no more plausible than the hypothesis that smoking causes coffee drinking, or that they have a common cause, so the original hypothesis is now unsupported by evidence. The explanation that smoking causes heart disease screens off the coffee-heart disease connection, appropriating all of its evidence. Worse, the coffee-heart disease connection has a mark against it, since it led to erroneous inferences while the smoking-heart disease explanation did not.

The moral is that scientists will think that their preferred explanation for the lack of progress in the social sciences appropriates all of the evidence for free will, rendering it gratuitous, and will claim that the hypothesis of free will has led to erroneous inferences in the past. Religious people will point out that any evidence that a righteous, retributive God exists constitutes indirect evidence for free will—evidence that these theories do not appropriate, but of course some scientists think they can explain this other evidence too. Thus the battle is joined, each side elaborating a worldview that

---

[135] See Wesley Salmon, *Scientific Explanations and the Causal Structure of the World* (Princeton Univ. Press, 1984), p. 44.

attempts to appropriate all of the evidential claims made by the opposition. Philosophers who enter the fray are likely to get caught in the crossfire. However, the fact that the original explanations were mutually consistent suggests that peacefully coexistence can be had, if anyone wants it.

5.2.2 Is Free Will Intelligible?

A more serious difficulty with the free will thesis is its relative unclarity. After all, failure to find nontrivial causes for human actions is at most negative evidence that they are uncaused. Does anyone know what free will is, what it amounts to, or what would constitute positive evidence for it? In order not to duplicate the discussion of the relative unclarity of religious explanations in chapter 3, here I focus on the counterargument that the very concept of free will is part-and-parcel with an antiquated "folk psychology" that ought to be revised or eliminated.

Stephen Stich and Patricia and Paul Churchland have been crusading for the elimination of folk psychological concepts such as 'will', 'belief', 'desire', etc., arguing that science will enable us to give an account of human action that makes no essential use of them.[136] While the term 'will' has already disappeared from the scientific literature for the most part, the issue is whether it will be replaced by something substantially similar in extension and intension, being only more precise and more in accordance with contemporary science's understanding of brain processes. In other words, does anything exist in reality substantially corresponding to our notion of will?

Current discussions of parallel distributed processing as a model of brain activity frequently conclude that decision-making in the brain is not localizable, but a function of the entire organic structure, or at any rate a large portion of it. If so, this would undercut attempts to reduce or localize the function of willing to some manageably small part of the brain which might be entirely analyzable in terms of the stimulation of identifiable nerve fibers. Hence the elimination of will through reduction to specific, localizable processes does not appear promising. Localizability is not the only issue, of course. Eliminating other concepts such as belief, desire, intention, deliberation, and option would leave us without a language to describe the will or its activities. Stich argues that talk of beliefs is unscientific, and that beliefs and desires are not useful scientific terms because they lack such

---

[136] Stephen Stich, *From Folk Psychology to Cognitive Science* (MIT Press, 1983); Paul Churchland, "Eliminative Materialism and Propositional Attitudes," *Journal of Philosophy* 78 (1981): 67–89; Patricia Churchland, "A Perspective on Mind-Brain Research," *Journal of Philosophy* 77 (1980): 185–207.

pragmatic virtues as context-free generalizability. Paul Churchland calls folk psychology a degenerating research program.[137]   But these pragmatically and scientistically oriented attacks are irrelevant to the immediate issue, although they might bear on the viability of social sciences employing folk psychological terms.   When adjudicating an issue over which science and religion conflict, what makes for good science is not in point.   I do not oppose modeling psychological processes computationally.   This research will surely yield valuable information even if it doesn't accomplish everything imagined by its visionaries.   My point is that the ultimate success of such models in eliminating folk psychological terms is not a foregone conclusion, and I see no reason to reject free will simply on the basis of scientism plus a promissory note—the scientific version of "a hope and a prayer."

Dennett advances a slightly more moderate position, holding that the notions of belief and desire have instrumental value insofar as they allow us to predict and explain behavior in ways that could not be done without adopting the intentional stance.   He denies that they are ultimately real—no entities in the head substantially corresponding to beliefs and desires.   Rather, he compares their metaphysical status to a person's center of gravity, or the earth's equator.[138]   He finds an obstacle to ontologizing beliefs and desires in making sense of irrational or counternormative behavior, which also is a problem for attributing responsibility.   If the boy knows arithmetic, the price of the lemonade, and the amount of money the man gave him, then how could he give him only 11¢ change instead of 13¢?   Yet this kind of thing happens everyday.   If we describe the situation in terms of beliefs and desires, Dennett says, we inevitably end up with an inconsistency—something that is irreducibly senseless or absurd.   The same applies to will: Did he will to shortchange him?   How much money did he will to return?

Given the status of free will here as parasitic here on a particular view of God, the simplest course is to subordinate our judgments of what a person wills to judgments of the acts for which he is responsible.   Since we normally do not hold a person responsible for actions that are inadvertent, as this appears to be, we can agree with Dennett that there is no fact of the matter what the boy believed or willed.   That does not prove that beliefs, desires, and wills don't exist any more than immature, half-baked, and other borderline cases of apples proves that apples don't exist.   Similarly, so long as the

---

[137]   *From Folk Psychology to Cognitive Science,* pp. 127ff.; "Eliminative Materialism and Propositional Attitudes," p. 75.

[138]   *The Intentional Stance,* pp. 15–28, 52–3, 71–2.

primary threat to folk psychology is posed by its inability to describe or account for bizarre cases of abnormal brain function, as Patricia Churchland's examples suggest,[139] Quine's "maxim of minimum mutilation" suggests that the scope of folk psychological terms merely be limited so as not to apply in those cases.

Dennett will insist that this only postpones the dilemma. How are we to account for cases in which the beliefs, desires, and willing are fully matured, yet the person still does what is wrong? The problem of how a person can knowingly do wrong dates to ancient times and is a problem for all psychology, not just for free will. Here's another: should a person suggest that some of her thoughts during deliberation had external causes, many clinical psychologists would ascribe to her "delusions of passivity,"[140] while Dennett asserts that all such thoughts ultimately have external causes. Both of these are problems for psychologists to thrash out among themselves, not a problem for free will. In general, I think the appearance that there is a problem here is created by making fairly strong assumptions of rationality in combination with an equally strong claim that the actions of others can only be interpreted through the principle of charity. That is, once it is shown that some absurdity in the explanatory account is unavoidable, philosophers tend to assume that the account itself must be at fault, and so seek a better one. Although principles of charity have been fashionable recently, they also seem overdone.[141] Perhaps people do act absurdly on occasion, but this is not proof against their having beliefs and desires.

Dennett describes beliefs and desires as part of an intentional stance in which we assume that the actor is a rational agent. If the actor behaves irrationally, then we have that much less reason to ascribe beliefs and desires to him, but otherwise the actor appears compelled to do what rationality dictates. However, rationality need not yield a univocal "optimal" result under every set of circumstances, and a person may not always have an option which fits his beliefs or desires best. If a person had to choose between a supererogatory and a reprehensible act, there might be no fact of the matter which act is "rational" or "corresponds to his beliefs and desires"—hence no

---

[139] *Neurophilosophy*, pp. 222–34.

[140] Graham Reed, *The Psychology of Anomalous Experience*, revised ed. (Buffalo: Prometheus, 1988), pp. 119–23.

[141] David Henderson, "The Principle of Charity and the Problem of Irrationality," *Synthese* 73 (1987): 225–52; "A Solution to Davidson's Paradox of Irrationality," *Erkenntnis* 27 (1987): 359–69. See also Christopher Cherniak, *Minimal Rationality* (MIT Press, 1986).

obvious cause—yet it does not follow that neither act deserves praise or blame. If Dennett is insisting that we give a fully adequate naturalistic (causal) explanation of how it is possible for a person to know that an action is wrong and still do it, he is begging the question against free will. My interpretation of free will makes it possible that some ultimate questions regarding why people do what they do cannot be answered in scientific terms, but this does not automatically preclude justified reward or punishment for those people.

5.2.3 Free Will, Deliberation, and Responsibility

Still, some explanation is necessary of what a will, or a free will, is supposed to be. We may think of the will as applying at the culmination of a process of deliberation, when the results of that process are implemented in the form of some action. If this is what the will is, then what can it mean for such a will to be free? Dennett asks the ad hominem question in terms of why anyone would want such a will to be free, whereas it should be evident from the foregoing that the real issue is whether it really is free, regardless of whether anyone desires or benefits from that freedom. So the question of what it means to be free is crucial here.

Dennett points out correctly that one cannot conceive of the will as implicated only once the process of deliberation is over, because the choices made during deliberation regarding which theories, observations, and consequences to consider, as well as how much weight to assign them, are as much an act of willing as any action implemented as a result.[142] Furthermore, one *wants* the considerations adduced during deliberation to shape the practical result—otherwise deliberation is pointless. Yet if this applies at the nexus of every choice made in the deliberative process—i.e. (i) that it be rationally related to what preceded, and (ii) that the reasons supporting it must also have caused it—at what point would freedom even be appropriate? Don't we end up with an endless regress of reasons acting as causes?

Let us distinguish here between reasons operating as causes and reasons operating as after-the-fact rationales. It is always possible to adduce a rationale for an action afterwards, but philosophers disagree on whether such reasons justify an action when they did not function in bringing it about. Granting that some reasons do act as causes, let's call them *precipitating* reasons. Dennett is saying that we choose the precipitating rationale upon which we act just as much as we do the action itself, which threatens to start

---

[142] *Brainstorms,* pp. 295–7.

us off on an endless regress of reasons acting as causes, leaving no room for free will. However, here one could make a Wittgensteinian point that our reasoning or justification only goes back so far, regardless of whether the reasons are precipitating or adduced after the fact. Beyond a certain point we act without reason, although not necessarily wrongly. This could happen if either our reasons are caused by something that is not a reason, or if they are not caused at all. Presumably, this is the point at which free will would come in, but Dennett doesn't carry his analysis this far back into the deliberative process. If our reasons for acting do not regress to infinity, then how is it a conceptual confusion to suppose that sometimes necessitating causes of action don't either? This may undermine Kant's notion of a necessary connection between free will and reason, but the existentialist program of connecting freedom directly to an arational power of choice seems more apt regardless. By fragmenting the overall deliberative process into many smaller deliberative processes, Dennett has only multiplied the opportunities for this arational power of choice to operate.

Dennett states, "the important claim that one could have done otherwise under the circumstances is not plausibly construed as the claim that one could have done otherwise given *exactly* the set of convictions and desires that prevailed at the end of rational deliberation."[143] This is precisely what is in question. Strangely, Dennett offers no reason for supposing that determinism is more plausible as a general thesis than indeterminism. Some religious people would go on to suggest that what is physically indeterministic is nevertheless determined in some way subjectively, or by the agent's "character," perhaps conceived along Cartesian dualist lines. While I have no theory to offer in defense of this idea, the common rejoinder that such a supposition would make a completed science of the mind impossible has no force in a dispute between religion and science.

Saying that people have a free will need not commit one to saying that all or even most of their actions are undertaken freely. There may be degrees of freedom corresponding to the proportion of actions engaged in freely, or the strength of external causation, even as common sense suggests that children and adults have varying degrees of responsibility. Ultimately, the process of deliberation could be construed broadly as encompassing a whole lifetime. Attributions of responsibility also require more than simply establishing that an action was causally necessitated by factors external to the brain. We normally require at least that the subject be aware how she could

---

[143] *Brainstorms*, p. 295.

have behaved differently, and why an alternative action was worth considering. Elaborating the problem in greater detail suggests that one would need a God's eye view of the matter to make full determination of what actions are free and what actions a person can be held responsible for. Incompatibilist conceptions of free will are largely metaphysical in character—they are concerned with the way the world is, not with direct pragmatic consequences of freedom for public policy, so talk of a God's eye view is harmless here. These metaphysical issues prevent comparative evaluation of scientific and religious points of view on purely empirical grounds, but call attention to a fundamental compatibility in the competing theories that could be the basis of a peaceful settlement between religion and science.

5.3   NATURALISM AND REDUCTIONISM

Naturalists and reductionists would eliminate from our ontology not only any notion of the will, but the very possibility that a God exists who influences the world or is immanent in it. Recall that in Hempelian terms, a reductive explanation does not explain an *event* but another *theory*—the theory that is "reduced." It is standardly assumed that the "reducing" theory or laws are formulated in terms closer to those of physics, or employ theoretical entities at a smaller scale than the target theory. One rationale for reductionism is implicit in the western analytic tradition of taking large problems and "analyzing" them, or showing how they are composed of smaller problems, each of which can be solved more easily. The assumption is that the large problem is "nothing but" the smaller problems in a certain combination. If the whole is nothing but a certain arrangement of its parts, then whole theories and theoretical entities may also be analyzable or reducible to a combination of smaller theories postulating smaller and simpler entities. Hence the reducing theory is assumed to operate at a smaller or more localized level than the theory being reduced. Theories involving the existence of God posit the largest of all entities, and their use and verification present the greatest of all problems. Hence if any theory were ever a likely candidate for reduction or elimination, religious theories should head the list.

Reductionism does not draw its strength primarily from metaphysics but from epistemology. A standard religious tradition claims that God exists at all times and all places, and is at least partially the cause and sustainer of all things. Therefore, no belief that God exists could be mistaken, nor could any experience that indicates God's presence be unreliable. Given that God uses the natural world as an instrument for realizing his will, establishing a natural cause of an event cannot show that God is not a more distal super-natural cause of the same event, or that it was not part of God's plan or purpose. Reductionists reply that once one isolates a natural cause for belief in God, one has grounds to argue that the belief in God would have existed whether or not God exists. But religious people rightly respond that we have no idea how the world would be different if God's existence were other than what it is. It is too big a counterfactual to evaluate. Perhaps natural causes also would not exist, or their effects would be different. Then their status as reliable indicators of God's existence would not be undercut.

When we turn to epistemology, our concern shifts from which beliefs are true to which beliefs are justified, and from God's nature and existence to how we can determine God's nature and existence. If everything is a reliable indicator of God's presence, then God is never differentially present, but God *is* differentially manifest to people and these manifestations are supposed to be a source of knowledge about God. When we do not know in advance that God has a certain property, if it can be shown that God's manifesting that property has a wholly natural cause, then we have a problem explaining why we don't take this manifestation as a reliable indicator of the natural cause, rather than of God's having the property in question.

This is where Swinburne's principle of credulity and Plantinga's "proper basicality" are supposed to come in, but Proudfoot complains that these are all otiose protective strategies in a context of inquiry. That is, their effect is to immunize a certain point of view from falsification by shifting the burden of proof from the believer to the skeptic. Reductionists argue that whenever an experience can be shown to reliably indicate a natural cause, then it provides no information or evidence regarding God's nature or existence. Reductionists claim not to be similarly immunizing their explanations from falsification because they still entertain the possibility that alternative naturalistic explanations are correct, and would accept competing religious explanations if independent evidence for them could be adduced. But this appearance of asymmetry does not withstand scrutiny. Plantinga and Swinburne could claim equally that they are not protecting any pet religious hypothesis from competition with other religious theories or explanations, and they do entertain naturalistic explanations but deny that they contradict or count as evidence against religious ones. Each side adopts a methodology that partially immunizes it from criticism from the other side. I think this makes both approaches unnecessarily ideological, but getting into the subject more deeply requires an abstract theoretical account of how reductionism works and where its ontological significance comes from. I start with an example of a putative scientific reduction.

5.3.1   Persinger's Explanation of Beliefs in God

Recently the neurologist Michael Persinger claimed to have solved the riddle of why people believe in God. His finding was that all such behavior is explainable in terms of the usual evolutionary and cultural factors, plus his theory that experiences of God occur when and only when relatively inconspicuous seizures of the brain's temporal lobe occur—seizures known as temporal lobe transients (TLTs). "With a single [electrical] burst in the temporal lobe, people find structure and meaning in seconds."[144] This does not explain what brings about TLTs, or why the resulting perceptions have the phenomenological qualities they do, but some factors that increase or decrease their likelihood are known, and explanations of some of their qualitative aspects are at least initially plausible. If these loose ends could be tied up neurologically, the genesis and content of all beliefs in the existence of God might be explainable without any essential mention of a God whose existence or appearance brought them about. Assuming a causal theory of knowledge, and that the explanations were constructed so as to safeguard adequately the religious concern for truth as correspondence, a person might reasonably conclude that they are all illusory, and that religious explanations based on them are spurious.

Most philosophers of religion would not "stoop into the gutter" to reply to such crudely reductionistic accounts as Persinger's, but a brief reply may be instructive. The fact that some observers saw a green afterimage after watching the sunset did not prove that everyone claiming to see the green flash saw only an afterimage. Even so the fact that stimulating a temporal lobe causes an experience of meaning does not prove that every experience of meaning is reducible to or explainable in terms of stimulus to the temporal lobe. Moreover, one expects something to be going on in the brain at the time people experience meaning, or have meaningful experiences, but that does not prove that the experiences do not have the meaning ascribed, or that the experiences are unreliable indicators of meaning.

There is a broader lesson to learn here. The twentieth century has been replete with discoveries that contributed to our understanding of some outstanding problem, whether physical or philosophical. Naturally the discoverer of the method or technique responsible for the breakthrough wants to apply it to other outstanding problems to see if it can solve them as well. Unfortunately, discoverers often jump to the unwarranted conclusion that because they were able to solve one problem with their technique or method,

---

[144] *Neuropsychological Bases of God Beliefs* (New York: Praeger, 1987), pp. 10–17.

almost every major problem in their field will fall to it as well. Invariably they are mistaken. The most outstanding recent philosophical example of this tendency was the pioneering logical work of Frege, Russell, Whitehead, Wittgenstein, and others, and the early breakthroughs that resulted from it, which led philosophers by the droves to assume imperialistically that all outstanding philosophical problems are susceptible to logical analysis or they aren't really problems at all. Not only were they mistaken, but because of institutional inertia this blind alley was pursued far longer than it should have been, and the result was a regrettably colossal waste of effort. The current success of connectionism in modeling processes such as pattern recognition, and the rush of philosophers to assume that all kinds of cognitive processes can be explained in connectionist terms, or that the mind is "nothing but" a vast and complicated neural network, has the earmarkings of repeating the same pattern. Grandiose, imperialistic assumptions are almost invariably too simplistic to be true, but wishful thinking is so seductive that each new generation of potential imperialists can hardly resist their enticement. Persinger's reductionism that seems too crude to merit a response actually exemplifies a pattern of reasoning that is prevalent in science and philosophy, though rarely identified as such. Discovering an interesting correlation between TLTs and experiences of meaningfulness, he supposes that he can now explain all manner of related experiences by means of TLTs.

Like most "debunking" literature, Persinger's work is highly polemical and speculative, uninhibitedly making hasty and sweeping generalizations, undocumented claims, and ad hominem appeals to anti-religious prejudice. This is a shame, because debunking can serve a vital philosophical role in keeping people honest.

The trump card of reductionists is that it does not matter whether this or that reductive attempt is successful, because the promise always exists that a successful reduction will be forthcoming as our knowledge of the brain and behavior grows. It only takes one successful reduction to doom religious explanation, granting that theoretical reduction is accompanied by ontological reduction. I will return to this promissory aspect of reductionism, but first it is necessary to be more explicit about the kind of reductions involved here, and the abstract theory underlying ascriptions of ontological significance to them. Since I must be brief, readers wishing to learn more should consult Patricia Churchland's *Neurophilosophy*.

5.3.2 Interlevel Reductions and their Ontological Significance

At least intuitively, there are a number of scales or ontological levels at which scientific investigations are conducted and explanations offered. If traced through the life sciences, these would include the subatomic, atomic, molecular, and cellular levels, as well as the levels of tissue, organ, organism, society, and ecosystem. Inorganic levels could be defined geophysically and astrophysically. Either way, one can speak of causal theories and explanations as emanating from or clustering around distinct scales, each corresponding to roughly autonomous fields of investigation.

This ontological notion of levels comes from taking a model-theoretic or semantic view of scientific theories. On a syntactic or proof-theoretic view one may also have levels, but they are quite distinct and function differently. Under that view, observation sentences make up the lowest level, with each higher level being more theoretical, or further removed from observation. The highest level, which might be thought to contain Newton's laws or Maxwell's equations, has no observational consequences of its own, and has the highest level of immunity from falsification. This notion of "higher" and "lower" tends to be the inverse of the model-theoretic notion, since observations are made at the macro level, which now becomes the lowest level. Newton's laws do not have a fixed level in the model-theoretic sense, since they supposedly govern the behavior of all matter from particles to galaxies. But when one moves toward lower model-theoretic levels one is inevitably moving away from observation and toward entities that are ever more theoretical. On the other hand, causal explanations run across proof-theoretic levels since they connect observations with highly theoretical entities. Hence, different accounts of reduction are appropriate to the semantic and syntactic views. Contemporary accounts of reduction concern themselves primarily with ontological levels, since Quine's attack on proof-theoretic reductionism in "Two Dogmas of Empiricism" is widely regarded as conclusive against it.[145]

Broadly speaking, a reduction is simply the explanation of one theory by another, but in a stricter sense we are not interested in any kind of theoretical subsumption, but those with ontological significance. For example, finding that one set of phenomena follows a pattern found in other sets—say, that all can be modeled as linear harmonic oscillators—need not show that the entities posited in explaining any of them set are superfluous. We also are not interested in putative reductions in which the new theory uses substantially the same terminology and theoretical entities as the old. One really has theory replacement in this case. E.g., Einstein's notions of mass and time were similar enough to Newton's to warrant continued use of the same

---

[145] *Philosophical Review* 60 (1951): 20–43.

terms. While Einsteinian relativity is sometimes thought to reduce Newtonian mechanics, and Newton's theory of universal gravitation is sometimes called a reduction of Kepler's laws, it is really the *new* theory that reduces to the *old* theory in these cases, under certain limiting conditions.[146] Einstein's equations reduce to those of Newtonian mechanics when v/c is negligible, and distance is small compared to ct. Similarly, Kepler's laws are a special case of Newton's theory when there are only two interacting bodies.

The canonical form of a reduction with ontological implications is the reduction of ideal gas laws to statistical mechanics. In this case, referential terms from the higher theory, such as 'temperature' and 'pressure', are eliminated in favor of more precise terminology drawn from the lower level—e.g., 'mean molecular kinetic energy'. Temperature could no longer be treated as a sui generis property of objects after the reduction, the way it was before. The classical ideal for such a reduction is to give bridge principles defining all of the higher level terms using the language of the lower level theory, and then deduce the laws of the higher theory from those of the lower one. But it should not be surprising that this kind of project never gets carried out, since it conflates ontological and proof-theoretic notions of reduction. Marshall Spector points out that scientists are not very interested in pursuing such deductions per se, but in the pragmatic value of knowing that one set of concepts is eliminable in favor of another. But also it is not necessary or even customary to establish truth deductively within science; what is essential is that the statements of the old theory remain true and lawlike when their terms are substituted in accordance with the bridge principles. Even if the reduced theory may still be regarded as true and have pragmatic value, Spector points out that ontological status is not so much a pragmatic matter as it is a theoretical one. That is, it is still convenient to formulate explanations in terms of temperature and pressure, but no ontological significance can be drawn from a mere *façon de parler*.[147]

The ontological reduction just mentioned is an instance of the application of Occam's razor, the principle by which entities that are unnecessary to explain the world's phenomena are eliminated. If we initially posited God's existence for its explanatory value in a context of inquiry (Preface), then the elimination of any explanatory work for this concept would undercut

---

[146] Thomas Nickles, "Two Concepts of Intertheoretic Reduction," *Journal of Philosophy* 70 (1973): 181–201.

[147] Marshall Spector, *Concepts of Reduction in Physical Science* (Philadelphia: Temple Univ. Press, 1978), pp. 38, 53–6.

the basis on which it was offered. Hence, Occam's razor is not merely a pragmatic principle, irrelevant to truth as correspondence. A successful reduction effectively broadens the evidential base of the reducing theory by permitting it to claim the evidence for the theory being reduced as its own, which may leave the theory being reduced without independent evidence. Interlevel reductions do confer pragmatic advantages in scope and systematicity, but this is in addition to altering the evidential landscape.

The major stumbling block for Spector's view of the ontological significance of interlevel reductions is that few reductions go through smoothly as in the classical case of thermodynamics and statistical mechanics. Another ostensibly paradigmatic example of reduction is that of Mendelian genetics to molecular genetics, yet Philip Kitcher denies that the traditional reductionistic theses apply here.[148] In particular, he denies that there are (1) any general laws stemming from the genetics of Mendel and Morgan. Following the semantic view, he argues that classical genetics is more a collection of illustrations of patterns of reasoning which have evolved over time into a standard practice (351ff.). Also, (2) no bridge principles or replacement functions link the distinctive vocabulary of the former theory to the latter, nor (3) is it possible to derive the principles of Mendelian genetics from molecular biology, or show why the laws of gene transmission hold to the extent that they do (339). Kitcher points out occasional instances of conclusions of the higher theory being explained by appealing to the lower theory, but denies that this can be done for the theory as a whole (363). Under such a scenario, it is entirely possible that the explanatory value of the higher level theory is not entirely lost, and that the lower level theory does more to explain what the higher theory left unexplained than to explain the higher level theory itself.[149]

The problem is roughly that there is no effective way to define 'gene' or describe in full generality what a gene is using the language of molecular biology. Hence the possibility of carrying through a successful reduction effectively devolves on being able to enumerate all the different kinds of genes via a disjunction of their known molecular structures. Similar difficulties apply to the concepts of mitosis, meiosis, spindle, etc. But even if such

---

[148] "1953 and All That: A Tale of Two Sciences," *Philosophical Review* 93 (1984): 335–74. Page references in this subsection are to this work.

[149] See also William Wimsatt, "Reduction, Levels of Organization, and the Mind-Body Problem," in *Consciousness and the Brain*, ed. by Globus, et. al. (New York: Plenum, 1976), p. 225.

an enumeration were carried out, it would not be able to support counterfactual claims regarding yet unexamined genes that may be discovered or manufactured. Nor would it explain such elementary facts from classical genetics as why genes on nonhomologous chromosomes assort independently (345–8). In other words it would not perform adequately the function of a nomological generalization, yet it was this function that gave reductions their compelling virtues in the first place. When this happens, the language of the reduced theory is no longer dispensable as a *façon de parler,* and neither can there be any demonstration of the derivative status of its laws. Hence, there also is no longer a clear case for stripping the entities of the higher level theory of their ontological status. The reductionist must emphasize the "in principle" nature of his project here, even though genetics is supposedly already a successful instance of reduction. My point is that a principled basis for drawing ontological conclusions is lacking when reductions cannot be (or to date have not been) fully carried out, not that scientists actually disagree over how we ought to regard the ontological status of the entities postulated by Mendelian genetics.

Much of the reductionist threat to religious explanation is dependent on one's faith or confidence in the promissory note issued by reductionists that all of these details can "in principle" be worked out, and will be in the fullness of time. Again, no distinction is often observed between where reductions have not *in fact* been carried out and where they are incapable *in principle* of being carried out, although this issue has attracted some interest in contemporary philosophy. The distinction is methodologically unmotivated for science. The ideological aspect of reductionism is apparent in the lack of any indication even in principle why the natural kinds of the higher level should happen to correspond to any definable congeries of natural kinds of the lower level, so as to make them eliminable. If an explanatory account cannot be given across levels, then what is the basis for supposing that nothing exists at the higher level that is "emergent" over the lower level, and hence a distinct ontological entity? Subscribers to physicalism are committed to the existence of many such reductions crossing all levels from the atom to the ecosystem. Just as one day does not a summer make, so a few isolated reductions do not establish physicalism.

As for the value of the promissory note, not much of the capital of science is being devoted to paying down the principal, as opposed to other projects of greater interest or importance. The person who finds the question of the nature and attributes of God important cannot defer taking a stand on this issue until the promissory note is redeemed—he does not have enough lifetimes for that. Confronted with the risks that even suspension of belief cannot evade, he lacks a comfortable way to dismiss the issue. A promissory note does not constitute evidence that can take the place of an act of faith; it merely represents an alternative faith disguised as something more secure.

5.3.2   The Preferred Naturalistic Worldview

Naturalism and reductionism are part of a standard metaphysical worldview that is widely heralded for its simplicity and intelligibility. One element of this worldview is the impingement concept of causation by which causal processes are continuous—i.e., action at a distance is impossible. Can God be the explanation for anything he didn't cause? Yet God-matter causation transparently violates the continuity requirement. There are actually two continuity issues to address: spatio-temporal continuity, and continuity across the metaphysical divide between material and immaterial entities. If the issue were merely spatio-temporal continuity, one might defend the continuity of God-matter causation by invoking omnipresence. The more worrisome question is the metaphysical divide that separates the immaterial from the material. How can any immaterial being affect the material world?

Understanding the question in terms of epistemic possibility, one might argue that immaterial beings can affect the material world because, for all we know, we are immaterial beings and we have such effects all the time.[150] That is, while we all have bodies, we hear of people having out-of-body or near-death experiences in which they remain conscious but their consciousness assumes a subjectively apparent location outside the body. Such people invariably take a detached stance toward their physical selves, referring to it as "my body," while using 'I' to refer to their consciousness. What matters here is not whether these people are telling the truth, or whether such experiences actually occur, nor am I defending Cartesian dualism or life after death. What is in question is their possibility, not their actuality. The point is that for all we know, OBEs and NDEs may be veridical, or something like Cartesian dualism may be true, in which case for all we know we may be essentially immaterial consciousnesses, and our physical bodies inessential concomitants. Then the answer to how an immaterial entity can affect the material world is as simple as asking the interlocutor how she manages to move a finger. Like riding a bicycle, explaining how one does it is virtually impossible, yet we may know how to do it just the same.

It is hard to derive metaphysical comfort from epistemic possibilities, however. My preferred response is to distinguish the ideal of a *complete*

---

[150]   This argument was suggested to me by Alvin Plantinga.

explanation—one that provides every relevant causal or explanatory detail for the entire history of the phenomenon's genesis—from everyday, *incomplete* explanations—the partial explanations used in practice. I further subdivide incomplete explanations into *prosaic* and *ultimate* explanations. An ultimate explanation assures us that the details that were left out all fall within our preferred metaphysical framework or worldview without attempting to supply them, whereas a prosaic explanation provides no such assurance. That is, an ultimate explanation would make it clear that a complete explanation is "metaphysically possible"—that only pragmatic limitations of human finitude prevent a complete explanation from being given. I take the standard metaphysical preferences underlying naturalism to include that explanations be completable by citing causal processes that are

> (1) real, or observer independent (where all real causal processes supervene on, or are composed of physical objects)
> (2) continuous
>   (a) spatio-temporally
>   (b) metaphysically
> (3) appeal to no irreducibly "brute" or unexplainable facts.

With this distinction in hand, it can be conceded that all explanations appealing to God are prosaic rather than ultimate explanations—they cannot be brought into the preferred metaphysical worldview. But I claim that no ultimate explanations are possible for anything, hence this is no more a problem for religious explanation than for any explanatory program. Rather, it is a problem for the standard metaphysical preferences.

What makes ultimate explanations impossible is Bell's theorem, a quantum mechanical result that unsettles our commonsense understanding of the material world. Stripped to its essentials, Bell's theorem presents the standard worldview with a trilemma: one must either formulate a "hidden variable" theory that (1) denies the ultimate reality or observer independence of physical particles at the quantum level—the particles that ostensibly constitute all physical and causal processes—or (2) denies that all causal interactions satisfy a locality condition that is essentially equivalent to spatio-temporal continuity. Otherwise, one must (3) give up on hidden variables and say that quantum level phenomena ultimately cannot be explained—they are brute facts about the world.[151]

---

[151] An accessible introduction to Bell's Theorem and its implications appears in Davies and Brown, eds., *The Ghost in the Atom* (Cambridge Univ. Press, 1986); for a more sophisticated discussion, see Cushing and McMullin, eds., *Philosophical Consequences of Quantum Theory*

On (2), Bell's theorem strongly suggests that for a great many events *E,* the products of events in *E*'s causal history can affect *E* from a distance. An analogy may help the reader to conceive this. It is theorized that most of the matter in the earth was formed about ten billion years ago when a nameless star undergoing gravitational collapse exploded into a supernova, expelling its matter into space. Bell's theorem suggests that causal processes currently taking place on the earth could instantaneously affect and be affected by processes which the rest of the expelled matter is now undergoing, even though this matter is now thousands of light-years distant. It essentially brings back action at a distance. This makes it effectively impossible to rule out anything in the universe as a potential cause of *E.* While jettisoning spatio-temporal continuity does not solve the problem of metaphysical discontinuity or dualism, once virtually anything in the universe becomes a potential causal factor, there can be no empirical grounds for excluding God. So long as only local or continuous processes can cause *E,* one in principle has access to *all* of the proximal causes of *E* and so can verify whether *E* occurs as theory indicates. Once virtually any entity in the universe is a potential cause of *E,* one can never verify or show decisively that any entity is causally unrelated to *E*—its influence in a specific instance may be confounded by another unknown entity. In such a case, why think that only very distant entities are involved in discontinuous causation and not God? It is merely a matter of prejudice—we would really have no idea what is causing what.

On (1), if matter itself is not an ultimately independent and permanent existent, then what is? Occasionally it is suggested that observers may be the only ultimate reality, but this implies dualism and subjectivism, so the more common answer is that a wave function or similar device possesses ultimate reality or observer independence.[152] Yet the wave function is itself an abstract and hence immaterial entity—a mathematical object some interpret as a probability distribution and Bell compares to a Maxwellian force field[153]—so the quantum theorist is still positing an immaterial entity which affects the material world. If the question now arises, "But *how* can an

---

(Univ. of Notre Dame Press, 1989).

[152] Defenders of the former position include N. D. Mermin, "Can You Help Your Team Tonight by Watching on TV?" in *Philosophical Consequences of Quantum Theory,* ed. by Cushing and McMullin, 38–59; and Eugene Wigner, "Remarks on the Mind-Body Question," in *The Scientist Speculates,* ed. by Good, 284–302 (London: Heinemann, 1962). For the latter, see John Bell, *Speakable and Unspeakable in Quantum Mechanics* (Cambridge Univ. Press, 1987).

[153] *Speakable and Unspeakable in Quantum Mechanics,* pp. 128, 171.

immaterial entity affect the material world?" the quantum theorist will reply that it does so because it has more reality than the material objects themselves. Interestingly, religious people pioneered this kind of answer for God long before physicists ever thought of it, only to be hooted and howled at.

Finally, (3) if one posits the quantum level as a realm of unexplainable "brute" facts, one is hardly in a position to cavil over the religious person's inability to explain how an immaterial entity can affect the material universe—it may be another brute or unexplainable fact. If science abdicates its explanatory function here, it leaves religious people with all of the informational virtues working in their favor, an endowment that can defray significant epistemic risks. But the clincher is that taking the "brute fact" way out does not evade (1) or (2) entirely, because their conjunction is still inconsistent with quantum mechanics. At best, it lets one say that, thanks to the correspondence principle, (1) or (2) may be rendered negligible by restricting explanations to ontological levels well above the quantum level.

If only prosaic explanations are possible, then our intuition that causal processes are continuous is just that—an intuition—and cannot be elevated into a requirement for explanatory adequacy. One cannot keep metaphysical gremlins out of the explanatory machine, so treating continuity as a valuable heuristic is the highest honor one can confer on it. If such be the case, countenancing God-matter causation is less a metaphysical crime than ruling it out on the basis of a supposedly commonsensical naturalism.

5.4   INFERENCE TO THE BEST EXPLANATION

Gilbert Harman pioneered the view that, at bottom, all scientific explanations are inferences to the best explanation.[154] Such a position should not seem outlandish, since we already noted the fundamental role of inference in giving scientific explanations. Granting this, why infer anything *other* than the best explanation? Who dares to suggest that Harman is wrong? Actually, Harman could better be characterized as holding that Peirce's notion of abduction is at the root of all scientific explanations, rather than the inductive reasoning that is the traditional staple of confirmation theory. I have no particular quarrel with this view, but mention it to point out the ideological

---

[154] "Inference to the Best Explanation," *Philosophical Review* 74 (1965): 88–95. See also the exchange between Robert Ennis ("Enumerative Induction and Best Explanation") and Harman ("Enumerative Induction as Inference to the Best Explanation") in the *Journal of Philosophy* 65 (1968): 523–33.

aspect of Harman's position: what appears to be a truism actually masks a controversial claim.

Quine says that when a native asserts as true an apparent contradiction, one should seriously consider the possibility that one's translation manual is incorrect or that the expression is idiomatic or syncategorematic, so that its meaning cannot be reconstructed adequately from the meanings of the component words.[155] The same could be said when analytic truths are asserted as if they contained substantive information. People do not pound on conference tables declaring "Business is business" just to assert the law of identity. Neither is this Clark Gable's purpose in telling his flame, "I want what I want when I want it." When a substantive claim parades in the guise of an analytic truth, it is likely an instance of ideology. Following my tripartite classification, this falls closest to the category of value-laden terminology, since it involves a controversial claim couched so as to appropriate the epistemic value of an incontrovertible truism. This is typical of claims that one is "merely inferring the best explanation."

I recognize some substantive inferences to the best explanation as legitimate, so an explication of their source of legitimacy is in order. Taking the phrase at face value, that an explanation is being inferred from a group of competitors on the grounds that it is best, three questions trouble me:

(1) Why draw any inference at all?
(2) What makes the inferred explanation best?
(3) How much better must the best explanation be, to justify inferring it over the others?

The second question hearkens back to my earlier point (chapter 3) that there is no univocal sense of 'best' applicable to all explanatory practice. Since this has already been discussed at some length, I dwell on the other two questions in what follows.

5.4.1   When Can This Inference Be Avoided?

From the standpoint of ordinary language, explanation may not seem to require inference. If I see a rock crash through my window with a note attached to it, I may infer that the underground has finally caught up with me. I do not say, however, that I *inferred* the rock crashed through my window when I *saw* it do so. If someone asks why all the broken glass on the floor, and I answer that the best explanation I have been able to infer is that this rock broke the window, she would reasonably conclude that I did not see it

---

[155] *Word and Object* (MIT Press, 1960), pp. 59, 69, 103.

happen. This scenario is not typical of scientific practice, however, and even the appearance that no inference is involved dissolves once one entertains skeptical doubts, so I don't believe this seriously undercuts the view that all scientific explanations are inferred. But for this special kind of case, one might answer the question of why infer anything at all by pointing out that we would never have any explanations otherwise. Hence, whatever reasons we have for seeking explanations in general count as reasons for inferring the best explanation.

This way of posing the question leads naturally to re-emphasizing the pragmatic orientation of the activity of explaining. If a person's why-question were motivated simply by curiosity, or "theoretically," it would be sufficient to inform him of the explanations that have been suggested or explored and their respective merits, and let him make of this information whatever he pleases. Drawing an additional inference to the best explanation seems unnecessary here, but it seems more appropriate when an imminent decision hinges on the inquiry's outcome. In preceding sections we saw how the process of founding a research program requires making inferences to the best explanation in order to establish working hypotheses (1.5.1; 2.3).

Showing that pragmatic concerns *force* such inferences to be drawn is nontrivial, but additional clarification of how the inferential process works will be needed to make this point. Consider, for example, the case of the annual springtime hole in the ozone layer over Antarctica. Pragmatically speaking, a lot hinges on which of the competing explanations for the phenomenon turns out to be best. Each proposed explanation is associated with some corresponding course of action that would comprise the most appropriate response if it were correct. If, for example, chlorofluorocarbons cause the ozone hole, then global restrictions on their production, use, and disposal need to be implemented immediately, but if it has other causes then other courses of action would be more appropriate.

The evidence favoring the chlorofluorocarbon hypothesis may not be strong enough to justify drastic action at this time. If not, it would be more appropriate to deny that the chlorofluorocarbon hypothesis satisfies even minimal standards for explanatory adequacy. But before setting high minimal standards of adequacy, one must bear in mind the risks associated with suspending judgment. The risk of not *now* inferring the chlorofluorocarbon hypothesis is that if it actually is the cause, the window now open for preventing global catastrophe may be shut by the time our evidence is better. Let us say, then, that a proposed explanation is *minimally adequate* if the evidence in its favor would be sufficient to warrant action rather than suspension of judgment as things stand, other things being equal, before other explanatory possibilities are taken into account. This is essentially the status that must be achieved to have a proto-explanation (1.5). It does not mean the explanation is probable; it may mean only that the cost of implementing the corresponding action is very small. In what follows, I assume that only minimally adequate hypotheses count as potential, plausible, or competing explanations. I also assume that comparisons among competing explanations, customarily considered important in determining their adequacy, figure only in the final inference to the best explanation drawn from the minimally adequate pool.

This gives rise to three possible scenarios. Perhaps none of the explanations available are minimally adequate. In that case, one would have grounds for inferring no explanation at all, pending further study. Or perhaps the pool has only one minimally adequate member. Then we would have a situation similar to that discussed in connection with Olbers' Paradox (1.5.2), in which the various inferences to the *best* explanation are essentially inferences to the *only* explanation then plausible. While such an inference may not be objectionable, this scenario trivializes the notion of inferring the best explanation, and emphasizes that the reason it is the only explanation may be due to our lack of imagination rather than its truth.

So suppose the pool has more than one member—suppose there are five potential explanations for the Antarctic ozone hole, and corresponding courses of action appropriate to each. It still may not be necessary to infer a "best" explanation if one could fashion a pragmatic response that parallels the "theoretical" response mentioned previously. That is, perhaps one can hedge one's bets by adopting as the most appropriate overall strategy a synthesis of salient elements from the five independent plans. In this fashion one might arrive at a maximally prudent plan of action while making no commitment regarding which explanation, if any, to infer. There are drawbacks to this ecumenical approach. It would not work if the courses of action were in such conflict that the maximal strategy could not preserve enough of each to provide an adequate response if that explanation were correct. It also seems that one cannot avoid making some inferences just to determine which explanations to include on one's "short list." Moreover, it gets expensive trying to hedge one's bets all the time. Nevertheless, the possibility of an ecumenical approach undercuts any general argument that inference to the best explanation is unavoidable or innocuous.

5.4.2 What Are We to Infer?
I think our primary interest in drawing inferences to the best explanation is not to argue that the best explanation is true so much as that the other expla-

nations may be disregarded. If the best explanation for the window breaking is that it was struck by a stray baseball, then I don't need to concern myself that it was an attempted break-in, or that the underground has finally caught up with me. This conclusion is supported by my "semiconductor" analogy for explanation, which suggests that it is always easier to determine that one explanation is false rather than that its rival is true. The process of elimination is often the path of least resistance. Inferences to the best explanation need not be drawn to rule in, because presumably the best explanation already receives adequate attention as something that one's subsequent actions must allow for. Referring to the other examples in chapter 1, Harré was probably less interested in establishing the meteorite hypothesis than in arguing that we need not concern ourselves that intelligent space aliens were behind the incident. He is suggesting that no cause for alarm be taken from this isolated occurrence. Likewise, Folkman's inference was based on experiments which were carefully designed to rule out the explanatory alternatives then countenanced. The statements of peer reviewers who did not recommend his research for funding indicated not so much doubt regarding his explanation as doubt that he would be able to isolate the causal factors involved, or that his project was more worthy of funding than competing ones.

If inferences to the best explanation are drawn to rule out, then they disguise in language that appears incontrovertible a more controversial inference—one away from sub-optimal explanations. A standard rationale for dismissing suboptimal explanations was mentioned briefly in 5.2.1. The evidence for an explanation normally includes the phenomenon it explains, so the existence of an alternative explanation for the same phenomenon will weaken the first explanation's evidential base. Presumably, the best explanation will still be pretty good despite such weakening, but the evidence for an explanation that is weak to start with may evaporate under such competitive pressure. The appropriateness of this rationale depends on a number of factors, however. Suboptimal explanations may draw on independent sources of evidence which the best explanation cannot appropriate. Whether an explanation should be dismissed also depends on its degree of inferiority to the explanation touted as best. For example, the best explanation might be less likely than the combined disjunction of the suboptimal explanations. Or the cost of implementing the actions appropriate to some suboptimal explanations may be small enough to be a warranted outlay, despite their lower probability. The expression encourages us to ignore both them and the possibility that their suboptimal status may not be adequate grounds for their dismissal. In a case in which only one explanation meets minimal standards of adequacy, the inference would be more aptly described as being to the *only* explanation, calling attention to the fact that an alternative to drawing such an inference exists—namely, develop more explanatory hypotheses.

Another conclusion follows. Inferences to the best explanation are especially inappropriate when the competing explanations are not mutually exclusive, or could all be correct. It is unfortunate that the pragmatic difficulty of hedging one's bets may not be allayed by the news that each proposed explanation is independently sufficient to bring about the phenomenon in question, but that difficulty may be unavoidable. Religious explanations given in terms of the purposes or intentions of God will generally be compatible with causal scientific explanations, and hence not the kind that can be eliminated by an inference to the best explanation. Given differences in the value systems by which explanations are evaluated, the commonplace rejection of religious explanations by scientists via inference to the best explanation will typically be parochial to science. Oftentimes, scientists are neither properly positioned nor equipped, nor is it their particular concern, to determine whether a given phenomenon tells us anything about God's will. Thus, their rejection of such explanations as "outside their jurisdiction" need not cast aspersions on their epistemological credentials. Even when religious explanations are comparatively unlikely, if the cost of implementing action based on them is not great, rejecting them on the basis of their suboptimal status may still be unwarranted.

There remains one type of scenario in which inferences to the best explanation are both nontrivial and appropriate. First, there must be more than one minimally adequate explanation under consideration. Second, the explanations must be mutually inconsistent, or conflicting at least to the point that the appropriate responses corresponding to each cannot all be carried out. Finally, the best explanation must be so superior to the other explanations to justify disregarding them. At this point I am not prepared to venture how great this superiority must be.

CHAPTER 6

ASSESSING NEAR-DEATH EXPERIENCE REPORTS

Most of the argument so far has been directed at clearing away objections to religious explanations. The argument in chapter 4, however, suggests that there can be no canonical religious explanations, because the kind that a person might reasonably accept will depend on that person's evidential background. I do not say 'socio-cultural' background because I do not assume that religious experiences or religious explanations are exclusively or primarily the product of socio-cultural factors, although such factors are surely influential. But anecdotal evidence in a person's possession also plays a role in determining the kinds of religious explanations she will accept, given that much of religious experience broadly construed has an anecdotal basis. Therefore, no category of religious explanations I might propose can be expected to command universal assent. Through the effects of anecdotal evidence, the religious community has become balkanized in a way quite unlike the effect of scientific specialization. For example, not only do the members of religious communities not generally recognize the authority or expertise of their counterparts in other communities, they often adopt belief systems that openly contradict them.

    An odd consequence is that my abstract description of the conflicts between religion and science over values, the effects of scientific ideology, and the role and importance of anecdotal evidence, may command broader agreement among religious people than any religious explanation I might propose. Epistemic principles are less divisive than differences in substantive belief, doctrine, or experiential claims that have doctrinal implications. In giving a substantive example of religious explanation, therefore, I expect to arouse more disagreement among religious people than in all other chapters combined; nor do I expect much support or sympathy from those who are not religious. It is a thankless job, yet the preceding exercise would be pointless without examples of how it could be put into practice in constructing religious explanations. The next two chapters undertake this task, first by giving a substantive example of potential religious explanations, and then by describing in more general terms how the process of constructing religious explanations works.

6.1 INTRODUCTION

The phenomena for which I propose a religious explanation are near-death experiences (NDEs). People who have NDEs frequently give them religious interpretations, especially when the experiences involve communicating beings. A typical religious interpretation would be that one had an encounter with God, or that God was in some sense the source, or had a specific purpose or reason for bringing the experience about, e.g., redirecting the person's life. Moreover, most NDEs *could* be interpreted religiously, since the experiences are generally consistent with and often suggest (i) the existence of a supreme being similar to the conceptualizations of God prevalent in western cultures. The experiences also suggest (ii) the possibility that the "self" or consciousness may be somewhat autonomous of the physical body, and (iii) that consciousness may continue to exist after or "survive" bodily death. These are all claims that have long been maintained by religious traditions in the face of vigorous opposition and ridicule from scientists. I am not saying that most people who have NDEs interpret them religiously, or that they should, but it would have a salutary effect on the credibility of these traditions if such experiences stand up to critical scrutiny. It is significant that many people who have NDEs are not religious and do not interpret them religiously, because this makes the attribution of God to the experiences less subjective. My chief concern, however, is only to show how NDEs might be explained.

Near-death experiences have been reported at least since Plato,[156] but widespread recognition of them as a distinct genre of experience came only recently. Prior to the advent of cardio-pulmonary resuscitation (CPR), recovery from comatose states and/or states in which heartbeat and respiration

---

[156] See the "Tale of Er" which concludes *Republic,* Book X.

had ceased was quite rare, and it was widely assumed that the comatose experience nothing at all, as if they were in a deep, dreamless sleep. For the majority of comatose patients this is, in fact, true. But a significant number of those who are close enough to death to require CPR—perhaps a third—report a significant near-death experience.[157] Under the prototypical scenario a patient whose heart has stopped beating is being tended by medical personnel who are attempting to resuscitate him. The patient appears entirely unconscious but later reports particulars about what happened at the time that we would not expect an unconscious person to know. He also reports that at the time he was viewing the commotion apparently from a vantage point outside his body, often near the ceiling of the emergency room or ICU. He may have experienced going down a long tunnel, a synoptic review of his life, being in the presence of a brilliant light, or conversing with a dead relative or other being. At some point he decides or becomes aware that he must return to this "vale of tears." All the while he experiences a sense of profound unity and understanding and a total lack of pain or anxiety.[158]

This popular prototype belies the fact that there is no canonical definition for 'near-death experience', which makes it difficult to say that we are dealing with a single phenomenon, or that it is different from related psychological phenomena. One issue is whether NDEs occur only near death, but there is also disagreement regarding what constitutes nearness to death. Is it when the subject believes she is close to death, or believes she has died? Or is it when a physician judges that death is imminent, or that death can be expected soon if medical treatment is not undertaken? Should such judgments be based solely on the body's physical condition or state—e.g., injury or disease—or take into account its circumstances—say, that it is falling off a cliff? Those who favor a subjective or psychological definition often find similarities between NDEs and *depersonalization,* a phenomenon commonly found in auto and mountain climbing accidents. Perceiving death to be imminent, the person feels distanced from his body, so that it seems that what

---

[157] Kenneth Ring, *Life at Death,* pp. 32ff., 191–2. To determine what counts as "significant," Ring developed a Weighted Core Experience Index based on ten factors common to Moody-type experiences. Sabom's prospective study of patients who had suffered cardiac arrest confirmed Ring's figure—see *Recollections of Death*—but it is on the high end of other estimates, which range to as low as 10%.

[158] For specific examples of NDE reports, see Raymond Moody, *Life After Life* (New York: Bantam, 1976); M. Rawlings, *Beyond Death's Door* (New York: Thomas Nelson, 1978); as well as *Life at Death* and *Recollections of Death.*

the body is suffering is really happening to someone else.[159] The injuries sustained need not be fatal or nearly fatal for this to happen. Such psychological NDEs lack religiously significant features, and possess a distinct phenomenology and different behavioral consequences from prototypical NDEs. To recognize this and other distinctions, investigators now tend to categorize experiences as NDEs on the basis of their content, or phenomenologically. Different scales are used to evaluate them, but the idea is that if an experience has enough of the features of a prototypical Moody-type experience, then it counts as an NDE; otherwise not. Ironically, physical nearness to death is no longer part of the definition of 'near-death experience'.[160]

NDEs also vary significantly in their reported content.[161] *Naturalistic* NDEs are essentially out-of-body experiences (OBEs) associated with death, involving self-visualization of the body, and visual and auditory perception of the immediate environment. This part of the experience most often is perceived very clearly and distinctly, and with considerable detail. If communication is attempted with others, it is with those whose presence is objectively real, and is almost invariably unsuccessful. *Transcendental* NDEs prototypically involve entering an area of darkness, or a tunnel, encountering and/or entering a light, a life review, and other visions of places that are exceptionally beautiful. There may be successful communication, but with beings that are apparent only to the subject. This part of the experience usually does not involve self-visualization of the body or perception of its physical environment. Those having transcendental NDEs are more likely to see return to this life as a choice consciously made, whereas those with naturalistic NDEs tend to connect their return to the performance of a particular resuscitative technique. The epistemological importance of this distinction is that only the naturalistic part of an NDE is independently verifiable, but the transcendental part is what particularly invites religious explanation. Many NDEs combine both kinds of content, however.

---

[159] See, e.g., *Recollections of Death*, pp. 9–10, 160–3; and Russell Noyes, "Near-Death Experiences: Their Interpretation and Significance," in *Between Life and Death*, ed. by Kastenbaum (New York: Springer, 1978).

[160] See Glen Gabbard, Stuart Twemlow, and F. Jones, "Do 'Near-Death Experiences' Occur Only Near Death?" *Journal of Nervous and Mental Disease* 169 (1981): 374–7; Glen Gabbard and Stuart Twemlow, "Do 'Near-Death Experiences' Occur Only Near Death?—Revisited," *Journal of Near-Death Studies* 10, 1 (1991): 41–7.

[161] *Recollections of Death*, pp. 27–36; 41–52. Page references herein are to this work.

6.2   AETIOLOGICAL HYPOTHESES

The primary philosophical issue concerning these experiences is their objectivity, or *veridicality*. Does anything exist in reality corresponding to the contents of these perceptions? If so, is the reality largely what it is perceived to be? Those who claim objectivity would answer in the affirmative; skeptics often underline their doubts by refusing to dignify these phenomena with the word 'experience', calling them *hallucinations*. Of course, they *are* hallucinations if this means only that they are perceptions not shared by people who are seemingly well-situated to perceive the same thing. Whether they are also hallucinations in a sense that implies their unreality is what is at issue. Many physiological, psychological and sociological explanations have been offered for NDEs, but all are far enough from being adequate that it is still premature to rule out the objectivity of NDEs. Indeed, this conclusion is fairly widespread among both critics and advocates.[162] Aetiological hypotheses that have received attention include:

    anoxic hallucination
    drug-induced hallucination
    hypercapnic hallucination
    semi-conscious state
    altered state of consciousness
    conscious or subconscious fabrication
    endorphin release
    temporal lobe seizure.

Accepting some of these explanations would not necessarily rule out religious explanations, and those who defend their objectivity aren't necessarily ascribing to them religious significance. However, they are ascribing objectivity to nonnatural, nonmaterial entities not normally countenanced by scientists. The purpose of this section is to sort through and examine these considerations, and the conflicting claims arising from them.

6.2.1   Concepts and Causes of Hallucination

Many discussants of NDEs do not clarify what is meant by the term 'hallucination', and at least four concepts are commonly used. 'Hallucination' is

---

[162] See, e.g., D. Scott Rogo, *Return from Silence* (Northamptonshire, England: Aquarian Press, 1989); Mark Woodhouse, "Five Arguments Regarding the Objectivity of NDEs," *Anabiosis—The Journal of Near-Death Studies* 3 (1983): 63–75; Carol Zaleski, *Otherworld Journeys* (New York: Oxford Univ. Press, 1987); *Recollections of Death.*

sometimes defined descriptively as what happens when a person senses and believes to be real what other unimpaired people in her immediate vicinity do not sense or believe to be real. This definition is easily applied and neutral regarding the reality of object experienced, but many scientists prefer to omit talk of the subject's beliefs, defining hallucinations as "[any] waking sensory experience having no identified external stimulus." Historically, clinical psychologists defined hallucinations as "the unshared sensory experiences of persons who are mentally ill."[163] Philosophers usually use 'hallucination' to make the normative claim that what the subject perceives is not real, however. Not only is there no "identified external stimulus"; there may be no external stimulus at all.

These are not merely different attempts to conceptualize the same phenomenon; rather, they effectively circumscribe different phenomena. For example, the kinds of hallucinations typically experienced by the mentally ill generally keep to rigid patterns, occur repeatedly during manifest illness, and are accompanied by such other symptoms as loss of awareness of normal surroundings and disturbance of consciousness. But the visions associated with near-death and paranormal experiences are usually isolated, and are not connected to mental illness, loss of contact with normal surroundings, or other psychiatric symptoms.[164] The different definitions also contain different evaluative components. Conflating factual and evaluative elements in one word does not always cause problems, but when one kind of vision becomes widely shared by a great many people its unreal status becomes less clear, since commonality of experience is a standard benchmark of reality. Excluding the mentally ill, people who experience hallucinations come to recognize their unreality later, if not at the time of occurrence, but this does not normally happen with NDEs.[165]

Questions of evidence and veridicality can be approached from either an internalist or an externalist perspective. For internalists, any explanatory dismissal of an experience as hallucinatory is formally ad hominem. Citing

---

[163] Ian Stevenson, "Do We Need a new Word to Supplement 'Hallucination'?" *The American Journal of Psychiatry* 140 (1983): 1609–11.

[164] D. J. West, "Visionary and Hallucinatory Experiences: A Comparative Appraisal," *International Journal of Parapsychology* 2 (1960): 89–100.

[165] Stuart Twemlow and Glen Gabbard, "The Influence of Demographic/Psychological Factors and Preexisting Conditions on the Near-Death Experience," *Omega* 15 (1984–85): 225; Ronald Siegel, "The Psychology of Life After Death," *American Psychologist* 35, 10 (1980): 914, 927.

a cause or aetiology for a reality claim, or placing it in a "diagnostically re-lated group," as for any line of reasoning, does not constitute an evaluation of it based on its merits. If a person with a drug overdose hallucinates that he is conversing with God, the fact that he has drugs in his system does not prove that he is mistaken. As C. D. Broad once said, "One might need to be slightly 'cracked' in order to have some peep-hole into the super-sensible world."[166] Of course, one might still remove such a claim by argument. For example, Anthony Kenny denies the possibility of experiences of God by reasoning that it is impossible to converse with an "everlasting, unchang-ing, and ubiquitous" being.[167] But simply to point out that the incidence of reported conversations with higher beings is greater among those who in-gest hallucinogenic drugs than among the population at large is inconclusive as to whether said beings are real. Even if one's ability to sense material objects were impaired, that would not necessarily impair one's ability to per-ceive or communicate with immaterial or "spiritual" entities.

Nevertheless, the difficulties in formulating any reasonable criterion of internal justification, especially with respect to religious experiences, does not offer much hope of making a positive case for the evidential status of such experiences, or the viability of religious explanations of them. An ex-ternalist or reliabilist account seems more promising. There are, unfortu-nately, no apparently reliable indicators of the presence or agency of God, since there is no solution to the problem of finding a basis on which to ex-tend credulity to religious experiences, and no religiously accepted basis for drawing an appearance/reality distinction. There are, however, lots of testa-ble physical and psychological hypotheses regarding how these experiences come about, and if it could be shown that the experience would have been roughly the same if these factors were the same, then apparently the person would have experienced the presence of the same transcendental being under those circumstances, whether or not the being were differentially present or causally active. In such an epistemic context, religious explanations could be discounted, because what was ostensibly experienced does not indicate re-liably what caused the experience. Put crudely, God is not a TLT, and TLTs are not worthy of worship (5.3.1), so if God-experiences occur when and only when TLTs occur, why should we believe they are really experiences of God and not experiences of TLTs? If no aetiological factors such as TLTs are found, however, then a religious explanation becomes more likely.

---

[166] "Arguments for the Existence of God, II," p. 164.

[167] *Faith and Reason* (Columbia Univ. Press, 1983), p. 60.

As a general rule, assessing reliability requires placing the phenomenon into a reference class or natural kind. Lumping NDEs together with all hallucinatory phenomena, as Terence Hines does, makes them seem more unreliable than if considered as a separate category. Hence it is important to examine the ways in which NDEs resemble other hallucinations, both in content and aetiology. The hallucinations to which they are most often compared are associated with anoxia or hypoxia (lack of oxygen in the brain), hypercapnia (excess carbon dioxide in the brain), and drug-induced hallucinations. Drug intoxication and cerebral anoxia are perhaps the most frequently cited agents in explanations of NDEs proposed by skeptical scientists.[168] I examine these in turn in the remainder of this subsection.

Not all NDE patients are victims of intoxication or anoxia; in some cases there is no obvious physical impairment. Most frequently, NDEs are reported among cardiac patients who are being administered oxygen at the time, in an attempt to resuscitate them. One would not expect such patients to be anoxic, at least for the duration of the NDE. In fact, one person being administered oxygen during his NDE actually "observed" a doctor putting a needle into his femoral artery to do a blood gas analysis. The resulting analysis, as verified by his medical records, showed his blood oxygen level to be above normal and his carbon dioxide level to be below normal (105–11, 178). That in itself does not show that anoxia did not precipitate the NDE, since many patients are not receiving oxygen at the onset of cardiac arrest. Even so, experimental subjects deprived of oxygen through high elevation or in air chambers do not report experiences similar to NDEs. Rather, their mental and physical abilities became progressively muddled and confused. They require greater effort to carry out their tasks, suffer from mental laziness and irritability, and experience difficulty in concentrating, reasoning, and remembering.[169] This contrasts sharply with the clarity of awareness and mental functioning typically reported by those having NDEs.

As for drug intoxication, although some subjects come near death as a result of drug overdoses, interest in this possibility derives more from the

---

[168] Ernst Rodin, "The Reality of Death Experiences: A Personal Perspective," *Journal of Nervous and Mental Disease* 168 (1980): 259–63; James Alcock, "Psychology and Near-Death Experiences," in *Paranormal Borderlands of Science*, ed. by Frazier, 153–69; Siegel, "The Psychology of Life After Death;" *Pseudoscience and the Paranormal*, pp. 68ff.

[169] See Y. Henderson and H. W. Haggard, *Noxious Gases and the Principles of Respiration Influencing their Action* (New York: American Chemical Society, 1927); Ross McFarland, "The Psychological Effects of Oxygen Deprivation (Anoxaemia) on Human Behavior," *Archiv fur Psychologie* 145 (1932); *Recollections of Death*, p. 176.

common practice of administering morphine or other pain-killing drugs to alleviate chest pain in cardiac patients, and the greater depth of our knowledge of drug-induced hallucinations. Nevertheless, drug-induced hallucinations are often delusional insofar as the verifiable part of their content is concerned, which has not been found with NDEs (169).

Finally, there is the possibility that such experiences are brought on by hypercapnia. Here some of the hallucinations show striking parallels to NDEs, and have been associated with other signs of extreme neurological dysfunction similar to those of a patient who appears at or near death.[170] Here also Michael Sabom's countervailing evidence is at its weakest, consisting only of the previously mentioned anecdote of the NDEer who saw his femoral artery tapped to test blood gases—a test that found below normal levels of CO_2 (176–8). Increased CO_2 levels in tissues and the capillaries that supply them will not immediately affect CO_2 levels in major arteries once the blood stops circulating, nor will they be immediately affected by it once the heart is restarted, and this difference is probably more pronounced in cerebral tissue than elsewhere because of its high rate of metabolism.[171]

The claim advanced by Hines is that, whatever their aetiology, NDE hallucinations are relevantly similar in form and content to those of impaired individuals, and therefore probably involve a common underlying physical condition. While emphasizing their similarity to other kinds of hallucinations, Hines also emphasizes their diversity in discounting the possibility of interpreting NDEs objectively. This raises a logical point. Since NDEs are at best a proper subclass of all hallucinations, it is impossible that they have greater heterogeneity than the larger group. In fact, most who study NDEs find their cross-cultural homogeneity uncontroversial and striking. Indeed, this is one of the most puzzling aspects of the phenomenon, since as a rule hallucinations tend to be quite diverse and idiosyncratic.[172]

Judgments of similarity between NDEs and hallucinations might easily be based on the kinds of commitments or assumptions that cannot be taken

---

[170] L. J. Meduna, "The Effects of Carbon Dioxide upon the Functions of the Brain," in *Carbon Dioxide Therapy* (Springfield, IL: Charles Thomas, 1950), pp. 23–8.

[171] See Michael Gliksman and Allan Kellehear, "Near-Death Experiences and the Measurement of Blood Gases," *Journal of Near-Death Studies* 9, 1 (1990): 41–3.

[172] Twemlow and Gabbard, *op. cit.; Recollections of Death*, p. 168; Brian Bates and Adrian Stanley, "The Epidemiology and Differential Diagnosis of Near-Death Experience," *American Journal of Orthopsychiatry* 55 (1985): 548–9; Michael Grosso, "Toward an Explanation of Near-Death Phenomena," *Journal of the American Society for Psychical Research* 75 (1981): 37–60.

for granted in assessing religious claims vis-à-vis scientific ones. Thus, Hines illustrates the diversity among NDEs by pointing out that some are not pleasant and beautiful but are more like experiences of hell. While this is indeed a major sensory difference, it would hardly suggest to a religious person that there is no common underlying reality for both experiences—one they could both be *about*. Ronald Siegel is more specific in the similarities he finds between the content of NDEs and drug-induced hallucinations. He claims that both commonly include tunnels, bright lights, vivid colors and geometric forms. But near-death experiencers rarely report geometric forms. In Ring's study, few subjects volunteered mention of tunnels, and those who experienced a bright light said that it did not hurt their eyes, apparently contradicting Siegel's naturalistic explanation in terms of neuronal discharges in the eye and related structures. Bright lights in LSD hallucinations are not ascribed personal qualities nearly so often as in NDEs.[173]

6.2.2 Alternative Psychological Hypotheses
Siegel suggests that NDEs be classified as altered states of consciousness. He writes:

> These experiences can include transcendence of space and time; awe, wonder, and a sense of sacredness; a deeply felt positive mood, often accompanied by emotions of peace and tranquility; a feeling of insight or illumination or of understanding some universal truth or knowledge . . . .

Continuing to cite mostly his own work as his source of authority (what else can you do when the world is going mad?), he concludes that these states of consciousness "are triggered by a variety of stimuli that result in massive cortical disinhibition and autonomic arousal."[174]

What is an altered state of consciousness? A standard definition is[175]

> any mental state(s), induced by various physiological, psychological, or pharmacologic maneuvers or agents, which can be recognized subjectively by the individual himself (or

---

[173] Bates and Stanley, *ibid.* See also Kevin Drab, "The Tunnel Experience: Reality or Hallucination?" *Anabiosis* 1 (1981): 126–153.

[174] "The Psychology of Life After Death," pp. 923–5. Nathan Schnaper supports Siegel in this assessment—see "Comments Germane to the Paper Entitled 'The Reality of Death Experiences' by Ernst Rodin," *Journal of Nervous and Mental Disease* 168 (1980): 269.

[175] Arnold Ludwig, "Altered States of Consciousness," *Archives of General Psychiatry* 15 (1966): 225.

by an objective observer of the individual) as representing a sufficient deviation in subjective experience or psychological functioning from certain general norms for that individual during alert, waking consciousness.

This is broad enough to accommodate not only NDEs, but any scientific mindset, if only its holder does not occupy it constantly and either is aware of its "deviance" or is observed by "objective" persons who are. Scientists maintain that their "deviant" behavior is actually better than normal human behavior, and they may be right. But this undercuts the normative status of average behavior, without which altered states of consciousness pose no threat to the objectivity of NDEs.

Siegel's thesis that NDEs are similar to altered states of consciousness seems wrong in two respects. First, there are marked divergences in content between NDEs and such commonly studied altered states as OBEs, depersonalization, LSD hallucinations, and (meditation-induced) cosmic consciousness. Second, the degree of homogeneity among NDEs as a group appears to be much higher than for other altered states of consciousness.[176] Still, this aspect of Siegel's critique is not far from the mark. In reviewing some of the literature, Stuart Twemlow and Glen Gabbard note that the primary difference demonstrated between those who have NDEs and those who are equally near death but do not is their attention absorption ratings, which are unusually high for the NDE group. 'Absorption' is defined as "a full commitment of available perceptual, motoric, imaginative and ideational resources to a unified representation of the attentional object,"[177] and is typified by a person who becomes highly "absorbed" when watching a movie. High attention absorption ratings have been correlated with a capacity to alter consciousness and with hypnotic susceptibility. Is this bad? Some psychologists associate hypnotic susceptibility with less rigid and better balanced personalities and increased ability for concentration. Hines associates it with less ability to distinguish reality from unreality.

If eliminative materialists doubt that a direct physiological correlate for beliefs or desires exists, where would that leave images of tunnels, or feelings of transcendence, wonder, or insight? Add the fact that some people having NDEs are physically unimpaired at the time, while many suffering

---

[176] Bates and Stanley, *op. cit.*; *Recollections of Death*, pp. 160–3. In the case of OBEs, the divergences are with the transcendental aspects of NDEs.

[177] Twemlow and Gabbard, *op. cit.*, p. 230; see A. Tellegen and G. Atkinson, "Openness to Absorbing and Self-Altering Experiences ("Absorption"), a Trait Related to Hypnotic Susceptibility," *Journal of Abnormal Psychology* 83 (1974): 274.

from drug intoxication and cerebral anoxia report no such experiences, and there seems to be no straightforward causal relationship here. A person who assumes that NDEs must have some overtly physiological cause may take this to imply that the causes are just more complex. That is fine so long as the ideological nature of this commitment is recognized; it is not a uniquely rational perspective.

Hines offers another reason for rejecting the veridicality of NDEs. Whenever we are unconscious our senses continue to register impressions from the external world, filtering out the less important ones. A mother will awake at the sound of her baby's cry but not for louder noises. Experiments show that subjects can distinguish words which were played from a recording while they were anesthetized from miscellaneous other words, when presented with them subsequently, at least to a degree well above chance.[178] Yet this is hardly comparable with the spontaneous recall of conversation and events that has been repeatedly documented in NDEs. In one study, anesthetized subjects could not remember a single word without prompting.

Indeed, the richness of this kind of evidence was what convinced the skeptical cardiologist, Sabom, that these experiences were veridical (83–4):

> At this stage in my career, I had personally directed and participated in well over a hundred [resuscitations from cardiac arrest]. I knew what a resuscitation consisted of and how it would appear to an onlooker. I had been eagerly awaiting the moment when a patient would claim to have "seen" what had taken place during his resuscitation. Upon such an encounter, I had intended to probe meticulously for details which would not ordinarily be known to nonmedical personnel. In essence, I would pit both my experience as a trained cardiologist and the description of the resuscitation in the medical chart against the professed visual recollections of a lay individual. Thus, I was convinced, obvious inconsistencies would appear which would reduce these "visual" observations to no more than "educated guesses."

To set a base rate for educated guessing he used a control group of twenty-five patients with backgrounds similar to those reporting NDEs.

> . . . [they were] seasoned cardiac patients with an average duration of known heart disease exceeding five years . . . . While in the CCU [coronary care unit], each of these patients had had the opportunity to observe closely at his bedside a cardiac monitor to which he was attached, a cardiac defibrillator, and intravenous needles and equipment. Moreover, each patient had admitted to regular viewing of a home television set prior to this admission . . . which [also] could have contributed to their knowledge of CPR.

---

[178] K. Millar and N. Watkinson, "Recognition of Words Presented during General Anaesthesia," *Ergonomics* 36 (1983): 585–94.

Asked to describe in detail what they would expect to see in such a situation, 80% of the respondents made a major error in their accounts. By contrast, of the six of 32 patients having naturalistic NDEs who were able to describe details of their resuscitation, none made a major error, based either on Sabom's expertise or their medical records (85ff., 113ff.).

Sabom offers three other arguments against the semiconscious state hypothesis. First, surgical patients who through hypnotic regression are able to recall snippets of conversation that took place during their surgery do not recall visual images, let alone the detailed ones typical of NDEs. Second, semi-conscious states are commonly induced in patients undergoing cardioversion to correct abnormalities in heart rhythm. The patient's senses are dulled with intravenous valium to minimize the pain of the electric shock, yet these patients still report distinctively uncomfortable and unpleasant feelings—"It's like having everything torn out of your insides." Those with NDEs feel no unpleasantness whatsoever in connection with the administration of CPR. Finally, some patients have experienced both an NDE and a semi-conscious state during a near-death crisis, and report the experiences to be markedly different (154ff.).

Other psychological hypotheses can be summarized more briefly.

(1) *Conscious fabrication:* Presumably, this would happen if people expected to gain attention or notoriety for themselves. Sabom found that most subjects are reluctant to reveal the contents of their experiences to members of the medical community, fearing ridicule, or even referral for psychiatric treatment. Such fears are often well-founded. Subjects who did reveal the contents of their experiences generally denied sharing them with many acquaintances for the same reason (157).

(2) *Subconscious fabrication:* Without a consistent pattern that might imply a direct link—e.g., to a subconscious need to deny death—this is hard to verify. Even persons who had both multiple near-death crises and multiple NDEs may show no marked similarity in the contents of their NDEs. Or if the subject had only one NDE, it may not have been during one of his closer brushes with death (159–60).

(3) *Prior expectation:* Ring actually found a negative correlation between those who had some prior knowledge of NDEs and those who report NDEs themselves. In spite of the attention they have received nationally, Sabom found most of his patients reporting experiences (who were generally from Florida's rural north) to be ignorant of the phenomenon prior to their own experience (158, 166ff.).

Alcock and Hines claim that the sense of floating near the ceiling should not surprise anyone, inviting us to remember where we were when we ate dinner last night. It is difficult for me to believe, however, that a person cannot distinguish an immediate perception from a recall image, or that people performing this exercise become confused about whether they were having an OBE last night. Details of the dinner setting comparable to the details reported by those having NDEs do not often come to mind.

6.2.3 Alternative Physiological Hypotheses

Another possibility is that NDEs are related to releases by the brain of large quantities of *endorphins* at times of overwhelming trauma. Endorphins are substances similar to morphine that can cause a state of painlessness so profound as to be comparable to what those having NDEs report. Experiments demonstrating this effect through injections of endorphins, however, found that it lasted from 22 to 73 hours, whereas those having NDEs report sensations of even overwhelming pain returning immediately once the experience is over and they have resumed ordinary consciousness (171-2). NDEs typically last only a few minutes although an hour may elapse before the patient resumes consciousness. *Temporal lobe seizures* have also been suggested as causing NDEs (5.3.1). Electrical stimulation of the temporal or parietal lobes may cause visual or auditory illusions or hallucinations, flashbacks, feelings of detachment, fear, sadness, or loneliness, or forced thought. One does not find forced thought or distorted perceptions of the environment in NDEs, however, nor are the emotions felt usually negative. The flashbacks associated with NDEs take the form of multiple significant events in rapid succession, not the random, isolated, insignificant events of a seizure.

In sum, Sabom did not find any adequate explanation for the incidence of NDEs. Since almost any interesting scientific hypothesis is likely to have some evidence against it, I would think that a few of the above possibilities are still worth investigating—particularly the hypercapnia hypothesis. Also, even though anoxia, endorphin release, temporal lobe seizure, and hypercapnia produce different effects from NDEs in isolation, it remains possible that combining them would produce a similar effect. On the other hand, the possibility that NDEs are veridical experiences also warrants consideration. It may constitute the best explanation for many instances of the phenomenon. Since many people come to a point of subjectively deciding to return to this life, one interesting avenue of inquiry might involve determining, if possible, whether they reach these decisions prior to the beginning of improvement in their condition as measured by the medical practitioners attending them. Such a temporal priority seems necessary for a causal relationship between decision and subsequent improvement to exist. If the temporal relation were reversed, then that aspect of the experience must lack causal reality.

6.3   THE SIGNIFICANCE OF NDES

Even if NDEs have more reality than mere hallucinations, they are still far different from what we normally consider real. The problem is not lack of contiguity in space and time of the experiencers per se. Most of those who have observed Neptune over the years have also been significantly separated in space and time, yet nobody questions Neptune's reality. What makes NDEs different from most reality claims is the failure of replicability "on demand" or "at will." Yet here we have a value that is parochial to science to a significant degree. There are many checks which one can perform in the course of an experience to confirm that one's cognitive abilities are functioning properly. If successful, they lend support to the veridicality of what one is experiencing regardless of whether the experience can itself be replicated. Even so, the problem of interpreting these experiences is a major one. What follows in this section are miscellaneous observations on the problem of interpretation and significance.

What people experience near death often exerts a powerful influence on their subsequent lives. Frequently they become more conscientious morally or more religiously oriented. Hines remarks of this phenomenon, "These personality changes testify to the power of the misinterpretation of what is actually happening to the individual."[179] If demonstrating psychopathology counts as evidence against the veridicality of NDEs, then failure to find any evidence of psychopathology, or the discovery of salubrious effects for the experiences, should also count as inductive evidence in their favor. I do not claim that these *should* count as evidence—in my view, pathology is a pragmatic consideration that is strictly irrelevant to whether entities exist in reality corresponding to the contents of perception (3.4). I advance this argument for the benefit of those who believe that evidence of psychopathology would argue against veridicality. If they are right, then finding a lack of psychopathology in the experiencers is evidence of the veridicality of their NDEs in the same sense that examining ravens and finding them black is evidence that ravens are black.

So salutary are the effects of NDEs on the experiencer's subsequent lives that at least one investigator has expressed a desire to replicate them "artificially" so as to make their therapeutic value more widely available.[180]

---

[179]   *Pseudoscience and the Paranormal*, p. 70.

[180]   Russell Noyes, "The Human Experience of Death Or, What Can We Learn from Near-Death Experiences?" *Omega* 13 (1982–83): 255–6.

Those who have had NDEs tend to show less interest in drugs, or in paranormal or psychic phenomena than the population at large.[181] The rash of interest in NDEs during the late 70s alarmed psychologists because of how wonderfully the experiences and the after-life were being portrayed. It was feared that people would try to experience the same thing for themselves by putting their own lives in jeopardy or attempting suicide. Such a trend never materialized, but those who study NDEs subsequently scrutinized cases of attempted suicide. Kenneth Ring and Stephen Franklin found "Chiefly those suicide attempters that do *not* undergo an NDE . . . are likely to try it again—not those who report an NDE."[182] They concurred with Bruce Greyson that there has not been a single well-documented case of suicidal intent persisting or increasing following an NDE.[183] This is remarkable given the fact that those who attempt suicide, taken as a group, are 50 to 100 times more likely to commit suicide subsequently in comparison to the general population, and having an NDE usually results in a reduced fear of death.

The only part of an NDE that can be independently confirmed is the naturalistic part, but the part with greatest religious significance is the transcendental part. As mentioned, the naturalistic part may have religious significance in suggesting that consciousness is at least partly autonomous of the body, though it does not particularly invite religious interpretation. Even if all the physiological, pharmacological, and psychological explanations mentioned in this section fail, how would the veridicality of naturalistic experiences explain anything? How is it even possible? Ring and Sabom both conclude that most likely a genuine out-of-body experience is involved, and that any adequate explanation of NDEs would have to account for how it is possible for consciousness to exist apart from the body.[184] This conclusion is not forced, and even if consciousness can exist separately from the body, the two may continue to influence one another. In one case, a woman having an naturalistic NDE during a grand mal seizure from toxemia of pregnancy reportedly "watched" her convulsing body in clear detail. After the doctor administered a shot of phenobarbital, her visual perceptions no longer seemed so clear, however (170–1).

---

[181] Twemlow and Gabbard, *op. cit.*, pp. 227, 230.

[182] "Do Suicide Survivors Report Near-Death Experiences?" *Omega* 12 (1981–82): 205–6.

[183] "Near Death Experiences and Attempted Suicide," *Suicide and Life-Threatening Behavior* 11 (1981): 10–16.

[184] *Life at Death*, p. 221; *Recollections of Death*, pp. 184–5.

Well, before they had given me the shot, I could see everything that was going on and it was very sharp in detail . . . . But after they gave me the shot, it was almost a depressing feeling. I couldn't see everything as well as at first. It was like the clarity was gone from the picture. I couldn't hear things as well. It was just getting darker and it was like I was fading away . . . . I went to sleep and woke up the next morning.

A number of naturalistic experiencers seem to return to their body automatically in connection with the performance of some medical procedure, also suggesting that, even if separated, consciousness and physical body continue to influence one another.

Finally, one cannot help coming back to the following question: What significance should be attributed to experiences many of which occur when the body is seriously impaired or not functioning normally? This hardly seems to be the ideal setting for making observations about the true nature of the world, or for grasping clearly the distinction between reality and unreality. An experimenter would not consider observations made while his faculties were thus impaired to have scientific value. Thus, Bertrand Russell argues, "From a scientific point of view, we can make no distinction between the man who eats little and sees heaven and the man who drinks much and sees snakes. Each is in an abnormal physical condition and therefore has abnormal perceptions."[185] Why treat as *important* observation reports that are obtained under such circumstances?

Here is a case in which what is scientifically important and what is religiously important differ, so that a scientific value system cannot be taken for granted. What happens at or near death is very important, both religiously and commonsensically, regardless of the circumstances. The very choice of "abnormal perceptions" as the appropriate reference class for such experiences is heavily loaded with parochial values. Lest this still seem irrational vis-à-vis the workings of science, consider contemporary high-energy physics research aimed at limning those ultimate constituents of the physical universe, quarks. This is the kind of work upon which Quine and other philosophical descendants of Russell would base their ontologies. One cannot interest physicists in studying the material out of which everyday objects such as chairs and lamps are made, because they believe that only when particles—and not just any particles, but leptons—are excited to 20 GeV or more, are their interactions ontologically revealing. Thus, the objectivity of science cannot simply be characterized as interest in what is everyday, common, or the norm, the way Aristotle's science was. If you want to uncover

---

[185] *Religion and Science* (London: Oxford Univ. Press, 1935), p. 188.

the ultimate underpinnings of reality you may need to look in places that are bizarre by ordinary standards—such as in huge underground tanks lined with photoelectric cells (for neutrinos). Yet nobody dismisses such research casually by saying, "If you do abnormal things to matter, undoubtedly you will get abnormal results." The physicist wants to know why she gets precisely the abnormal results she does. The same applies in religious circles: if one wants to learn something about God—the ultimate ontological entity for most western religions—one expects to find that knowledge where God is encountered, however unusual such circumstances may be otherwise.

6.4   NDES AND RELIGIOUS EXPERIENCE

What makes NDEs of distinct interest for religious epistemology is

(1) their relative homogeneity;
(2) our ability to identify the circumstances in which they are likely to occur well enough to permit the use of scientific instrumentation on those who have them at the time they are having them;
(3) the resulting quantity and quality of evidence and theoretic competition, which lends additional credibility to any religious hypothesis that it does not rule out;
(4) independent means of verifying some of the claims of the experiencers, as a check on their reliability.

For the sake of clarity, I restrict the term 'religious experience' in what follows to experiences that are not NDEs.

For an inference to the best explanation to have significant force, there needs to be a field of competing explanations, and this in turn requires an abundance of evidence that bears on each one. That is, the credibility accruing to the "best" explanation is positively correlated with the number of competing explanations under consideration, as well as with the credentials of the theories standing behind them. It is difficult to develop and test scientific hypotheses adequately when one has nothing available except anecdotal evidence. Any given occurrence could have almost an unlimited number of explanations, and testing is greatly facilitated when one can subject the entities involved to systematic measurements using scientific instruments. For such transient phenomena as religious experiences this also requires an ability to determine the circumstances under which they are likely to occur.

Scientific accounts of religious experiences generally stress psychoanalytic and socio-cultural factors, which are the only ones easily assessed when one lacks access to the subject at the time the experience is occurring. Such explanations rely on psychological profiles or an assessment of the subject's cultural environment as their primary source of information. These theories and the evidence they draw on are notoriously weaker than many of their scientific brethren, and their general lack of credibility undermines the credibility of hypotheses whose successful competition with them would be their chief asset. In the case of NDEs, however, the availability of both an abundance of scientific instrumentation and of trained personnel in the environment in which they most frequently occur (hospitals), and the predictability of the experiences themselves, which is much higher than for religious experiences generally, makes it more practical to test and dismiss a multitude of scientific hypotheses. Insofar as such hypotheses are found inadequate, the hypothesis that God is in some sense their source (at least for the transcendental portion) gains more credibility than it is ever likely to get by competition with psychoanalytic and sociological hypotheses alone. Let me stress the theoretical or "in principle" aspect of my argument; direct, scientific tests of veridicality even for naturalistic experiences appear a long way off.[186]

Another major problem with religious experiences is their heterogeneity, which seems to lead to a multiplicity of mutually inconsistent interpretations that are apparently culture-dependent. Swinburne claims a common underlying reality can be found with which the great majority of all religious experiences are consistent, but others disagree.[187] So long as the cross-cultural homogeneity of NDEs remains remarkably high, it confers a measure of objectivity on NDEs which religious experiences generally lack. Such a lack suggests that religious experiences are more often merely a matter of interpretation, prior expectation, top-down processing, and/or acculturation. All of these factors are recognizable as common sources of error, and hence work to defeat the experience's evidential value. Commonality of experience being one benchmark of reality, the homogeneity of NDEs gives one the beginnings of an appearance/reality distinction that is generally impossible to draw for religious experiences as a whole. If this homogeneity holds up to further scrutiny, and it may not, then we would seem to have a difference here with special epistemological significance. Giving an explanation of NDEs does amount to imposing an interpretation on them, yet it could have broad scope, rather than being subjective or capricious.

---

[186] Cf. Janice Holden and Leroy Joesten, "Near-Death Veridicality Research in the Hospital Setting: Problems and Promise," *Journal of Near-Death Studies* 9, 1 (1990): 45–54.

[187] *The Existence of God,* pp. 265–6; Flew, *God and Philosophy,* pp. 126–7; Michael Martin, "The Principle of Credulity and Religious Experience," p. 86.

6.5   A SUGGESTED EXPLANATION FOR SOME NDES

One need not interpret NDEs as fully objective to give them a religious explanation. Indeed, I argue that one should not, because 'objective' implies a literal interpretation that appears untenable. Oftentimes people experience deathbed visions of a close relative—since deceased—coming to comfort them or show them the way to the next realm. This may occur either as part of an NDE or at other times when death appears imminent. The relative is often reported as appearing "just the way I knew her, years ago." I cannot imagine any reason to believe that a person who has since entered the beyond would continue to *be* or *exist* in just the same manner as in earthly life—why should the resurrected body *be* like the physical body, to the point of wearing the same clothing? But I can readily imagine why God might want the person to *appear* the same as in earthly life—namely, to make her recognizable to the percipient. So if an appearance/reality distinction is to be drawn, part of what the experiencer is catching hold of is an appearance that is somewhat far afield from the underlying reality. I am not saying that the appearance is necessarily illusory or the result of an intention to deceive. Rather, the degree of mediation between it and reality is greater than what we normally associate with objectivity. NDEs might better be compared to a play or movie in which the one-person "audience" interacts with the actors.

Visions of heaven or hell may help to illustrate my point. Although I sympathize with people who claim literally to have seen or experienced hell or heaven, I note that these are often the same people who claim that they were literally dead, and that they knew this with certainty. We simply do not agree that they were dead—otherwise we would call them 'death experiences' rather than 'near-death experiences.' Understood literally, death precludes return to this life, nor have there been any instances of a person fitting the modern medical definition of death—no brain activity for twenty-four hours—being revived and having an NDE. My point is that near-death experiencers exhibit a tendency to describe their experiences in terms that cannot be interpreted as both literal and true. Also, not everyone who has these experiences ultimately accepts their authenticity or guidance. Hence some are aware that reality and experience are not the same. Perhaps, as James says of religious experiences, one cannot interact effectively with transcendental communicating beings if one does not believe them to be real, or treat them as if they were real. Neither can one appreciate a movie without suspending disbelief for a moment and going with the flow. My point pertains to how we should understand the ultimate ontological claims involved, not what attitude is necessary to have or benefit from an NDE. Seeing a great movie can change a person's life for the better, and the "truth" of the vividly conveyed message may be part of the reason why, as with NDEs. This does not commit us to concluding that reality in the movie *exists* in precisely the way it *appears*.

My suggested religious explanation, then, is that God authors the transcendental content of some NDEs, that the experiences are indicative of a supernatural reality and contain information about that reality, but that the relation of experience to reality is a mediated one of representation, not unmediated contact. Perhaps God stages such experiences for the percipient's edification. Skeptics often satisfy themselves with explaining away a number of NDEs in physiological or psychological terms while leaving the rest unaccounted for, arguing that it is unreasonable to expect them to explain everything to make their universally dismissive case. I make no comparable claim of universality, but the existential claim that a significant number of NDEs are susceptible to religious explanation. Others may have wholly naturalistic aetiologies—God may have done nothing to bring them about.

In conclusion, our knowledge of NDEs is woefully incomplete, and the viability of religious interpretations for them is by no means assured, but the scientific study of NDEs could help us to reach this critical mass sooner. In some cases we have independent verification of the reliability of the subject's claims through medical records, professional expertise, and the fact that NDEs generally occur in the presence of other people who can corroborate or dispute what the percipient claims to have seen and heard, at least for the naturalistic content of the experience. There may also be independent verification of the presence or absence of agents which could serve as sources of delusions. All of this makes it possible to assess the reliability of both the subject and of the experience form itself with a measure of independence, and without relying simply on subjective assessments of the person's credibility. These confer a major advantage on our ability to screen NDEs for potential sources of unreliability, in comparison to religious experiences generally, and hence give us a more substantial basis on which to venture credulity. Private experiences still involve sufficient conceptual and evidential problems to justify considerable caution. All viable hypotheses should be pursued. My point is that at this juncture, religious explanations are also worth pursuing. NDEs have some distinct advantages over religious experiences, both as a basis for belief in God and as a source of information about God—advantages that heretofore have been unappreciated by philosophers of religion.

CHAPTER 7

CONSTRUCTING RELIGIOUS EXPLANATIONS

7.1 HOW FAR HAVE WE GOTTEN?

The preceding chapters have been devoted to creating a space in explanatory practice in which religious explanations could fit, if such explanations were available. Most of the material in historical religious texts comes in anecdotal form, as does the informational value in contemporary religious experience. The standards of scientific practice which severely restrict the use of anecdotal material seem parochial to science, and more general principles which serve to preclude religious explanations seem overtly ideological. Still, for reasons given in chapter 4, this kind of information lends itself better to uses that are idiosyncratic, rather than highly structured socially. How this information is used is not immune from rational criticism—one must, for example, take care that the value of error-avoidance not be shortchanged. Rather, one cannot reasonably expect the substantive conclusions themselves to command a broad consensus. Thus, it would be impertinent for me to make sweeping proposals for religious explanations. Each individual who is so inclined must construct them for herself.

This idiosyncratic aspect furnishes grounds for pessimism regarding the ability of contemporary religious institutions to fill the space I have opened with satisfactory explanations. The intellectual climate in religious circles is rarely conducive to free inquiry or open theoretical competition, yet a context of inquiry was seen to be necessary to extend credulity to religious explanations as working hypotheses. There is also too much willingness among religious communities to impose gratuitous a priori restrictions upon their concept of God or our relation to him. I don't think that Gary Gutting could have reached his contrary conclusion that only full participation in a particular religious community ultimately enables one's religious beliefs to be justified, if he had taken account of the above considerations.[188]

My sympathies incline toward anti-realist interpretations of scientific theorizing such as van Fraassen's, simply because science employs so many pragmatic values over and above any need to determine correspondence to reality. When it comes to fitting a curve to a set of data points, scientists sometimes engage in wholesale disregard of recalcitrant data, especially if the data can be interpreted as "noise" from which an essential "signal" is extractable. Israel Scheffler argues that "running roughshod over a few purported facts is still consistent with objective control [for a] hard-won system," meaning not only that running roughshod over some data is permissible, but that scientists may do so and claim objectivity for their results.[189] It seems to me, however, given the nature and history of conflict between science and religion, that if anything gets run over roughshod by science, the interests of religion are likely to be the first to suffer. They are not part of the "signal" that science seeks to recover. If so, the resulting "objectivity" would be parochial to science.

Emphasis on correspondence rather than pragmatics forces one to pay closer attention to observation and do less grandiose theorizing, in the name of error-avoidance. But how helpful will this be when the amassed data are not easily organized or systematized? A curve that runs roughshod over some data will still be more informative than the naked data themselves. This confronts the religious person with a dilemma—either he can attempt to be informative but make himself vulnerable to charges of anti-realism, or he can stick closer to correspondence, but have little or nothing useful to say. Under this scenario the religious person seems forced to construct models. If he does not attempt to model God directly, then at least a model of our relation to God is called for. A model functions like a theory by serving as an intermediary between evidence and explanation. Thus, anecdotal evidence may serve as evidence for some hypothesis, but it still does not constitute evidence for an explanation until the explanation gives an account of why,

---

[188] *Religious Belief and Religious Scepticism* (Univ. of Notre Dame Press, 1982), pp. 172–3. He bases this on a major premise also open to question, that "the great world religions seem to be the main loci and sustainers of our access to God"; along with an appeal to a pragmatic justification of belief that, in my view, shortchanges the value of truth as correspondence.

[189] *Science and Subjectivity,* 2nd ed. (Indianapolis: Hackett, 1982), p. 87.

when, or how the event occurred. The model provides the larger pattern into which individual anecdotes, hypotheses, and other evidence fit.

Talk of model building is usually associated with anti-realism, because it emphasizes construction rather than discovery in epistemic contexts. Yet anti-realism is unsatisfactory from a religious perspective, because of the importance of God's metaphysical status. It is not sufficient that God be merely a mental construct for explaining what happens in the world, having only the instrumental reality of centers of gravity. The religious person cannot worship an instrumental God, no matter how useful the construct might be, insofar as it represents the work of her own hands. Therefore, in creating such models, it seems best that we view them as nothing more than approximations or representations of an external reality that is not fully perceived, given the limitations of our sensory apparatus. Evolutionary epistemology shows how to make sense of such a reality when it is physical: it is that which, over time, caused our sensory apparatus to acquire the form it now has. Problems of adaptation lack unique solutions, so adaptation is more a process of satisficing than optimizing—i.e., of finding some cheap and workable heuristic that helps one to "get by." If it has left us with only partial ability to cognize the physical world, perhaps our ability to cognize the divine world is similarly compromised. What the talk of model building does, then, is remind us of how much of our "knowledge" of God represents the contribution of our own cognitive apparatus, so that we do not become naively optimistic about how well it corresponds to reality.

Nevertheless, if the model-builder strives for the utmost fidelity, she may be in a position to wring an important concession from the anti-realist. Namely, she may assert that if reality *were* so constituted as to correspond in every detail to the specifications of the model, we would have no reason to expect the world to behave differently than it currently does. We do not know that the model is not literally true, or that the postulated entities do not exist, unless there is at least some point of infidelity between the model and the world it represents. This is a very demanding requirement on the religious model-builder—it requires her to construct a model of God, or of one's relation to God, consistent with the totality of our evidence. That is, while retaining the logical structure of a map, such a religious interpretation must be capable of cohering with our understanding of everything that exists and happens in the world. Providing such a total interpretation is an enormous task, but the religious model builder ultimately has little alternative.

Modeling our relation to a transcendent God presents another difficulty. Seemingly, either *no* natural language predicates apply to a transcendent God (language having evolved chiefly for natural world applications), or if *some* are, then *all* are via one analogy or another. Recall that Schoen attempted to evade this difficulty by means of functional attribution:[190]

> By knowing that God is that which provides for his needs, Fred can conclude that God is not a rock, a threatening cloud, or a bump in the night on the straightforward grounds that things such as these are incapable of supplying food, clothing, and shelter.

Granting that God sometimes performs fatherly functions, why shouldn't he also perform other functions? What else did Jesus mean by analogizing belief in himself to a house built on a rock, if not that his words perform the function of a rock for such belief? He also analogized his return to that of a thief in the night, a rough functional equivalent of a bump in the night. Many biblical passages analogize God's threat of retribution to a threatening cloud.[191] So these represent aspects of our relation to God that appear just as genuine as the relation of a child to its father.

Modeling one's relation to God may be an exercise in futility, but it seems the best course given the value of a diversity of views. One cannot expect alternative explanatory paradigms to sprout out of the ground—they require periods of patient development. If the anecdotal and other evidence favoring the existence of a God-like entity approaches making it on-balance probable, developing appropriate models is necessary to achieve understanding. Theoretical modeling is the only game in town. So I proceed in the spirit of Jerry Fodor, who says, "The form of a philosophical theory, often enough, is *Let's try looking over here.*"[192] This does not completely eliminate the feeling that something gratuitous is going on, but it should remove the sense that it is an egregious departure from reasonable standards of philosophical practice.

This, then, represents how far we have come. Where might we go from here? To offer only a programmatic sketch of a model of God would require a book in itself, yet that would still fall far short of giving a total interpretation of the world. In order for our model to be informative, as pointed out with curve-fitting, it is necessary first to account for some of the world's major macro features before focusing on details. Therefore, the most that I can do here is adumbrate how the inquiry might profitably be pursued.

---

[190]   *Religious Explanations*, p. 86; see 1.6.

[191]   *Matthew* 7:24; *Luke* 12:39–40; *Exodus* 19:16, 20:18; *1st Samuel* 7:10, 12:17–18; *1st Kings* 18:38–46; *2nd Chronicles* 5:13–6:1; *Isaiah* 19:1; *Matthew* 26:64; *Mark* 9:6–7.

[192]   *Representations* (MIT Press, 1981), p. 31.

7.2   INTENTIONALITY MODELING

If one assumes that God is intelligent, powerful, and active in the world, then it should not be surprising that the world and much of what happens in it reflect the intentions of God. John (1:10) says of Jesus, as if to fault mankind, "He was in the world, and the world was made through him, and the world did not know him." Perhaps mankind's sinful nature is at fault for this, but one naturally wonders whether God did not intend that Jesus be unrecognizable by most of the world, and the same could be wondered about the authorship of many natural and religiously significant events. Of course, intentions not in harmony with God's may also play a role in shaping the world, whether they have human, demonic, or other origin. Nevertheless, a reasonable starting point would be to take what Dennett calls an "intentional stance" toward the world, or treat the world as an intentional system. Rather than acquiescing in the scientific popular prohibition of teleological explanations, Dennett reckons the ultimate viability of treating anything as an intentional system in terms of whether it enables us to predict or explain events within the system that we could not have otherwise. *Why* we could not does not matter. Explaining events in intentional terms justifies describing them in those terms, absent explanatory alternatives with equal predictive power.

That the world can be interpreted intentionally does not prove that the world actually was produced by those intentions. If anything, humans are habitually inclined to interpret even brute automata intentionally.[193] It is a strength of this approach that we are adept at it through habitual use—indeed, even small children quickly acquire a knack for using folk psychological terms (21, 48). Being able to determine the functions or intentions that artifacts and events can fulfill must have great survival value, but because of this we are apt to do so regardless of whether the intentions could possibly be real, to the point of pathology (91). Yet one can say that *if there were* any God-like entity acting in the world, and there may be, this seems a reasonable strategy for determining that being's nature. Perhaps susceptibility to intentional interpretation even constitutes prima facie evidence that there is some entity whose intentions these are, absent contrary evidence.

Dennett is a reductionist who denies the existence of intentions, taking an instrumentalistic stance toward such mental entities. He would find treating the world as an intentional system, or from the intentional stance, consistent with the pantheistic view that God is nothing other than the universe

---

[193]   *The Intentional Stance,* p. 37; Page references in this section are to this work.

itself—a universe that does not really possess intentions. Such pantheism is otiose to many religious people, but I want to stress its methodological short-comings lest anyone suppose that it is not only consistent with the intentional stance, but the most natural way of implementing it. Pantheism would crimp interpretation by requiring all of the intentions manifested in the world to be interpreted into a single coherent system. Humans are part of the world, but from the standpoint of reconstructing God's intentions, western religions deny that humans are part of God. Given that humans have many conflicting intentions and go to war over their differences, pantheism seems to require internalizing these conflicting intentions within God, making God at war with himself. From the standpoint of explanation or prediction, and certainly for localizing responsibility, restricting one's intentional interpretation to lesser scales seems more likely to be productive. That is, to find God's intentions, we should look first at the residual world formed by subtracting from the real world the effects of human intentions. One might subdivide further if more than one personality or set of intentions seems to be manifest in the residual system, as could happen if, say, a devil were also capable of affecting it. How the intentional landscape gets subdivided will depend on how fruitful each approach turns out to be, but will also depend on any evidence that the corresponding intentions are real.

Pantheism also seems defective in making the universe the source of the intentions it manifests. Science offers little reason to ascribe intelligence to matter in itself. That is, the intelligence of the brain resides primarily in how its matter is organized or structured, not the atoms it is made of. Nor can one locate within the universe a source of intelligence capable of having the intentions ascribed, since it has no functional equivalent of a brain. The universe is vast, and may have many emergent properties relative to those of the particles constituting it, but it would be a fundamental mistake to ascribe functions to it for which one cannot locate anything with such a functional capability.[194] Even computers (to which Dennett applies intentional language) are more complex than any known structure in the universe outside the brain itself, and no brain or computer is capable of implementing its intentions on more than a local basis. Thus, even interpreting the residual world as a manifestation of the intentions of God, with or without help from other personalities (demons, angels, etc.), it seems better to maintain the immateriality of God than identify him with any material substructure of the

---

[194]   William Bechtel, "Two Common Errors in Explaining Biological and Psychological Phenomena," *Philosophy of Science* 49 (1982): 549–74.

residual system. Nobody would identify God with the local cluster or super-cluster of galaxies, but hardly any properties of the universe are known to be emergent over properties of the local cluster. That is, if the universe were God's "body," clusters of galaxies would not comprise it the way that the parts of the human body comprise a whole greater than their sum, but more in the way that an ocean is comprised of various expanses, of which it equals the sum. Yet this greatness over the sum of the parts is necessary to make the universe worthy of worship, given that the local supercluster is not.

One charge brought against intentionality modeling is that it effectively anthropomorphizes God.[195] But it seems unexceptionable that we should attempt to understand God, as we do the world, using the tools of knowledge acquisition available to us, or with which we are adept. Since apparently we *are* adept at imagining functions for objects, or intentions that systems of events might realize, it matters little that the reality about God may be far different. Perhaps it transcends anything that can be captured in natural language. Applying talk of intentions to God is a way of making God intelligible to us to the extent that this is possible. It is not an objection that there may be aspects of God which such talk does not capture, or which transcend intelligibility by human standards. Protagoras is famous for having called man the measure of all things. It seems to me somewhat inevitable that we use ourselves as a measure of God's attributes, since we are quite incapable of using God either to measure God or to measure ourselves. We don't know how to wield that yardstick.

7.3   GOD THE FATHER AND THE PROBLEM OF EVIL

Perhaps the most common metaphor for the relation of an individual to God is that of a child to its father. This is the metaphor that Schoen attempts to parlay into a model—not just of any father, but of a rich and benevolent one. Near-death, numinous, and mystical experiences all typically suggest the goodness of the supreme being; indeed, it seems necessary that God be basically good if he is to be worthy of worship. But any model that is inconsistent with the presence of evil in the world would fall far short of counting as a total interpretation of the world as an intentional system. Some mileage can be gotten by supposing that God chastises us as any parent would his

---

[195] Kai Nielsen, *An Introduction to the Philosophy of Religion* (St. Martin's, 1982), pp. 18, 155. Gary Colwell replies in "The Flew-Nielsen Challenge: A Critical Exposition of its Methodology," *Religious Studies* 17 (1981): 323–42.

children, and thereby visits upon us calamities that seem bad from our limited perspective, but whose goodness would be apparent if we took a larger perspective. God does not want to spoil us as children, and so does not give us some of the things we ask for. Indeed, parents start weaning their children away from dependence on them almost from birth. Nobody wants to be weaned, so it should not be surprising that people often find God to be somewhat less than they had hoped.

This still seriously understates the amount and severity of evil in the world, which appears beyond the power of such an interpretation to accommodate. It also does not explain how the world came to be a place in which fathers must so often oppose their children's desires, and it is hard to find any criterion of reasonableness by which God answers most of the reasonable requests coming from his children. It might be better, therefore, to look at models that involve limitations on God's power or limitations on how we understand God's goodness. Given the necessity of arriving at a conception that makes God worthy of worship, I adumbrate in this section what I take to be the simpler and more natural approach of preserving the goodness of God at the expense of recognizing some limitation on his power. To an extent, this can be done within the confines of the father analogy, simply by recognizing in God more of the limitations that human fathers actually possess. Perhaps God is *not* particularly wealthy, at least with respect to the "goods of this world," or he may have other limitations that we fail to appreciate. However, I prefer to build these limitations into a model of our relation to God rather than into a model of God himself, in order to keep more explanatory possibilities open and avoid excessive controversy.

7.3.1   The "Wizard of Oz" Analogy

Freud at one time propounded a notorious theory regarding the genesis of religious belief, which goes something like this: as children we all believe naively that our parents are all-knowing, all-powerful, all-loving beings, because they seem to know everything and be able to do anything relative to our feeble capacities, and they never stop caring for us. As we get older, we realize that our parents are neither omniscient nor omnipotent as we once thought, nor wholly good. Needing the reassurance and security that comes from the infantile belief in ideal parents, and having nowhere to find it, we then imagine an immaterial God encompassing all of those qualities.

The popularity of this story far outstrips the amount of empirical evidence in its favor, yet I do not bring it up to criticize it, but to suggest turning it around. Some religious groups hold that the history of mankind is progressive, insofar as man's conception of and relation to God has been undergoing a process of development through cumulative experience, much the way all forms of knowledge develop or all ongoing relationships grow. This would be a dangerous perspective if it encouraged us to look down upon historical and primitive peoples as if they were our inferiors. But we can say that our progenitors were *technologically* and *informationally* underdeveloped in comparison to ourselves without making them our *moral* inferiors. Nor have we done anything to merit our informational and technological advantages: if it seems that we can see far, it may be because we stand on "the shoulders of giants."[196]

When the story is turned on its head, the notion of an omniscient, omnipotent, and wholly good God might be seen as a first stab at conceptualizing a God-like entity who has many remarkable powers, is apparently capable of seeing into the future (at least on occasion), and maintains a system of morality that has a broad and profound appeal. Indeed, belief in such a God has likely been justified at times as a proto-explanation—a working attempt at coming to grips with events that are difficult to understand or explain. However, given the logical and evidential difficulties attending this conception, a more thoroughly considered view might call for tempering these attributes which originally were ascribed without qualification. Perhaps our developing understanding of our relation to God could be characterized with what I call the "Wizard of Oz" analogy. As in the movie, people originally come to God expecting him to do great things and perform miraculous feats—throw mountains into the sea, and what not. In the end, God is exposed as a more limited being who at times may have misled us about his capabilities, although not maliciously. Still, there is a sense in which he is wonderful, and not comparable to the beings among whom he lives. True, there may be no way to translate or "cash out" that wonderfulness into tangible benefits, but perhaps our disappointment can be mollified somewhat by the fact that, for the very same reason, such a wonderful being is all the more accessible. If God is indeed trying to wean us away from dependence on him, as the father analogy suggests, it would be natural for our perspective to reflect an ever-diminishing role for God in relation to our own lives.

This model of our relation to God does nothing to explain how the world got created, who created it, or how the evil in it came to be here. Can a God be worthy of worship who is not personally responsible for Creation? Perhaps not, but I want to confine my modeling here to the direct contents of religious experience, rather than to matters requiring additional theory or

---

[196] Appropriating a well-known confession of Sir Isaac Newton.

interpretation. My analysis also should not be confused with the "demythologizing" theology of Rudolf Bultmann. I haven't denied the existence of an after-life, supernatural powers, or their occasional miraculous intervention in the course of nature.[197] But miraculous events are atypical of the relation between God and humans, and even the ability to perform miracles does not make one omniscient, omnipotent, or wholly good. Scientists perform many feats that seem miraculous to those who are less educated.

7.3.2   God the Provider

The brunt of the father analogy falls on the notion that God provides for us, which presents a difficulty from the standpoint of the problem of evil (see also 1.6). God may provide many things for us—perhaps more than we can know—but precisely because we don't know, it seems preferable to refrain from speculating. Anecdotes can always be offered regarding how God apparently helped a certain person in a time of distress, or how God failed to help someone else, and God's involvement in helping or hindering is debated endlessly. Once again, Hick suggests that all phenomena are religiously ambiguous.[198] But it seems typical of human experience, perhaps more typical than all evidence testifying to God's providence, that God does essentially nothing and the person must find a way through the crisis himself. Such experiences may not be called religious, but they remain an aspect of religious experience which models of our relation to God must take seriously.

Let me expand on this aspect for a moment. Matthew (6:28-9) says we ought not take thought for tomorrow, for "consider the lilies . . . , they neither toil nor spin, yet . . . Solomon in all his glory was not arrayed like one of these." Assuming that one can interpret this scripture either literally or figuratively ("spiritually"), I grant that one must depend on God for one's spiritual clothing. Perhaps one cannot even define or explain the concept of spiritual clothing apart from essential mention of God. But the desire for spiritual clothing has little to do with the problem for which this is offered as the solution. That is, few of my acquaintances who worry about how they will clothe themselves tomorrow are worrying about what spiritual clothes they will be wearing. The suggestion of Jesus may be that we *ought* to concern ourselves with that, which is probably true. But this does not resolve

---

[197] Bultmann considers beliefs in these to be naive and untenable in light of modern science. His writings are informed by such scientistic ideologies as the principle of sufficient reason—see *Jesus Christ and Mythology* (New York: Scribner's, 1958), pp. 15–8.

[198] John Hick, "Theology and Verification," *Theology Today* 17 (1960).

the question of what clothes, literally speaking, we will wear tomorrow. Regarding this, it simply will not happen that God clothes me as the lilies are clothed. It is unlikely that he will clothe me as Solomon was clothed. And it is at least unusual that, if left entirely up to him, he will clothe me as well as I can clothe myself. If so, and I care about how I am clothed, then I had better see to that myself. If I understand the tradition rightly, God first and foremost helps those who cannot help themselves, but one goal in doing this—not necessarily the only one—is to enable them to help themselves in the future.

This point stood out in a recent incident in which a Western reporter asked a middle-aged Jordanian Bedouin whether he thought the old ways or the new ways were better. "The new ways," he said. "Before we had to trust in God for when the rains came. But now, praise God, the water comes in the pipes!"[199] Piped water is reason for anyone to rejoice; the difficulty is in determining to whom the thanks are due. God may not be the proximal cause, but may be an important distal cause. If one knew who is really responsible, one would know whom to thank, but most of the time this knowledge eludes us.

I conclude that God's role as father and provider is often emphasized out of proportion to the evidence that God plays this role with corresponding frequency. I do not deny the appropriateness of the father analogy, but this role may be no more extensive than other roles that God plays. In the remainder of this chapter I suggest one supplement for the father analogy that is consistent with longstanding traditions in revealed theology. It should not be construed as more than a sketch, or as precluding alternatives. Before presenting it, additional stage setting is necessary.

7.4 MULTIPLE PERSONALITIES

Psychologists are not agreed on the existence of multiple personalities in the same person, or in the need for "multiple personality disorder" (MPD) as a disease category. Dennett theorizes that the existence of multiple personalities should not be surprising, however, and suggests an evolutionary model of how they could come about.[200] I agree that one could have a basis for

---

[199] He continued, "But the old ways were also better—our families were closer, our ties were stronger. Now they grow less and less every year."

[200] "The Origins of Selves," unpublished, 1989; *Consciousness Explained,* pp. 412–30.

postulating multiple personalities within a single being, although the extent to which it is a disorder is another matter. For example, biblical scholars generally agree that *Isaiah* was written by at least two different people. Here I assume for the sake of illustration that their conclusion is derived solely from textual evidence, rather than "external" considerations such as the age of the manuscripts, where they were found, etc. The textual evidence certainly suggests dual authorship, since the first 39 chapters have a markedly different writing style and thematic content than the last 27 chapters. Hence, if it turned out that a single individual were responsible for having written all 66 chapters, we would have a prima facie case for saying that he exhibited multiple personalities.[201]

One source of psychological skepticism of multiple personalities is skepticism about personalities themselves. Whatever else a personality may be, it should include "that which is contributed by the person to the determination of behavior," as opposed to that which circumstances or the environment contribute.[202] Behaviorists deny that the person contributes anything, and we saw Nisbett and Ross label the mistaken supposition that personality rather than situational factors causes behavior the "fundamental attribution error" (4.2.3). For methodological reasons described in chapter 5, psychologists commonly assume metaphysical determinism, which also inclines them to look for the causes of behavior outside any given personality. Moreover, the person's contribution is difficult to identify or isolate in practice.

'Personality' refers to a coherent, relatively stable system of dispositions to behavior covering a broad range of contingencies. These systems can also activate subsystems in appropriate circumstances, as when a person is "play-acting" or performing a functional role. This makes it difficult to individuate personalities or specify circumstances under which the dispositions manifest themselves, creating a problem of testability or circularity for the corresponding theories. Without straightforwardly observable stimulus-response conditions, one must usually rely on the theory being tested to describe the test conditions, or circumstances in which the dispositions become manifest. One can reach many conclusions when allowed to argue in a circle; consequently there are a great many theories of personality. These

---

[201]   Nicholas Humphrey and Daniel Dennett make a similar point in "Speaking for Our Selves: An Assessment of Multiple Personality Disorder," *Raritan* 9 (1989): 68–98, in arguing for the theoretical possibility of multiple personalities within a single being.

[202]   William Alston, "Traits, Consistency and Conceptual Alternatives for Personality Theory," in *Personality*, ed. by Harré (Basil Blackwell, 1976), p. 91.

can be grouped into various disciplinary matrices—theoretical paradigms in the Kuhnian sense—but since there are at least nine such paradigms in current use (as logged by one recent textbook on personality), general talk about personalities tends to become inchoate.[203]

This makes the claim that personalities don't exist appealing from a pragmatic point of view, though not necessarily from the standpoint of truth as correspondence. Following a pattern which we have seen repeatedly in earlier chapters, psychologists often base their rejection of personality as a category on allegations that it lacks utility, rather than evidence that such systems of dispositions are illusory. Some evidence exists in the form of "consistency studies" which have produced negative results for specific dispositions, indicating that they are not stable if they exist. But these studies are open to a number of interpretations. For example, the instruments used to measure the alleged personality trait may not do so accurately, or they may not be correlated with it tightly enough to afford means of predicting it. Even if one trait turns out to be illusory, others might not be.[204]

In view of this, practitioners have found it more appropriate to approach MPD directly through criteria that ostensibly indicate its existence, rather than through general considerations of personality. Referring to the absence of multiplicity as personality *integration,* and acknowledging that multiplicity is sometimes a matter of degree, Richard Kluft has proposed six conditions as jointly sufficient for personality integration. These are:[205]

> continuity of memory
> absence of dissociation
> a subjective sense of unity
> absence of alter personalities under hypnosis
> moderation of the transference consistent with fusion
> presence of the previously segregated feelings, attitudes, and memories in the fused personality.

These criteria employ theoretical terms that require some explanation.

---

[203] Duane Schultz, *Theories of Personality,* 2nd ed. (Monterey, CA: Brooks/Cole, 1981), p. 4. Indeed, many contemporary textbooks on personality appear to be little more than summaries of sample theories taken from each of the disciplinary matrices the author chooses to recognize.

[204] "Traits, Consistency and Conceptual Alternatives for Personality Theory," pp. 77–89.

[205] "Varieties of Hypnotic Intervention in the Treatment of Multiple Personality," *American Journal of Clinical Hypnosis* 24 (1981-2): 230–40.

In multiple personality disorder, there is typically an emotionally bland personality that is present most of the time and is called the "host." When situations arise in which the host personality cannot cope, or at other times that yet defy prediction, it gives way to one or more "alter" personalities, which are emotionally exaggerated to the point of being functionally one-dimensional, but are often recognizably different by such seemingly objective criteria as voice, accent, handwriting, and preferences regarding clothing, friends, and locales that they frequent. The most palpable evidence that these personalities are not integrated is that at least one apparently draws on pools of memories to which some of its counterparts lack access.[206] Although there is ample anecdotal evidence for the phenomenon, most of the systematically gathered evidence has been obtained using hypnosis.

An essential feature of multiple personalities, dissociation is widely regarded as a matter of degree.[207] Almost all hypnotic phenomena illustrate dissociation—i.e., they show that more than one system of control is in operation. In posthypnotic amnesia, for example, a person is incapable of recalling memories that are recoverable if hypnotized again. More generally, in Ernest Hilgard's words, "dissociated systems can be identified as relatively coherent patterns of behavior with sufficient complexity to represent some degree of internal organization."[208] Nevertheless, such control systems are never fully autonomous, or completely free of one another's interference. One might think of dissociated systems of the multiple personality sort as maximally coherent sets of the kinds of behavioral dispositions that normally constitute personality, but such dispositions need not relate to a person's ability to remember or the specific contents of her memory. Rather, memory discontinuity seems to be a common *symptom* of multiplicity which is being substituted for a lack of objective criteria. Setting this symptom aside, many people might appear to manifest more than one personality to a degree, were it not for prevailing resistance among psychologists to the personality category in general, and multiplicity in particular. The crucial question would be whether the various control systems are competing with one another, or

---

[206] See "Speaking for Our Selves"; Ernest Hilgard, *Divided Consciousness,* expanded ed. (New York: Wiley, 1986), p. 27. Usually it is the host personality that has little or no access to the alters' memories, while the alters at least claim to have access to those of the host.

[207] Ernest Hilgard, "Dissociation Revisited," in *Historical Conceptions of Psychology,* ed. by Henle, Jaynes, and Sullivan (New York: Springer, 1973), p. 216; Peter McKellar, *Mindsplit* (London: Dent, 1979), p. 27.

[208] *Divided Consciousness,* p. 18; "Dissociation Revisited," p. 212–3.

struggling for hegemony. Control subsystems coexist more-or-less harmoniously in a well-integrated personality, occupying functional nodes in a stable, control hierarchy. If consciousness emerges from a "pandemonium," however, as recently suggested by Dennett, then stable, well-integrated personalities may not be the paradigm of normalcy after all.[209]

Providing better criteria for multiplicity is still difficult. One possible way would be to design an appropriate kind of Turing test. In the original Turing test a standardized output format was posited as a means of testing for the existence of intelligence, or personhood, on the other side of an epistemic barrier. Perhaps a similar test could furnish a suitable criterion for multiple personalities. Let psychiatrists be the judges. A standardized computer terminal interface would perhaps make it too difficult to search the subjects for clues regarding personality integration, but at least a visual barrier between subject and judge would be necessary to prevent the judge's knowledge of the physical source of the output from contaminating his judgment of the number of personalities involved. The epistemic barrier presented by the *Isaiah* case illustrates how such a test might lead to ascriptions of multiplicity. My point is that, to the extent we do recognize personalities as a category that has not been reduced or eliminated in favor of more precise terminology, there seems to be no a priori reason for supposing that more than one could not be manifested by the same person.

There is also ample historical tradition for making such attributions. Hilgard compares dissociative states of the multiple personality kind to historically alleged cases of demon possession.[210] Socrates also speaks as if his body has a mind of its own, so that if it were not for his soul, "these bones and sinews would have been in the neighborhood of Megara or Boeotia long ago" (*Phaedo* 99a). In *Romans,* Paul paints a dramatic picture of personal pathos suggestive of the existence of multiple personalities, concluding:

> For the good that I wish, I do not do; but I practice the very evil that I do not wish. But if I am doing the very thing I do not wish, I am no longer the one doing it, but sin which dwells in me. I find then the principle that evil is present in me, the one who wishes to do good. For I joyfully concur with the law of God in the inner man, but I see a different law in the members of my body, waging war against the law of my mind, and making me a prisoner of the law of sin which is in my members. Wretched man that I am!

---

[209] *Consciousness Explained,* pp. 234–52.

[210] *Divided Consciousness,* pp. 19–21, 40.

Elsewhere he describes the personalities dwelling within him as old and new natures, the new nature being that which is supposedly the more god-like. Perhaps it is here if anywhere that one might find more direct and dependable manifestations of God's existence—being the supposed cutting edge of the war against evil. Much of the New Testament appears devoted to disabusing us of the notion that the battle lines between good and evil are to be drawn between nations, between religions, or even between one person and the next. Rather, the penchant to do evil resides within every person and is supposedly the object of God's efforts to purify and sanctify—efforts that this penchant naturally resists.

7.5   THE NASCENCE ARCHETYPE

If Paul is correct that believers contain within them both newer and older selves, one might reasonably ask how the newer personality arrived on the scene. A natural answer would be that this happens in a way similar to how the old nature arrived—via birth. John quotes Jesus as speaking of a new birth, or a rebirth. William James also finds nascence a common theme throughout mystical literature, both eastern and western.[211] This rebirth is almost universally said to be brought about or facilitated by God, though under many different interpretations of God's nature. The newness or new nature is then thought to manifest God within that person's life. All of this is reminiscent of a recurrent theme from Greek and Hebrew mythology according to which God (or the gods) occasionally uses people as a means of begetting offspring which are, in effect, half god and half human.

This leads me to supplement the father analogy with two other roles which God may frequently play in a believer's life—that of lover and of child. Space does not permit me to address the role of lover here, but there is ample textual support for it. But perhaps the greatest part of a person's relation to God is mediated by this newborn nature or personality, which I describe analogically as a case in which God plays more or less the role of child. Once again, I do not deny that God functions at times as a spiritual father; I merely point out that this model of our relation to God does not account adequately for a lot of religious experience, and other mundane facts pertaining to the existence of evil. I have no solution for the unclarity that results from complementarity in models (see 1.6)—viz., that no general rule

---

[211]   *The Varieties of Religious Experience*, p. 413.

exists for predicting what personality might manifest itself next, or when to expect God to function in the role of father, lover, or child.

Before carrying the analogy further, let me approach it from a different direction. As mentioned at the beginning of this chapter, it is more or less up to the individual to take up the gauntlet of exploring and elaborating religious explanations. The task is by no means easy, but the project does not lend itself to being deferred or turned over to a committee. Ultimate success is not assured, nor will ultimate failure necessarily be discovered quickly if it is to occur. In many ways, such a project starts at the moment it is conceived, and becomes the baby of the person who undertakes it. This is not to say that God is merely an idea, or that this is the only direction by which one might become related to God. It is not. But it is not far, epistemologically speaking, from having the idea that a God might exist to the belief that in reality God does exist, since the latter can only be known by mediation of the mind whose idea it was in the first place. Thus one of the pioneers of the concept of dissociation, Pierre Janet, once said "Things happen as if an idea, a partial system of thoughts, emancipated itself, became independent, and developed itself on its own account."[212] Again, the *physical* evidence for God does not seem incontrovertible.

Whichever way one approaches the issue, the child aspect of God is by way of analogy, but the effect on the person manifesting it is real. This does not prove that it has supernatural origins; indeed, age regression is commonly found in association with hypnosis.[213] But this is one place where direct manifestations of God's existence might be found. Identifying them as such would not be a matter of the apparent age of the nascent personality, but would require evaluating at least its goodness or wonderfulness. Should the new personality turn out to contain a spark of the divine, it would indeed represent the offspring of both God and the person in whom it is birthed. I think it is presumptuous of Paul to identify himself with the new nature, claiming to be the good side of his personality while blaming the bad side on sin working within him. The believer must exist first for God to become birthed within, which also makes more sense from the standpoint of Luke's saying that "the kingdom of God comes not with observation . . . for, behold, the kingdom of God is within you." The believer might then know God's manifestation in her life somewhat as Elijah allegedly did—namely, as a "still, small voice."

---

[212] *The Major Symptoms of Hysteria,* 2nd ed. (New York: Holt, 1920).

[213] See *Divided Consciousness,* chapter 3.

To the extent that God plays the role of infant or child in a person's life, the person plays basically the role of the breast that nourishes it—nursing, supporting, and protecting it. From the standpoint of religious traditions and texts, projecting humans in the female role relative to God is very common. In the *I Ching,* for example, the heavens are universally associated with male qualities and the earth with female qualities. Few traditions compare God to a mother rather than to a father, but many Old Testament passages suggest that all people are as women in the presence of God, and both Paul and John speak of the Church as "the Bride of Christ."[214] There are other reasons for symbolizing the relation of man to God as analogous to the relation of breast to infant. Even as in the vernacular the breast is called the "boob" (from 'bosom'?), so science fiction writers and others with a futuristic perspective often portray humans as the less rational of intelligent beings, more prone to emotion, thoughtlessness, and other human "foibles." Moreover, this is one of the features that makes humans so attractive, at least from our perspective. As humans, we could hardly stand to live *with* a rational automaton all of our life, let alone *as* one. The human breast has what it takes both to sustain life and make that life attractive and desirable. Finding Captain Kirk after having been surrounded by space aliens for a few stellar epochs would be almost like finding one's mother.

Why put up with a God that functions in our lives more often as a child than in other roles? Certainly, children constitute liabilities in many ways, and inviting them into one's life may not make much sense on a cost/ benefit basis. Children do not provide for their parents, but parents provide for their children, as Paul says. Yet there are values which even young children can contribute to an adult's life, which for want of a better word might be called "aesthetic." Also, with time children mature and one's investment in them bears fruit. And then—who knows?—perhaps they will care for us when we can no longer care for ourselves. If the issue is not whether to *have* children, but whether to have *this kind* of child, the obvious reply is that having a little angel might be preferable in many ways to the other kinds possible (little devils?). At any rate, whether belief in God is by choice or forced, it takes on the gravity that bearing children does in terms of commitment, or its momentous effect on one's immediate and subsequent life. Discussions of the rationality of religious belief often overlook this gravity. For example, in arguing for his famous wager Pascal suggests that the cost of religious belief is trifling. Without overlooking this gravity, the question

---

[214] *Isaiah* 19:16; *Jeremiah* 50:37, 51:30; *Nahum* 3:13; *Ephesians* 5:23–33; *Revelation* 21.

would never arise whether belief that God exists is analogous to belief that one's mother-in-law exists.

It is a familiar religious theme dating to Plato that since God is perfect, it is impossible for him to be improved by anything we do, nor does he particularly need or benefit from anything we might give him. Yet the standard Christian belief that Jesus is God suggests that he did need the nourishment of his mortal parents, and benefitted from them directly. This is not to say that they improved him morally, of course. Still, there is some precedent for supposing that God derives benefit or pleasure from people through their sacrifices. This benefit is characterized as nourishment under my model, as God, or the "God idea," grows within the individual. Children can be expected to need a considerable period of growth before they are able to accomplish anything important. Jesus had to learn to walk and talk like the rest of us. To the extent that God functions as a child in the believer's life, God is not functioning as omnipotent or omniscient. I am not sure how far one can go with this nascence archetype, but let me say this much. At a time when mathematics was thought to be an essential part of God's creation, it seemed more plausible to suppose that God knows all of the truths of mathematics. One could then rationalize God's unwillingness to reveal them to us by saying that he does not want to spoil our fun in discovering them for ourselves. But as it has become more apparent that the foundations of mathematics are somewhat arbitrary—that much of the structure involves artifices of human invention—it becomes less clear whether God even has any *interest* in the truths of mathematics, or why he *should*. If not, omniscience may be more a liability than an asset; perhaps God would prefer freedom from the drudgery of having to know everything.

As mentioned, infancy has a downside—young children make a home far different from what it would be otherwise. But charging Christian morality with being infantile is unfair insofar as the charge ignores many of the good values in children while focusing on the bad.[215] Specifically, when Persinger describes the belief that one has received a personal message from Almighty God as exemplifying childlike egocentrism—noting that it is found most commonly in sheltered or uneducated adults[216]—he is not only arguing ad hominem, but failing to recognize the virtue of childlike innocence while taking for granted the philosophical virtue of exposing the intellect to

---

[215] Among others, this charge has been made by Patrick Nowell-Smith in "Morality: Religious and Secular," *The Rationalist Annual, 1961* (London: Pemberton).

[216] *Neuropsychological Bases of God Beliefs*, pp. 20, 45.

"perpetual vivisection." Another psychologist suggests that if beliefs derived from religious experiences were not so pervasive, they would on their own merits be considered pathological.[217] Again, the same could be said of the behavior of children, if considered apart from knowledge of the fact that they *are* children. Persinger also describes religious belief as an "addiction" or "obsession," as if it were a consuming parasite upon those holding it.[218] All of this could also be said about the typical relation of mothers toward their children. Perhaps these scientists are revealing a bit of their own androcentrism here.

It was previously suggested that ideas sometimes take on a life of their own. Given the "maxim of minimum mutilation," one does not want to kill them off until they have had ample opportunity to prove themselves. If it is true that scientific mindsets do not provide an environment suitable for nourishing religious ideas—any more than scientific laboratories do—it is not obvious to me that this is the fault of the ideas themselves, rather than the fault of the mindsets and laboratories. However, the breast that protects and nourishes may also be guilty of overprotecting its personal or intellectual offspring. If such overprotection can sometimes be rationalized from the standpoint of one's considerable investment, this still seems a primary source of irrational belief. There is some justification for accusing religious people of this, since they are often reluctant to confront openly and fairly the question of whether the existence of God or the Holy Spirit is really manifest within them, or whether it is an idea lacking external reality. Popper's general approach has something to be said for it: rather than try to shelter one's beliefs from criticism, it is preferable to expose them to vigorous attempts at falsification. If God is real, then the God idea should thrive resiliently in an environment that is sometimes hostile, even as all living things must. The phenomena by which God's presence manifests itself must be robust. But the believer has some discretion, such as any parent would exercise, in determining when his offspring is mature enough to face this treatment.

---

[217] Graham Reed, *The Psychology of Anomalous Experience,* p. 122.

[218] *Neuropsychological Bases of God Beliefs,* pp. 5–7, 19, 27, 31.

REFERENCES

Philosophical and Religious Works

Ackermann, Robert. *Data, Instruments, and Theory.* Princeton Univ. Press, 1985.

Alcock, James. "Psychology and Near-Death Experiences." In *Paranormal Borderlands of Science,* ed. by Kendrick Frazier, 153–69. Buffalo: Prometheus, 1981.

Alston, William. *Perceiving God.* Cornell Univ. Press, 1991.

_____. "Perceiving God." *Journal of Philosophy* 83 (1986): 655–65.

_____. "Traits, Consistency and Conceptual Alternatives for Personality Theory." In *Personality,* ed. by Rom Harré, 63–97. Basil Blackwell, 1976.

Arbib, Michael, and Mary Hesse. *The Construction of Reality.* Cambridge Univ. Press, 1987.

Barbour, Ian. *Myths, Models and Paradigms.* New York: Harper & Row, 1974.

Bechtel, William. "Two Common Errors in Explaining Biological and Psychological Phenomena." *Philosophy of Science* 49 (1982): 549–74.

Bell, John. *Speakable and Unspeakable in Quantum Mechanics.* Cambridge Univ. Press, 1987.

Bradie, Michael. "Assessing Evolutionary Epistemology." *Biology and Philosophy* 1 (1986): 401–59.

Braude, Stephen. *The Limits of Influence: Psychokinesis and the Philosophy of Science.* London: Routledge and Kegan Paul, 1986.

Broad, C. D. "Arguments for the Existence of God, II." *Journal of Theological Studies* 40 (1939): 157–67.

Brody, Baruch, ed. *Readings in the Philosophy of Religion.* Englewood

Cliffs, NJ: Prentice-Hall, 1974.

Bromberger, Sylvain. "Why-Questions." In *Mind and Cosmos,* ed. by Robert Colodny, 86–111. Univ. of Pittsburgh Press, 1966.

Bultmann, Rudolf. *Jesus Christ and Mythology.* New York: Scribner's, 1958.

Burkhardt, Frederick, ed. *William James: The Will to Believe, and Other Essays in Popular Philosophy.* Harvard Univ. Press, 1979.

Cartwright, Nancy. *Nature's Capacities and their Measurement.* Oxford: Clarendon Press, 1989.

_____. *How the Laws of Physics Lie.* Oxford: Clarendon Press, 1983.

Cherniak, Christopher. *Minimal Rationality.* MIT Press, 1986.

Churchland, Patricia. *Neurophilosophy.* MIT Press, 1986.

_____. "A Perspective on Mind-Brain Research." *Journal of Philosophy* 77 (1980): 185–207.

Churchland, Paul. "Eliminative Materialism and Propositional Attitudes." *Journal of Philosophy* 78 (1981): 67–89.

Coady, C. A. J. *Testimony: A Philosophical Study.* Oxford: Clarendon Press, 1992. (4)

Colwell, Gary. "The Flew-Nielsen Challenge: A Critical Exposition of its Methodology." *Religious Studies* 17 (1981): 323–42.

Cook, Thomas, and Donald Campbell. "The Causal Assumptions of Quasi-Experimental Practice." *Synthese* 68 (1986): 141–80.

Cooper, Gregory. "Fitness and Explanation." *PSA 1988* 1: 207–215.

Cummins, Robert. *The Nature of Psychological Explanation.* MIT Press, 1983.

Cushing, James, and Ernan McMullin, eds. *Philosophical Consequences of Quantum Theory.* Univ. of Notre Dame Press, 1989.

Davies, P. C. W., and J. R. Brown, eds. *The Ghost in the Atom.* Cambridge Univ. Press, 1986.

Davis, Caroline Franks. *The Evidential Force of Religious Experience.* Oxford: Clarendon Press, 1989.

Dennett, Daniel. *Consciousness Explained.* New York: Little Brown, 1991.

_____. *Brainstorms.* MIT Press, 1981.

_____. *Elbow Room: The Varieties of Free Will Worth Wanting.* MIT Press, 1984.

_____. *The Intentional Stance.* MIT Press, 1987.

_____. "I Could Not Have Done Otherwise—So What?" *Journal of Philosophy* 81 (1984): 553–65.

_____. "The Origins of Selves." Unpublished, 1989.

Doppelt, Gerald. "Kuhn's Epistemological Relativism: An Interpretation and Defense." *Inquiry* 21 (1978): 33–86. Reprinted in *Relativism: Cognitive and Moral,* ed. by Michael Krausz and Jack Meiland, 113–46. Univ of Notre Dame Press, 1982.

Doyle, Arthur Conan. *The Coming of the Fairies.* London, 1922.

Dretske, Fred. "Précis of *Knowledge and the Flow of Information.*" *Behavioral and Brain Sciences* 6 (1983): 55–63.

Ennis, Robert. "Enumerative Induction and Best Explanation." *Journal of Philosophy* 65 (1968): 523–9.

Feyerabend, Paul. *Farewell to Reason.* London: Verso, 1987.

Flew, Antony. *God and Philosophy.* London: Hutchinson, 1966.

_____. "Theology and Falsification in Retrospect." In *The Logic of God: Theology and Verification,* ed. by Malcolm Diamond and Thomas Litzenburg, 269–283. Indianapolis: Bobbs-Merrill, 1975.

Fodor, Jerry. *Representations.* MIT Press, 1981.

Forgie, J. William. "The Principle of Credulity and the Evidential Value of Religious Experience." *International Journal for Philosophy of Religion* 19 (1986): 145–59.

Gardner, Edward. *A Book of Real Fairies: The Cottingley Photographs and their Sequel.* London, 1945.

Garfinkel, Alan. *Forms of Explanation: Rethinking the Questions of Social Theory.* Yale Univ. Press, 1981.

Gettier, Edmund. "Is Justified True Belief Knowledge?" *Analysis* 23 (1963): 121–3.

Gibson, Roger. *The Philosophy of W. V. Quine: An Expository Essay.* Univ. Press of Florida, 1982.

Gilman, Daniel. *Lines of Sight: An Essay on Mind, Vision, and Pictorial Representation.* Ph.D. Dissertation: Univ. of Chicago, 1988.

Glymour, Clark. *Theory and Evidence.* Princeton Univ. Press, 1980.

Goldman, Alvin. *Epistemology and Cognition.* Harvard Univ. Press, 1986.

Goodman, Nelson. *Problems and Projects.* Indianapolis: Bobbs-Merrill, 1972.

Grünbaum, Adolf. "Epistemological Liabilities of the Clinical Appraisal of Psychoanalytic Theory." *Noûs* 14 (1980): 307–85.

_____. "Is Freudian Theory Pseudo-Scientific by Karl Popper's Criterion of Demarcation?" *American Philosophical Quarterly* 16 (1979): 131–41.

_____. "Retrospective and Prospective Testing of Aetiological Hypotheses in Freudian Theory." In *Testing Scientific Theories,* ed. by John Earman, 315–47. Univ. of Minnesota Press, 1983.

Gutting, Gary. *Religious Belief and Religious Scepticism.* Univ. of Notre Dame Press, 1982.

Hacking, Ian. *Representing and Intervening.* Cambridge Univ. Press, 1983.

_____. "Experimentation and Scientific Realism." In *Scientific Realism,* ed. by Jarrett Leplin, 154–72. Univ. of California Press, 1984.

Hahlweg, Kai, and C. A. Hooker, eds. *Issues in Evolutionary Epistemology.* Albany: SUNY Press, 1989.

Harman, Gilbert. "Enumerative Induction as Inference to the Best Explanation." *Journal of Philosophy* 65 (1968): 529–33.

_____. "Inference to the Best Explanation." *Philosophical Review* 74 (1965): 88–95.

Harré, Rom. *The Principles of Scientific Thinking.* Univ. of Chicago Press, 1970.

Hempel, Carl. *Aspects of Scientific Explanation.* New York: Free, 1965.

_____. *Philosophy of Natural Science.* Englewood Cliffs, NJ: Prentice-Hall, 1966.

Hempel, Carl, and Paul Oppenheim. "Studies in the Logic of Explanation." *Philosophy of Science* 15 (1948): 135–75.

Henderson, David. "The Principle of Charity and the Problem of Irrationality." *Synthese* 73 (1987): 225–52.

_____. "A Solution to Davidson's Paradox of Irrationality." *Erkenntnis* 27 (1987): 359–69.

Hick, John. *Faith and Knowledge.* Cornell Univ. Press, 1957.

_____. "Theology and Verification." *Theology Today* 17 (1960).

Hines, Terence. *Pseudoscience and the Paranormal.* Buffalo: Prometheus, 1988.

Hobbes, Thomas. *Leviathan.* 1651.

Hobbs, Jesse. "A Limited Defense of the Pessimistic Induction." *British Journal for the Philosophy of Science* forthcoming.

Humphrey, Nicholas, and Daniel Dennett. "Speaking for Our Selves: An Assessment of Multiple Personality Disorder." *Raritan* 9, 1 (1989): 68–98.

Jaki, Stanley. *The Paradox of Olbers' Paradox.* New York: Herder & Herder, 1969.

James, William. *The Varieties of Religious Experience.* New York: Random House, 1929.

_____. *The Will to Believe, and Other Essays in Popular Philosophy,* ed. by Frederick Burkhardt. Harvard Univ. Press, 1979.

Kane, Robert. *Free Will and Values.* Albany: SUNY Press, 1985.

Kenny, Anthony. *Faith and Reason.* Columbia Univ. Press, 1983.

Kitcher, Philip. "1953 and All That: A Tale of Two Sciences." *Philosophical Review* 93 (1984): 335–74.

Kuhn, Thomas. *The Essential Tension.* Univ. of Chicago Press, 1977.

_____. *The Structure of Scientific Revolutions,* 2nd ed. Univ. of Chicago Press, 1970.

_____. "Reflections on My Critics." In *Criticism and the Growth of Knowledge,* ed. by Imre Lakatos and Alan Musgrave, 231–78. Cambridge Univ. Press, 1970.

Küng, Hans. *Freud and the Problem of God.* Yale Univ. Press, 1979.

Kurtz, Paul. "Is Parapsychology a Science?" In *Paranormal Borderlands of Science,* ed. by Kendrick Frazier, 5–23. Buffalo: Prometheus, 1981.

Lakatos, Imre. "The Methodology of Scientific Research Programmes." In *Criticism and the Growth of Knowledge,* ed. by Imre Lakatos and Alan Musgrave, 91–196. Cambridge Univ. Press, 1970.

Laudan, Larry. *Progress and Its Problems.* Univ. of California Press, 1977.

_____. *Science and Values: the Aims of Science and their Role in Scientific Debate.* Univ. of California Press, 1984.

Levi, Isaac. "Escape from Boredom: Edification According to Rorty." *Canadian Journal of Philosophy* 11, 4 (1981): 589–601.

Locke, John. *Essay Concerning Human Understanding.* 1690.

MacKinnon, Edward. "Scientific Realism: The New Debates." *Philosophy of Science* 46 (1979): 501–32.

Martin, Michael. "The Principle of Credulity and Religious Experience." *Religious Studies* 22 (1986): 79–93.

McDermott, John J., ed. *The Writings of William James.* Univ. of Chicago Press, 1977.

Mermin, N. David. "Can You Help Your Team Tonight by Watching on TV?" In *Philosophical Consequences of Quantum Theory,* ed. by James Cushing and Ernan McMullin, 38–59. Univ. of Notre Dame Press, 1989.

Millikan, Ruth. "Truth-Rules, Hoverflies, and the Kripke-Wittgenstein Paradox." *Philosophical Review* 99 (1990): 323–53.

Mitchell, Basil. *The Justification of Belief.* New York: Macmillan, 1973.

_____. "Theology and Falsification." In *New Essays in Philosophical Theology,* ed. by Antony Flew and Alasdair MacIntyre. London: SCM Press, 1955.

Mitroff, Ian. *The Subjective Side of Science.* Amsterdam: Elsevier, 1974.

Murphy, Nancey. *Theology in the Age of Scientific Reasoning.* Cornell Univ. Press, 1990.

Newton-Smith, William H. *The Rationality of Science*. London: Routledge & Kegan Paul, 1981.

Nickles, Thomas. "Two Concepts of Intertheoretic Reduction." *Journal of Philosophy* 70 (1973): 181–201.

Nielsen, Kai. *An Introduction to the Philosophy of Religion*. New York: St. Martin's, 1982.

Nowell-Smith, Patrick. "Morality: Religious and Secular." *The Rationalist Annual, 1961*. London: Pemberton. Reprinted in *Readings in the Philosophy of Religion,* ed. by Baruch Brody. Englewood Cliffs, NJ: Prentice-Hall, 1974.

Pickering, Andrew. *Constructing Quarks*. Univ. of Chicago Press, 1984.

Plantinga, Alvin. "An Evolutionary Argument Against Naturalism." In *Faith in Theory and Practice: Essays on the Justification of Religious Belief,* ed. by Elizabeth Radcliffe and Carol White. La Salle, IL: Open Court, 1993.

_____. "Justification in the 20th Century." *Philosophy and Phenomenological Research* 50 Supp. (Fall 1990): 45–71.

_____. "Reason and Belief in God." In *Faith and Rationality: Reason and Belief in God,* ed. by Alvin Plantinga and Nicholas Wolterstorff, 16–93. Univ. of Notre Dame Press, 1983.

Plato. *Republic*.

Popper, Karl. *Conjectures and Refutations*. New York: Basic, 1962.

Prevost, Robert. "Swinburne, Mackie and Bayes' Theorem." *International Journal for Philosophy of Religion* 17 (1985): 175–84.

Proudfoot, Wayne. *Religious Experience*. Univ. of California Press, 1985.

Putnam, Hilary. *Meaning and the Moral Sciences*. London: Routledge & Kegan Paul, 1978.

Quine, W. V. *Pursuit of Truth*. Harvard Univ. Press, 1990.

_____. "Ontology and Ideology Revisited." *Journal of Philosophy* 80 (1983): 499–502.

_____. *Theories and Things*. Harvard Univ. Press, 1981.

_____. *Ontological Relativity and Other Essays*. Columbia Univ. Press, 1969.

_____. *Word and Object*. MIT Press, 1960.

_____. "Ontology and Ideology." *Philosophical Studies* 2 (1951): 11–15.

_____. "Two Dogmas of Empiricism." *Philosophical Review* 60 (1951): 20–43.

Radnitzky, Gerard, and W. W. Bartley, eds. *Evolutionary Epistemology, Theory of Rationality, and the Sociology of Knowledge*. La Salle, IL:

Open Court, 1987.

Randi, James. "A Report on Project Alpha." In *Science Confronts the Paranormal,* ed. by Kendrick Frazier, 158–65. Buffalo: Prometheus, 1986.

Rogo, D. Scott. *Return from Silence.* Northamptonshire, England: Aquarian Press, 1989.

Rorty, Richard. *Philosophy and the Mirror of Nature.* Princeton Univ. Press, 1979.

Rosenberg, Alexander. *Sociobiology and the Preemption of Social Science.* Baltimore: Johns Hopkins, 1980.

_____. "Fitness." *Journal of Philosophy* 80 (1983): 457–73.

Roth, Paul. *Meaning and Method in the Social Sciences.* Cornell Univ. Press, 1987.

Roth, Paul, and Robert Barrett. "Deconstructing Quarks." *Social Studies of Science* 20 (1990): 579–631.

Rowe, William. "Religious Experience and the Principle of Credulity." *International Journal for Philosophy of Religion* 13 (1982): 85–92.

Rudner, Richard. *Philosophy of Social Science.* Englewood Cliffs, NJ: Prentice-Hall, 1966.

Russell, Bertrand. *Religion and Science.* London: Oxford Univ. Press, 1935.

Salmon, Wesley. *Scientific Explanation and the Causal Structure of the World.* Princeton Univ. Press, 1984.

Scheffler, Israel. *Science and Subjectivity,* 2nd ed. Indianapolis: Hackett, 1982.

Schoen, Edward. *Religious Explanations: A Model from the Sciences.* Duke Univ. Press, 1985.

Sheaffer, Robert. "Do Fairies Exist?" *The Skeptical Inquirer* 2 (1977): 45–52. Reprinted in *Paranormal Borderlands of Science,* ed. by Kendrick Frazier, 68–75. Buffalo: Prometheus, 1981.

Sober, Elliott. *Simplicity.* Oxford: Clarendon Press, 1975.

Spector, Marshall. *Concepts of Reduction in Physical Science.* Philadelphia: Temple Univ. Press, 1978.

Stegmüller, Wolfgang. *The Structuralist View of Theories: A Possible Analog to the Bourbaki Programme in Physical Science.* Berlin: Springer, 1979.

_____. *The Structure and Dynamics of Theories.* Berlin: Springer, 1976.

Stich, Stephen. "Could Man be an Irrational Animal? Some Notes on the Epistemology of Rationality." *Synthese* 64 (1985): 115–35.

_____. *From Folk Psychology to Cognitive Science: The Case Against Belief.* MIT Press, 1983.

Stoll, Clifford. *The Cuckoo's Egg: Tracking a Spy through the Maze of Computer Espionage.* New York: Doubleday, 1989.

Suppe, Frederick. *The Semantic Conception of Theories and Scientific Realism.* Univ. of Illinois Press, 1989.

Suppes, Patrick. "What Is a Scientific Theory?" In *Philosophy of Science Today,* ed. by Sidney Morgenbesser, 55–67. New York: Basic, 1967.

Swinburne, Richard. *The Existence of God.* Oxford: Clarendon Press, 1979.

_____. "The Christian Wager." *Religious Studies* 4 (1969): 217–28.

Thompson, Paul. "The Structure of Evolutionary Theory: A Semantic Approach." *Studies in the History and Philosophy of Science* 14 (1983): 215–29.

Toulmin, Stephen. *The Philosophy of Science: An Introduction.* London: Hutchinson, 1967.

Trusted, Jennifer. *Free Will and Responsibility.* Oxford Univ. Press, 1984.

Van Fraassen, Bas. *The Scientific Image.* Oxford: Clarendon Press, 1980.

_____. "Empiricism in the Philosophy of Science." In *Images of Science,* ed. by Paul Churchland and Clifford Hooker, 245–308. Univ. of Chicago Press, 1985.

_____. "A Formal Approach to the Philosophy of Science." In *Paradigms and Paradoxes,* ed. by Robert Colodny, 303–66. Univ. of Pittsburgh Press, 1972.

_____. "Glymour on Evidence and Explanation." In *Testing Scientific Theories,* ed. by John Earman, 165–76. Univ. of Minnesota Press, 1983.

Van Inwagen, Peter. *An Essay on Free Will.* Oxford: Clarendon Press, 1983.

_____. "Dennett on 'Could Have Done Otherwise'." *Journal of Philosophy* 81 (1984): 565–7.

_____. "Ability and Responsibility." *Philosophical Review* 87 (1978): 201–24.

Wigner, Eugene. "Remarks on the Mind-Body Question." In *The Scientist Speculates: An Anthology of Partly-Baked Ideas,* ed. by I. J. Good, 284–302. London: Heinemann, 1962.

Williams, Mary, and Alexander Rosenberg. "'Fitness' in Fact and Fiction: A Rejoinder to Sober." *Journal of Philosophy* 82 (1985): 738–49.

Wilshire, Bruce, ed. *William James: The Essential Writings.* Harper & Row, 1971.

Wimsatt, William. "Reduction, Levels of Organization, and the Mind-Body Problem." In *Consciousness and the Brain: A Scientific and Philosophical Inquiry,* ed. by Gordon Globus, et. al., 205–67. New York: Plenum, 1976.

Wolterstorff, Nicholas. *Reason within the Bounds of Religion,* 2nd ed. Grand Rapids, MI: Eerdman's, 1984.

Woodward, James. "Are Singular Causal Explanations Implicit Covering-Law Explanations?" *Canadian Journal of Philosophy* 16 (1986): 253–80.

Woolgar, Steve. *Science: The Very Idea.* Chichester: Ellis Horwood, 1988.

Wuketits, Franz, ed. *Concepts and Approaches in Evolutionary Epistemology.* Dordrecht: Reidel, 1984.

Scientific Works

Argyle, Edward. "Ball Lightning as an Optical Illusion." *Nature* 230 (1971): 179–80.

Barringer, D. M. "Note on the 'Green Flash'." *Popular Astronomy* 57 (1949): 252–3.

Bates, Brian, and Adrian Stanley. "The Epidemiology and Differential Diagnosis of Near-Death Experience." *American Journal of Orthopsychiatry* 55 (1985): 542–9.

Beecher, Henry K. "Surgery as Placebo: A Quantitative Study of Bias." *Journal of the American Medical Association* 176 (1961): 1102–7.

Benson, Herbert, and David McCallie. "Angina Pectoris and the Placebo Effect." *New England Journal of Medicine* 300, 25 (1979): 1424–9.

Berger, K. "Kugelblitz und Blitzforschung." *Naturwissenschaften* 60 (1973): 485–92.

Blinderman, Charles. *The Piltdown Inquest.* Buffalo: Prometheus, 1986.

Borgida, E., and R. E. Nisbett. "The Differential Impact of Abstract vs. Concrete Information on Decisions." *Journal of Applied Social Psychology* 7 (1977): 258–71.

Buckhout, Robert. "Eyewitness Testimony." *Scientific American* 231, 6 (1974): 23–31.

Comrie, L. J. "The Green (?) Flash (?)." *Journal of the British Astronomical Association* 58 (1948): 280. Reprinted in *Popular Astronomy* 57 (1949): 42–3.

Culliton, Barbara. "Harvard and Monsanto: The $23-Million Alliance."

Science 195 (1977): 759–63.

Davies, P.C.W. "Ball Lightning or Spots Before the Eyes?" *Nature* 230 (1971): 576–7.

Drab, Kevin. "The Tunnel Experience: Reality or Hallucination?" *Anabiosis* 1 (1981): 126–153.

Eliade, Mircea. "Cultural Fashions and the History of Religion." In *The History of Religions: Essays on the Problem of Understanding,* ed. by Joseph Kitagawa, 21–38. Univ. of Chicago Press, 1967.

Folkman, Judah, and Michael Klagsbrun. "Angiogenic Factors." *Science* 235 (1987): 442–7.

Gabbard, Glen, and Stuart Twemlow. "Do 'Near-Death Experiences' Occur Only Near Death?—Revisited." *Journal of Near-Death Studies* 10, 1 (1991): 41–7.

Gabbard, Glen, Stuart Twemlow, and F. Jones. "Do 'Near-Death Experiences' Occur Only Near Death?" *Journal of Nervous and Mental Disease* 169 (1981): 374–7.

Gardner, Martin. "Mathematical Games." *Scientific American* 223 (1970): 120–3.

Gliksman, Michael, and Allan Kellehear. "Near-Death Experiences and the Measurement of Blood Gases." *Journal of Near-Death Studies* 9, 1 (1990): 41–3.

Greyson, Bruce. "Near Death Experiences and Attempted Suicide." *Suicide and Life-Threatening Behavior* 11 (1981): 10–16.

Grosso, Michael. "Toward an Explanation of Near-Death Phenomena." *Journal of the American Society for Psychical Research* 75 (1981): 37–60.

Hamill, R., T. D. Wilson, and R. E. Nisbett. "Insensitivity to Sample Bias: Generalizing from Atypical Cases." *Journal of Personality and Social Psychology* 39 (1980): 578–89.

Harrison, E. R. "The Dark Night-Sky Riddle: A Paradox that Resisted Solution." *Science* 226 (1984): 941–5.

Henderson, Y., and H. W. Haggard. *Noxious Gases and the Principles of Respiration Influencing their Action.* New York: American Chemical Society, 1927.

Hilgard, Ernest. *Divided Consciousness: Multiple Controls in Human Thought and Action,* expanded ed. New York: Wiley, 1986.

_____. "Dissociation Revisited." In *Historical Conceptions of Psychology,* ed. by Mary Henle, Julian Jaynes, and John Sullivan, 205–19. New York: Springer, 1973.

Holden, Janice, and Leroy Joesten. "Near-Death Veridicality Research in the

Hospital Setting: Problems and Promise." *Journal of Near-Death Studies* 9, 1 (1990): 45–54.

Janet, Pierre. *The Major Symptoms of Hysteria,* 2nd ed. New York: Holt, 1920.

Kahneman, Daniel, and Amos Tversky. "Subjective Probability: A Judgment of Representativeness." *Cognitive Psychology* 3 (1971): 430–54.

Kelley, H. H., and A. J. Stahelski. "Social Interaction Basis of Cooperators' and Competitors' Belief about Others." *Journal of Personality and Social Psychology* 16 (1970): 66–91.

Kluft, Richard. "Varieties of Hypnotic Intervention in the Treatment of Multiple Personality." *American Journal of Clinical Hypnosis* 24 (1981–2): 230–40.

Ludwig, Arnold. "Altered States of Consciousness." *Archives of General Psychiatry* 15 (1966): 225.

McFarland, Ross. "The Psychological Effects of Oxygen Deprivation (Anoxaemia) on Human Behavior." *Archiv fur Psychologie* 145 (1932).

McKellar, Peter. *Mindsplit: The Psychology of Multiple Personality and the Dissociated Self.* London: Dent, 1979.

Meduna, L. J. "The Effects of Carbon Dioxide upon the Functions of the Brain." In *Carbon Dioxide Therapy,* pp. 23–8. Springfield, IL: Charles Thomas, 1950.

Merton, Robert. *The Sociology of Science.* Univ. of Chicago Press, 1973.

Millar, K., and N. Watkinson. "Recognition of Words Presented during General Anaesthesia." *Ergonomics* 36 (1983): 585–94.

Moody, Raymond. *Life After Life.* New York: Bantam, 1976.

Nisbett, Richard, and Lee Ross. *Human Inference: Strategies and Shortcomings of Social Judgment.* Englewood Cliffs, NJ: Prentice-Hall, 1980.

Noyes, Russell, Jr. "The Human Experience of Death Or, What Can We Learn from Near-Death Experiences?" *Omega* 13 (1982–83): 251–9.

_____. "Near-Death Experiences: Their Interpretation and Significance." In *Between Life and Death,* ed. by Robert Kastenbaum, 73–88. New York: Springer, 1978.

O'Connell, D. J. K. *The Green Flash and Other Low Sun Phenomena.* New York: Interscience, 1958.

Persinger, Michael. *Neuropsychological Bases of God Beliefs.* New York: Praeger, 1987.

Rawlings, M. *Beyond Death's Door.* New York: Thomas Nelson, 1978.

Reed, Graham. *The Psychology of Anomalous Experience,* revised ed. Buffalo: Prometheus, 1988.

Ring, Kenneth. *Life at Death: A Scientific Investigation of the Near-Death Experience.* New York: Quill, 1982.

Ring, Kenneth, and Stephen Franklin. "Do Suicide Survivors Report Near-Death Experiences?" *Omega* 12 (1981–82): 191–208.

Rodin, Ernst. "The Reality of Death Experiences: A Personal Perspective." *Journal of Nervous and Mental Disease* 168 (1980): 259–63.

Sabom, Michael. *Recollections of Death: A Medical Investigation.* New York: Harper & Row, 1982.

Schnaper, Nathan. "Comments Germane to the Paper Entitled 'The Reality of Death Experiences' by Ernst Rodin." *Journal of Nervous and Mental Disease* 168 (1980): 269.

Schultz, Duane. *Theories of Personality,* 2nd ed. Monterey, CA: Brooks/Cole, 1981.

Siegel, Ronald. "The Psychology of Life After Death." *American Psychologist* 35, 10 (1980): 911–31.

Singer, S. "Ball Lightning." In *Lightning,* Vol. 1, ed. by R. H. Golde, 409–36. London: Academic Press, 1977.

Stevenson, Ian. "Do We Need a New Word to Supplement 'Hallucination'?" *The American Journal of Psychiatry* 140 (1983): 1609–11.

Taylor, Shelley, and Suzanne Thompson. "Stalking the Elusive 'Vividness Effect'." *Psychological Review* 89 (1982): 155–81.

Tellegen, A., and G. Atkinson. "Openness to Absorbing and Self-Altering Experiences ("Absorption"), a Trait Related to Hypnotic Susceptibility." *Journal of Abnormal Psychology* 83 (1974): 268–77.

Twemlow, Stuart, and Glen Gabbard. "The Influence of Demographic/Psychological Factors and Preexisting Conditions on the Near-Death Experience." *Omega* 15 (1984–85): 223–35.

Wesson, Paul, K. Valle, and R. Stabell. "The Extragalactic Background Light and a Definitive Resolution of Olbers' Paradox." *Astrophysical Journal* 317, 2 (June 15, 1987): 601–6.

West, D. J. "Visionary and Hallucinatory Experiences: A Comparative Appraisal." *International Journal of Parapsychology* 2 (1960): 89–100.

Winslow, John, and Alfred Meyer. "The Perpetrator at Piltdown." *Science 83* (Sept. 1983): 32–43.

Woodhouse, Mark. "Five Arguments Regarding the Objectivity of NDEs." *Anabiosis—The Journal of Near-Death Studies* 3 (1983): 63–75.

Zaleski, Carol. *Otherworld Journeys.* New York: Oxford Univ. Press, 1987.

INDEX

A

abduction 163

acquisition of information xx, xxi, 17–19, 31–53, 58–60, 64–71, 83, 85, 89, 107, 140, 163, 191
   centrality to science 59–60
   tension with truth 17, 31, 66–71, 75, 85–6, 89, 93, 148, 168
   top-down processing 47

ad hoc hypotheses 16, 48, 57

ad hominem fallacy 36, 150, 155, 174, 210

aether, electromagnetic 49, 110

age regression 207

Alcock, James 77, 181

Alston, William 69, 122, 125, 127–8, 202n

altered states of consciousness 178–9

anecdotal evidence
   See evidence

anesthesia, effects 180–1

angina 38–41, 96

anoxia
   See near-death experiences, proposed explanatory hypotheses

Anselm xx

anti-realism
   See instrumentalism
   See truth

Arbib, Michael 3n, 144n

archival context 74–5, 93

Argyle, Edward 114–6, 127

Aristotle's cosmology 23

Aristotle's science 185

atmospheric refraction 112–3

attention absorption 179

avoidance of error xxi, 5, 31–59, 64, 68–9, 75, 85–6, 93, 100–2, 110–1, 140, 187, 191–2
   contribution of law of noncontradiction 58–9

B

balkanization 129, 169

ball lightning 110, 113–8, 121, 135

Barbour, Ian 27n

Barrett, Robert 132n

Bates, Brian 177n, 178n, 179n

Bayesian theory 86

Bedouin example 201

Beecher, Henry 39

behaviorism 18, 54, 73, 90, 134, 145, 202

belief
   justified 37–8
   obligated 37, 123–7
   permitted 37, 123–7
   religious xxii
   voluntarism 36
   warranted 38, 125